Early Nineteenth Century Punjab

Early Nineteenth Century Punjab

Historical Analysis of European Travellers' Literature

Kulwinder Singh Bajwa

Commonwealth

Early Nineteenth Century Punjab : Historical Analysis of European Travellers' Literature

Edition : **2027**

ISBN 978-81-311-0250-3

Published by :
COMMONWEALTH PUBLISHERS (P) LTD.
4831/24, Govind Lane,
Ansari Road, Darya Ganj,
New Delhi - 110002
Ph. : 23242541, 23272541
e-mail : commonwealthpublishers2016@gmail.com

Distributed by :
ARJUN PUBLISHING HOUSE
4831/24, Govind Lane,
Ansari Road, Darya Ganj,
New Delhi - 110002
Ph. : 23242541, 23272541
e-mail : arjunbooks2001@gmail.com
arjunpubhouse@gmail.com

Laser Typesetting by :
Dimple Computers
Delhi

Printed at :
Milan Enterprises
Delhi

Dedicated
to
my
friends

Foreword

All through the centuries of Punjab has played a very important role in the history of our country. Recent research shave shown that it was probable the firs place in India to have any human habitation. As per the presentations of knowledge, the first civilization to rise in this reason was the Indus valley Civilization in which the Punjab constituted a major territorial unit. The Indo-Aryans, the most significant of our ancestors, on their advent into India, settled first of all in the plains of the Punjab. It was here on the banks on the rivers that the first Vedic humans were composed by the *maharishis* of those good days. After some Century came and Greeks. Some of them experienced strong resistance at every step in the Punjab. They had to go back from banks of the *Beas*. This was soon follow by the rise of Chandragupta Maurya with the help of Punjabis, conquered the whole of northern India; he established great empire of India with its north-western frontier extending far beyond chaconne of Kabul. The post-Mauryan period was marked by a long series of inroads by certain central Asian tribes like *Sakas*, *Kushans* and, after a few centuries, *Hunas*. Obviously, they cost a great deal of devastation in the land. But they did not come to return, and after a time when they settled down, they did make a contribution to the variegated *Punjabi life*. At the end of the ancient period of our history, the Punjab witnessed the establishment of the powerful and extensive *Hindushahi* Kingdom which put up a heroic resistance to the tide of the Turkish invasions starting from the tenth century.

With the Turks' advent the Punjab passed under the influence Islamic civilization. The mutual clash and contact of the two civilization–Hindu and Muslim, let to many important changes in the life, of the People of Punjab as well as India, of which by far the most significant was the birth Sikh movement later half of the fifteenth Century. On the foundations lay down by Guru Nanak Dev ji and his nine successes, Guru Gobind Singh, being the last of the line, raised the revolutionary organization known as the Khalsa. This Khalsa, as is when today, valiantly faced all the terrible ordeals into which the hostility of the Mughal Government of the Punjab and the Afghan invaders from the north-west had thrown them, and the ultimately came out successful and establish their independent rule that is commonly termed the rule of the twelve Sikh *Misals*. Some years later, Maharaja Ranjit Singh rose as the lion of the Punjab and set up a mighty sovereign state compromising, besides the Punjab plains, the tracts of Kohistan, Kashmir, Ladakh and Peshawar.

In 1849 the Punjab was annexed to the British empire of India. Henceforward till the end of the British rule in 1947, the people of the Punjab earned the reputation of being the sword-arm of India on he one hand and on the other were second to none in making supreme sacrifices in the cause of the country's freedom from foreign domination. To now the history of this period the European Travels literature Historical Analysis (Early nineteenth Century, is the most significant source of history; so credit goes to Dr. K.S. Bajwa who has done a commendable job while writing this book for the young scholars who can peruse further research in this field. The above mentioned effects and references to the historic role of these foreign travels, though very scanty, should be sufficient to underpin the urgent need and worth of the subject. In view of this Dr. Bajwa has produced the present volume in a details and systematic manner and that on the basis of the consequences thereof another volume on the subject in comprehensive from can be produced that, by exploring new data and posing fresh problems, may pave the way of still higher studies in the same field. The present volume is the first concrete step in the road to that goal. It is hope that the young scholars will feel inspired and encouraged to take up further studies on this very subject and produce elaborative history.

The present work throws ample light on the changes that appeared as the result thereof in the diverse spheres of life-political administrative, social, religious, economic and artistic– have all been examined, in greater or lesser degree, in this book. It occupies a most significant phase in the long and detailed Punjab history, as it was during this period that a new culture entered the country, especially the Punjab and made deep impact upon the mode of living and thinking of the people of this region. The changes that appeared as a consequence thereof in the different walks of life-political administrative, socio-religious, economic, etc. have been examined, in greater or lesser degree, in this work. To the best of my Knowledge there is at present no other book on the subject having the same elaborate analysis.

Though several short comings may come to the notice of the readers, but such shortcomings are not unnatural in a pioneer work of this kind. In spite of all the shortcomings that may be there, I am formally of the view that the work will be of immense value to student, general readers and research scholars. For this successful attempt Dr K.S. Bajwa, who prepared and finally completed the original plan deserve my heartiest congratulations. I do hope that the momentous task undertaken by him will be further explored, re-interpreted and produced by some young scholars in the discipline history.

Dr. Joginder Singh

Professor of History
Namdhari Chair
Guru Nanak Dev University, Amritsar

PREFACE

European travel literature occupies a significant place among the contemporary sources in English. Over half a dozen travellers visited the Punjab during the reign of Maharaja Ranjit Singh. Their nationalities varies so much as their objectives. Also because of their specific historical context, they provide us useful information and rare insight into on the socio-political conditions of the early 19th century Punjab. In order to reconstruct meaningfully the socio-political history of the period, these sources can play a significant role. But it could only be possible if they are historically analysed.

Almost all the modern historians of the early 19th century Punjab in general and Maharaja Ranjit Singh in particular have extensively used the evidence presented by the European travellers. Such trend is indicative of the value of this form of historical literature. But a perusal of their works uncritically. Also, these works have not been taken in their totality. Each one of them has invoked the evidence of these travellers to suit his view point without looking into the objective of the travellers. These sources are used only to delineate certain aspects of the history of the Punjab.

For instance, N.K. Sinha has used the evidence of Alexander Burnes to underline Ranjit Singh's humanity, to show that the Afghan Governor of Attock was rather cheaply purchased by Ranjit Singh, to indicate the terms Ranjit Singh wanted to impose on Shah Shuja as the price of this support; and for informations on Ranjit Singh's bridge over the Indus; his friendly relations with a few of the Amirs of Sindh; has encouragement to silk textiles of Multan; his attitude towards the Akalis; his 'benevolent despotism' and the fair and unfair means by which the Jamwal brothers consolidated their power. Evidence of Baron Charles Hugel has been used to show Ranjit Singh's interest in the conquest of Ladakh; the increasing power of Jamwal brothers and the action of Jamrud in which Hari Singh Nalwa was killed. Similarly Victor Jacquemont's evidence has been used to lay emphasis that Ranjit Singh was aware of his inability to contend with the British; to underline the superiority of Sikh arms over the Afghans; to suggest that in 1831 Ranjit Singh was thinking of expansion towards North as well as south; to underline Prince Sher Singh's friendly relations with the European and French officers who were not on good terms with Prince Kharak Singh, and to highlight the prominent position of Raja Gulab Singh. But the evidence provided by the travellers was used uncritically. Sinha's only aim is to achieve his nationalistic end.

Such trend (tendency) is wanting in other historian's as well. Even modern historian like Fauja Singh fails to use these source critically. He does not try to co-relate evidence from other sources logically in order to understand the implied meaning. For example, in his book *Some Aspects of State and Society Under Ranjit Singh,* he co-relates Jacquemont's observation that he did not found any beggar in the areas through which he passed with the observations of European Travellers regarding the splendour of the Maharaja's court without going into their logical connection. On the basis of illogical co-relation of these observations he concludes that "all these valuable came from outside as a result of the country's favourable balance of trade", without realizing that the conclusion has no logical connection with the former. Hence, it is essential to analyse them historically.

No study on the subject is available except an M. Phil. dissertation entitled; *European Travellers to the Kingdom of Ranjit Singh* (1830-39) by Maninder Sandhu. Besides, there is an article by the same researchers based on the concluding chapter of her dissertation, entitled, "European Travellers to the Punjab", *Journal of Regional History,* Amritsar, Vol. V, 1985. The dissertation does not include all the representative works of early 19th century European travellers to the Punjab. Also it is somewhat a re-production of their observations without questioning to their evidence. Even in doing so, at many places the statements of these travellers are misunderstood and therefore misrepresented. For instance, on page 50 of his *Journal*, Jacquemont have made reference to the mode of payments to the courtiers of the kingdom of Lahore. But the researcher take it as 'a payments made to the revenue collectors'. On page 12 of her dissertation she says : 'commenting upon the system of payments, Jacquemont states that Ranjit Singh did not pay a regular salary to the revenue collectors. They received part of their pay in kind and the remainder in cash'. But Jacquemont on page 50 of his *Journal* says that : 'The irregular payment which his courtier received was made up by *Jagirs* or by royal bonds on the state debtors, who were either defaulters or criminals who had been fined'. Furthermore, on page 35 she says: 'The revenue derived by Ranjit Singh from Peshawar was nine lacs of rupees a year. In addition to it, he derived a yearly tribute of 60 horses and bara rice'. However, the observation made by Burnes with reference to the administration of Peshawar in 1830s; on page 319, Vol. II of his account is as: "It is governed by Sirdar Sultan Mohammad Khan, who share its revenues with two other brothers, Peer and Saeed Mohammad Khan. A large portion of the country is alienated to different individuals, and the net revenue falls short of nine lacs of rupees per annum. The younger brother enjoy three lacs, and the chief defrays from the remainder the entire expenses of the country, the tribute to the Seiks, and likewise supports clear that the researcher do not make any difference between the position of the territories directly administered by the state and of the vassal chiefs. Such treatment shows a lack of critical and analytical approach to the sources. The travel literature is not taken in totality and in the context of its times. Hence, the need for a meaningful, unified and critical analysis of travel literature.

For the present study, the travel accounts of William Moorcroft (English), Victor Jacquemont (French), Alexander Burnes (English), Charles Masson (English), Baron Charles Hugel (German) and Godfrey Thomas Vigne (English) have selected. All of them except Moorcroft visited the dominions of Maharaja Ranjit Singh Between 1830-39 which is rather significant period. For by 1830s the kingdom of Lahore was at the zenith of its glory, the work of conquests and consolidation was almost complete. With the defeat and death of Sayyid Ahmed in 1831 at Balkot, Maharaja was free to move his troops towards north or south. Now south received his attention and he started thinking seriously about the conquest of Sindh. This period was equally important for the British, French, German and Russian imperialistic designs. The immediate danger to the security of the kingdom of Lahore appeared to be from the British, for the Afghans were not in a position to have a collision with the Sikhs at their own. By this time, the British East India company too had virtually controlled the whole of India and was thinking seriously to reach to 'the natural line of defence'–the Indus. But at the same time the company's official wanted to preserve outward neutrality and show respect to the Treaty of Amritsar (1809). To fulfill their desired end, the British, therefore, thought of collecting much needed information through the agency of these travellers, so that they could form a definite policy to be pursued not only towards the kingdom of Lahore but also towards Sindh and Afghanistan. In this backdrop the evidence provided by the European travel literature on polity, economy and society in the early 19th century Punjab are being understood in a historical perspective.

Seven chapters have been devoted to this study. Chapter first aims at discussing the lives, works and milieu of the European travellers. The historical context in which they visited the dominions of Maharaja Ranjit Singh has been studied in the second chapter. Both the chapters are mutually exclusive and helps us to understand the purpose and nature of interest of the travellers in visiting the kingdom of Lahore. This constitute chapter third. In chapter fourth, fifth and sixth an attempt has been made to discuss the evidence on polity, economy and society. On the basis of the study an attempt has been made to understand the significance of the European travel literature in the form of concluding chapter.

Several persons and institutions helped me during the course of my research; I take the opportunity to acknowledge their cooperation. I am grateful to the staff of Sikh History Research Department, Khalsa College, Amritsar; National Library, Calcutta; India Office Library, London; Punjab State Archives, Patiala; Dr. Ganda Singh collections, Punjabi University, Patiala; Guru Ram Dass library, Guru Nanak Dev University, and the Library of the Department of History, Guru Nanak Dev University, Amritsar. I am extremely grateful to my supervisor Dr. S.S. Sagar for his keen interest in my work from its inception to completion. My thanks are also due to Prof. S.S. Hans, Prof. Gurdev Singh (Head), Department of History, Guru Nanak Dev University, Amritsar. Other members of the staff of the Department of history, Guru Nanak Dev University, Amritsar also helped me with their valuable suggestions. I am thankful to all of them.

Kulwinder Singh Bajwa

Contents

1

European Travellers : Lives, Works and Milieu

Over half a dozen European Travellers visited the kingdom of Lahore during the reign of Maharaja Ranjit Singh. They belonged to distinct nationalities and travelled for different purposes and interest. Four of them : William Moorcroft, Alexander Burnes, Charles Masson and Godfrey Thomas vigne were English. Victor Jacquemont was a French while Baron Charles Hugel was a German. Their accounts relates to many facets of life in the kingdom of Lahore. For full appreciation of their observations on the polity, economy and society of the Punjab, it is imperative to look into their lives, works and milieu.

I

William Moorcroft (1767-1825)

William Moorcroft was born in May 1767 at Lancashire; and educated for the medical profession at Liverpool.[1] At the age of eighteenth, upon the completion of his studies his attention was diverted to a different pursuit, and he finally settled in London. In a letter written from Kashmir to a friend in London he said, "whilst a pupil of Dr. Lyon, the colleague of Dr. Currie, at the Liverpool infirmary, the attention of the physicians and surgeons of that institution was suddenly and strongly called to a formidable epidemic disease amongst the horned cattle of a particular district, and was thought to be extending. It was agreed to depute a pupil to examine the disease upon the spot. The choice fell upon me, and in company with Mr. Wilson, the ablest farmer of the day, I performed my commission. As arising out of this occurrence, it is only necessary to remark, that two gentlemen, of whose judgment and patriotism I have the highest respect, took the trouble of endeavoring to show that if I were to devote myself to the improvement of a degraded profession, closely connected with the interests of agriculture, I might render myself much more useful to the country, than by continuing in one already cultivated by men of the most splendid talents. Convinced by their arguments, but opposed by other friends, and especially by my master, the matter was compromised by a reference to the celebrated John Hunter. After a long conversation with me, Mr. Hunter declared that if he were not advanced in years he himself would on the following day begin to study the profession in question. This declaration was decisive, and I followed the course of study which Mr. Hunter was pleased to Indicate.[2]

In those days there was no veterinary school in London, therefore, Moorcroft went to France for studying veterinary science. After completion of his study, he settled at London. For some years, in partnership with Mr. Field, he carried on a very lucrative veterinary practice. The nature of the profession, however, involved many occurrences unpleasant to a man of cultivated taste and warm temper and ad-midst intercourse with the persons of station and respectively, collision with individuals not always possessed either. Moorcroft, therefore, became disgusted with his profession, although, he seems to have realized an ample fortune by it, as his name appeared at 224 Oxford Street in Kelly's 'Dictionary' for 1800. However, he lost much of his wealth in some injudicious project for manufacturing cost-iron-horse-shoes by machinery. He, therefore, readily accepted an offer from the court of Directors of the East India Company to go out to Bengal as superintendent of their military stud.[3] In May 1808, Moorcroft left England for Bengal. As a superintendent of the East India Company at Pusa near Kanpur, he advocated the improvement of the native cavalry horses by the introduction of English or Turkoman bone and muscle, His preference for the Turkoman over the Arab horse appears to have directed his attention to the possibilities of commercial intercourse between British India and the countries beyond the Himalaya. In 1811–12 accompanied by captain (afterwards Major) Hyder Young Hearsey, he crossed the Himalaya by Niti Pass and made his way to the great plain between it and the Kuen Lun chain; he examined the sources and upper courses of the Satluj and the eastern branch of the Indus, and found the positions of Lakes Ravan and Mansarovara. He was the first British traveller to cross the Himalaya. An account of his journey was published in Asiatic Research.[4]

Seven years afterwards, in the end of October 1819, Moorcroft left Bareilly for an exploring expedition to Central Asia. The principal persons of his party were: Mr. George Trebeck in the capacity of general assistant, especially as draftsman and surveyor; Mr. George Guthrie as an apothecary; William Laidlaw, a geologist an mineralogist (was dismissed in January 1820); Mir Izzetullah Khan, a native gentleman of talent and information who had preceded him a few years before on the route Moorcroft proposed to follow; Gulam Hyder Khan, a native of Bareilly; Hafiz Muhammad Fazal ; two *pandits* as clerks; a sepoy guard; and servants and collies etc. He had with him a quantity of English goods, chiefly cottons, broad cloth and hardware to the value of about three to four thousands pounds, belonging to Messrs. Palmer & Co., and Mackillop & Co. of Calcutta.[5]

On 12th December 1819, he reached Joshimath and traversing the mountainous region entered into the plains. On 6th May 1820, he was at Lahore and was received with much courtesy and attention by Maharaja Ranjit Singh. He presented to the *Maharaja*, a pair of double-barrel and a pair of three-barrel pistols, a sword, the model of a cannon with carriage and all appurtenance complete, white churi tails and bags of musk from the mountains. The *Maharaja* was much pleased with the presents, particularly, with the pistols and cannon. Moorcroft's stay at Lahore was about eighteen days.[6] The *Maharaja* consented to his proceeding through Mandi, Kullu to Ladakh and his passing through Kashmir and appointed an attendant to accompany him to Kullu. On the eve of his departure, he was honoured with a dress of valuable shawls.[7]

He spent two years in the territories of Ladakh. He proposed important political arrangement to the independent states adjoining British India which were wholly unauthorized by the Government. During this period, Moorcroft spread no effort to obtain permission to enter Chinese Tartary, but he was unsuccessful, precisely due to the repressed attitude of the Chinese authorities, misinformed by the Kashmiri merchants who were monopolist of wool trade. However, disapproving his long sojourn at Leh, the Bengal government suspended his pay and allowances during absence.[8]

From Leh, Moorcroft proceeded to the valley of Kashmir, escorted by Surat Singh, deputed by Moti Ram, the governor of Kashmir. He entered the city on 3rd November, 1822, and took his abode at Dilawar Khan's garden. During his ten and a half month's stay at Kashmir, he spent a considerable time in inquiring into the management of the shawl-wool goat and the various processes of the Kashmir shawls manufacture.[9] Following the Rajauri-Mirpur-Jhelum route, he entered Rawalpindi. Proceeding on the line of route previously pursued by Mountstuart Elphistone in his diplomatic mission to Kabul in 1809, Moorcroft reached Kabul on 19th June 1824. His request for a letter of introduction to the King of Bokhara was turned down by British government. He, nevertheless, made his way from Kabul to Bokhara and met 'with as much kindness from the King as could be expected from Mir Hyder, a selfish sensual, and narrow-minded bigot'. He remained at Bokhara nearly five months.

After various difficulties, arising from the meanness and cupidity chiefly of the monarch himself, he started his return journey to Hindustan.[10]

On his way back, about 4th or 5th August, 1825, Moorcroft, crossing Oxus determined to deviate from the road to got to Maimana, where he understood it was likely that he should be able to make important additions to his stock of horses. "Before I quite Turkistan", he wrote from Bokhara, "I mean to penetrate into that tract which contains, probably, the best horses in Asia, but with which all intercourse has been suspended during the last five years. The experiment is full hazard, but *Le jeu vaut bien la chandelle"*.[11] However, he was taken by robbers. He died on 27th August 1825. According to other accounts, he died of fever, and still others of poison at Andekhui. His body was brought on a camel to Balkh and was buried outside the walls. As Trebeck, his fellow traveller was too ill when his body reached Balkh to investigate the case, nothing could be said about the circumstances of his death. At the time of his death his age was about sixty.[12]

He undertook this task without any accredited authority or political designation. The enterprise was taken at his own risk and expenses.[13] However, he was permitted to receive his allowances as superintendent of his stud. In all, spent about six years in travelling from the British frontier in the hills to the city of Bokhara. Out of these six years, two years, two and a half months were spent in the dominions of Maharaja Ranjit Singh.[14]

A sudden demise of Moorcroft deprived the party of a leader. The property being left without responsible owner was seized upon by Ata Khan, the Maulvi at the holy shrine of Mazara. However, the son of Nazir Ahmed managed to secure some of his horses, a part of his other belongings, and also most of his papers. These were given to Charles Trebeck at Kabul.[15] Although, Moorcroft himself had relinquished the right over information to the government that it might have been collected in case of his fall.[16] As his pay had been suspended, there was a debate in India and England about the ownership of these papers. Finally, the government decided to release his pay as the consequence of it the papers became the property.[17] These papers were edited by H.H. Wilson in two volumes, same time in 1837 entitled, *Travels in the Himalayan Provinces of Hindustan and the Punjab; in Ladakh and Kashmir, in Peshawar, Kabul, Kundoz, and Bokhara, from 1819-1828.*

The zealousness and hardihood with which he performed

his journey, is in itself an indicative of his character. His scientific attainments were strictly professional. He had neither, the necessary training nor the means to investigate the mysteries of Nature. Neither he was an antiquarian like Charles Masson, nor an Oriental scholar, yet, he could use some of the Eastern dialects and took interests in the remains of antiquity, he could find enroute. On all occasions, rural economy and manufactures, remained the chief objects of his discussion. He was convinced that much could be learnt from the Easterns, in the same way much could be taught to them. The capabilities of the countries, he visited, and the advantages to be derived from the cultivation of their products, impressed him so much, that he seriously made up this mind to settle, his return, in the lower range of the Himalaya and devote the rest of his life to the occupations of a peasant. But due to his untimely death, he was deprived of his plans; in other words his plans could not materialized.[18]

He was a true nationalist, determined to sacrifice everything for the benefit of his country. On the suspension of his pay he wrote to Palmer, "Is it intended to punish me for the delay in my mission? I have to high an opinion of the government to suppose they can have been so influenced and the check, however, originating shall not weigh upon my measures, although, on account of my children, I could wish to avoid encroaching on my past savings: yet even this shall not be exempt, if it be necessary to the completion of my objects. The accumulation of property can never afford such gratification to my mind as the reflection of having been, in some degree, accessory to the benefit of my country, and of this retrospect no human power can deprive me".[19]

His contribution to the annals of geographical information was entirely new in the annals of geographical research.[20] His journey from Joshimath to Srinagar (Gharwal) and thence to Lahore, his march by way of Katoch, Kullu and Lahaul to Leh as well as the details relating to the principality of Ladakh, was Alexander Burnes travels only confirmed the information, tapped by Moorcroft in his journey from Kashmir to Bokhara.

II

Alexander Burnes (1805-1841)

Alexander Burnes was born on 16th May 1805. His father, James Burnes, a man of character and ability, was provost of Montrose and a town clerk. He belonged to the same family as Robert the poet, his great grandfather and the poet's father having been brothers. Alexander Burnes took his schooling at Montrose Academy; his main interest was in classics and mathematics. At the age of sixteen, he was appointed, through the influence of Joseph Hume, to an Indian cadetship, and joined the Bombay native army in 1821. His subsequent advancement was rather rapid.[21]

In May 1822, he passed an examination Hindustani which fitted him for an interpreter ship. In January 1823, he was gazetted interpreter of the first battalion at Surat. In May, the same year, he was made regimental adjutant with an allowance of 500-600 rupees per month. His new duties were not allowed to interference with his programmes of language study. Soon after he qualified as an interpreter in Persian, the language of diplomacy in the East, as French was in the west. He was choosen Persian interpreter to a field force of 8,000 men under order to cross the Indus in 1825. However, the force did not advance and Burnes spent his time in surveying Cutch and produced a map of an unknown track, besides writing a voluminous report on his travels.[22]

By 1829, his reputation was such that Sir John Malcolm, Governor of Bombay and himself no mean traveller, had no hesitation in supporting Burnes' application for permission to explore the Rajputana desert. He was granted permission and set out for Jaisalmer. However, he was recalled by Lord William Bentinck, for the statesmen at Calcutta took fright, lest the appearance of a British officer in the wild of Rajputana might lead the locals to conclude that company was about to annex their territory. An angry and very frustrated Burnes returned to Bombay. However, he was made assistant to the Political Resident at Cutch.[23]

In 1830, Burnes was dispatched on a compulsory mission to Lahore; in charge of a present consisting of a batch of English horses, sent by the king of England to Ranjit Singh. He sailed from Mandvee on 21st January, 1831 and crossed the Satluj for Ludhiana on 26th of August, 1831. He accomplished this difficult, rather dangerous mission, with great success, within seven months. He arrived at Lahore on the 18th of July, 1831, and stayed for one month. From Ludhiana he went to Simla, to submit in person, the report of his voyage from sea to Lahore. William Bentinck listened to his story with great interest, and was told that his report was 'a model of its kind'.[24]

Encouraged by the treatment meted out from the Governor-General, Burnes took an opportunity to ask permission, to visit Afghanistan, and thereafter to travel by way of Balkh, Bokhara and Samarkand to the shores of the Caspian Sea. The approval was granted shortly afterward, and on 23rd, December, 1831, he was furnished passport at Delhi. On the 3rd January 1832, he started from Ludhiana. He visited Ranjit Singh at Lahore, Sultan Muhammad in Peshawar, Dost Muhammad Khan in Kabul, the brigand chief of Kunduz, the Shah of Persia. Although, denied access to Nasurullah Khan, the Amir of Bokhara, Burnes succeeded in establishing excellent relations with his chief minister, the Koosh Begee, and was more fortune than William Moorcroft in the treatment he received at Bokhara.[25]

On the 18th January, 1833, Burnes came back to Bombay, and reached Calcutta in February the same year. Thus, this long and difficult journey was completed within thirteenth months. During the course of their journey, Burnes and his companions travelled light, wearing native costume, and their only escort were men hired locally for the purpose, or provided for them by some local potentate.[26] However, this time, Burnes travelled as a private person, but not without the backing of the British Government.[27]

Burnes returned to England in 1833, and was well received in London, where his fame as an adventurous travellers had proceeded him. He received the gold medal of the Geographical Society of England, and the Silver medal of the Geographical

Society of Paris, the Athenaum Club admitted him as a member without ballot. Also, he had a privilege of audience with King William IV, for nearly an hour and a half. After listening about his travels and knowing what Russia was desiring to do, his Majesty said, "Really, Sir you are a wonderful man. You have done more for me in this hour than any one has been able to do."[28] However,, the year following he got published the results of his travels, which was an immediate and unprecedent success, selling 900 copies on the first day of publication. Subsequently it ran into several editions.[29]

Burnes returned to India in 1835, and resumed his duty as an assistant to the Resident in Cutch. On 26th , November, 1836, Lord Auckland sent him on a commercial mission to Kabul. He was well received by Dost Mohammad, the ruler of Kabul. However, his commercial mission speedily changed into political one. For Dost Mohammad wanted British help against the Sikhs and the Persians, but Burnes was not authorized to promise anything. Meanwhile, Captain Vitkievitch, the Russian envoy arrived with full authority to promise almost anything, the Amir wanted for. Disparaged by the situation, Burnes returned in utter despair. The reason for this was that Lord Auckland had decided to replace Shah Shuja on the throne of Kabul, with the help of the Sikhs.[30] A grand army 'Army of the Indus' was sent against Dost Mohammad Khan and Burnes was asked to smooth the advance of British army through Sindh.[31]

After the installation of Shah Shuja on the *masand* of Kabul, Burnes was made knight of his new Order of Cavalry, the 'Order of the Durrani Empire'. The British Government made him lieutenant-Colonel; and raised him to the dignity of knighthood, besides making him resident subordinate to Sir William Hay Macnaghten, without any power or responsibility. His advice was not even listened by Macnaghten. He spent much of his time in enjoying himself, for he knew well the language of the people, and had managed to cultivated friendship with the leading Afghans, with equal access to the Afghan ladies.[32] But he became identified in the Afghan eyes as one of the main protagonists of British intervention in

Afghanistan. He was assassinated in Kabul on 2nd November 1841.[33]

Divergents views are being held by his critics, about his dealing of the Afghan situation. One set of people supports him while the others condemned him saying that he was wanting in steadiness of purpose, sound judgement and moral self-restraint. Henry Durand goes to the extent of saying that "the man was hated as a treacherous cause of the invasion and occupation of the country."[34] However, Burnes' cannot be blamed for British disaster in Kabul, for he had a better understanding of the Afghan mind, and he had suggested to superiors at Calcutta to support Dost Mohammad Khan. But it was Lord Auckland who on the advice of his foreign secretary, Macnaghten, decided to support Shah Shuja. Also, he had accomplished much while still young and inexperienced; nor can it be denied that he possed a remarkable ability to understand the Oriental mind and to adopt himself to Oriental society. Above all, he was a man of unusual accomplishment, an acute observer and a devoted servant of his country. "It was the hard fate of Alexander Burnes to be overrated at the outset and underrated at the close of his carrer."[35]

III

Charles Masson (1800–1853)

Charles Masson's real name was James Lewis. He was a son of George Lewis, a London tradesman living in Aldermanbury. James Lewis was born on February 16th, 1800 in Aldermanbury according to his own account and the baptismal register's under date March 23th, 1800 of the church of St. Marry, the Virgin, Aldermanbury. He was fairly educated. He enlisted himself in the East India Company's Army on 5th October, 1821. He served in the Bengal Artillery from July 6th, 1822 to July 4th, 1827.[36]

Masson was employed in classifying and sketching General Hardwick's geographical specimens, which suggests that he was a person of sufficient intelligence and talent. However, he was with his regiment at the seize of Bharatpur which fell in January 1826. While stationed in the vicinity of Bharatpur,

Masson deserted the army and made his way across Bikaner and Bahawalpur into the Punjab with a companion named Richard Potter. Potter proceeded to Lahore and entered the service of Maharaja Ranjit Singh under the name of John Brown. Masson, perhaps fearing detection went all alone to Peshawar, Jelababad and Kabul.[37]

Having safely made his way into Afghan territory by the end of 1826 the first stage of his leisurely wandering took him to Kabul, Ghazni and Kandhar in all of which he made lengthy stays. In January 1829, he set off for Shikarpur in Sindh. For the next year and a half he made his way back and forth through Sindh and the Punjab. From Shikarpur, he travelled through Khairpur, Fazilpur and Multan as far as Lahore, where he was hospitably received by Ranjit Singh's French General Allard, However, unwilling to enter the Sikh service, he left Lahore before pressure could be exerted to hold him there. Thence he proceeded, via Peshawar, Fazilpur and Shikarpur into lower Sindh. He visited Hyderabad and Thatha before taking ship at Karachi on a vessel bound for the port of the Persian Gulf.[38]

After his brief visits to Muscat and Qish, Masson finally embarked in June 1830 at Bushire, where he became the guest of the British Resident, Major David Wilson. At his suggestion, Masson proceeded to Tabriz where he was received by John Campbell, who encouraged him to return to Afghanistan and provided him with funds. From Tabriz he travelled to Muscat via Baghdad, Basra and Bushire in the company of several British officers, yet he escaped detection. In April 1831, he parted from his companions in Muscat and sailed in an Arab coastal craft as far as Karachi. From Karachi Masson made his way to Sonmiani, whence he undertook a leisurely trip to Kalat. At Sonmiani he attached himself to a large Karila bound for Kandhar and by May 1832, he was back in Kabul which was to become his home for the next six years.[39]

In Afghanistan Masson embarked upon his antiquarian researches into the history of the area. Before the visit of Alexander Burnes to the Court of Kabul, he had obtained from Begram 1865 copper coins and 14 gold and silver ones.

Meanwhile, his activities had attracted attention of the officials of the East India Company. However, the Company began to pay Masson a retainer for his services as an antiquarian, an arrangement which seems to have been settled soon after his return from Bamiyan. He received an ex-gratia payment of Rs. 1,500 and an annual stipend of Rs. 1,000 on condition of handing over whatever coins and *objects d'art* he had found. In time the coins would exceed 30,000 while works of art would include one of the most exquisite masterpieces of Gandhara Buddhist metalware, the Bimran casket, now in the British Museum.[40]

Masson's intimate knowledge of Afghanistan and his personal connections with some of its most prominent figures, made him fit for becoming a most promising British agent in that country. On the recommendation of Alexander Burnes and C.M. Wade, the then political Agent at Ludhiana, he was granted a royal pardon in February 1835 and was appointed company's accredited Agent at the court of Dost Mohammad. Wade wrote to him on 5th March, 1835, "I have the pleasure to inform you that His Excellency the Right Honourable the Governor-General in Council has been pleased to appoint you our agent at Kabul, on a salary of 250 rupees per mensum".[41] From this time forward Masson embarked upon political activities detrimental both to his antiquarian pursuits and his Afghan friendship. He took his new duties very seriously and furnished lengthy accounts of events, of which he was in many instances an eye-witness.[42]

However, Masson left Kabul in April 1838, when the so called 'commercial mission' to the court of Dost Mohammad, headed by Alexander Burnes failed. At Peshawar he sent off a letter of resignation, although Burnes subsequently persuaded him to withdraw it. Lord Auckland, the Governor General assured him of employment on the projected expedition to Kabul, with a salary increase to Rs. 500 per mensum, but Sir William Macnaghten subsequently cancelled the appointment and ordered him to remain in Peshawar. Throughout the summer and autumn he waited news of the appointment which he regarded as his due but it never came. Auckland allegedly thought highly of him but it seems that Macnaghten did not. He was still subordinate to Wade and this in particular, irked him.[43] Tired of waiting his appointment, Masson left Peshawar in the autumn and made his way to Thatta by circuitous route, bitterly resentful of the treatment which he had received. In Thatta he stayed with Henry Pottinger, the political Agent at Sindh. There he prepared the material which was later incorporated into *Ariana Antiqua*, edited by H.H. Wilson and published at Company's expense in 1841. Here he also worked on his *Narrative of Various Journeys* which Pottinger took with him to England to be published in 1842.[44]

At last, Masson decided to return to Kabul through Baluchistan. However, he did not get further than Kalat, where he was embroiled in a local uprising. He was taken prisoner by the rebels, who sent him to Quetta to negotiate with the local political officer. The latter had him imprisoned under most harsh conditions and it was not without some difficulty that he obtained his release. Back in England, he sought compensation from the Company for wrongful imprisonment, but without success. He did, however, manage to obtain his due arrears in pay and allowances, and further ex-gratia payment of 1,000 pounds for his collections of antiquities and coins. From beginning to end his official connection with the Company had remained a source of misunderstanding and unhappiness, but at least it had brought him a pardon and freedom to return home.[45]

In England, he married Marry Anne Kilby in the beginning of 1843. In 1847, he was trying to sell his collections of coins and proposing to renew archaeological exploration in the East on behalf of the Austrian Government. He died on December 5th, 1853.[46] Masson was basically an explorer. His career as an archaeologist and antiquarian were more successful than his political activities. His *Narrative of Various Journeys* was fairly praised by various scholars. According to Holdichs, the Narratives is "a record which is unsurpassed on the Indian frontier for the width of its scope of inquiry into matters political, social, economic and scientific and the general accuracy of conclusions."[47]

IV

Godfrey Thomas Vigne (1801-1863)

G.T. Vigne was born in 1801 at Walthamstaw Essex. He was the eldest son of Thoms Vigne of Walthamstaw Eseex. He joined Harrow school in 1817. On December 23rd, 1818, he was admitted to Lincolin's Inn, and was called to the bar in 1824. Nothing is known for next seven years of his career. However, he started his career as a traveller, for which he had a great reputation. In 1831, he went to the United States of America, visited New York, Washington, Cincinnati and thence proceeded down the St. Lawrence to Quebec. The account of his journey entitled *six months in America* was published at London in 1832.[48] On 16th October, 1832, he left Southampton for India. Not much is known about the ways and means through which he reached the North-West Frontier in India. However, he passed through France from Normandy to Marseilles and experienced a first seasoning to more than European heat in the quarantine ground of Malta.[49] After passing through Persia, he reached Bombay on 1st January 1833. Thus he spent two and a half month on the way.[50]

He spent a year and half in travelling through different parts of India. Around the middle of the year 1835, we find him at Subathu, as a guest of Dr. Gernard. From Subathu, he marched on to Shimla to stay with Capt. C.P. Kannedy, then political Agent at Shimla. At Meerut, on his way from Delhi to Shimla, Vigne had been informed that Maharaja Ranjit Singh had no objection of his crossing the river Satluj, to visit the province of Kashmir. From Shimla, he hastened to Ludhiana to be the guest of Capt. C.M. Wade the then political Agent. He stayed there until the requisite permission to cross the Satluj arrived from Lahore.[51]

At Ludhiana, Capt. C.M. Wade encouraged him to continue his journey through the valley of Kashmir to Iskardu, the capital of Little Tibet. In fact, Ahmed Shah of Little Tibet had written a letter to Wade in which he "expressed his anxiety that some English Sahib should visit him". Vigne made up his mind "in a moment".[52] On the evening of 1st June, 1835, Vigne left Ludhiana for his first mountainous journey. By the end of the same year or in the beginning of 1836, Vigne was back to Ludhiana, after visiting Kashmir and Little Tibet.[53]

Vigne again quitted Ludhiana for his journey to Afghanistan on 12th March, 1836, and appears to be back to India by the end of the same year, as we find him again in Little Tibet for the second time in 1837.[54] In Kashmir, he met Baron Charles Hugel and accompanied him to Lahore and thence to Ludhiana.[55] After staying sometimes at Ludhiana, Vigne again asked the *Maharaja* to permit him to visit Kashmir. The permission was granted but with due reluctance. Around the middle of 1838, he was again in Kashmir. However, by the end of 1838, he left the valley once for all and reached Ludhiana in March 1839 and thanked the *Maharaja* for his kindness.[56]

From Ludhiana, Vigne accompanied G. Churchill Quartermaster-General of her Majesty's Artillery in India, and sailed on 30th March 1839 from Ferozpur in the Indus. On 23rd of April 1839, they were at Hyderabad, and within thirty-eight days, on 7th of May, they reached Bombay. Thence Vigne sailed in the Atlanta steamer. On 3rd of June, he reached Aden; stayed at Alexandria in Egypt for a week. However, he reached England in September 1839. In all, Vigne spent six years, eleven months, and twenty days in his Asian travels. Out of these seven years, about four years were spent in or around the dominion of Ranjit Singh.[57]

In England, he got published the experience of his Asian travels entitled : 1. *A Personal Narrative of a Visit to Ghazni, Kabul, and Afghanistan, and of a Residence at the Court of Dost Mohammad with Notices of Ranjit Singh, Khiva, and the Russian expedition,* 1840. 2. *Travels in Kashmir, Ladakh, Iskardo, the Countries Adjoining the Mountain Course of the Indus, and the Himalaya, North of the Punjab*, 2 Vols, 1842.

As an author, Vigne was familiar with the works of Prinsep, Forster, Burnes, James Tod, Moorcroft, Elphinstone, Wilson, Masson, Hederson, Desidei, Bernier, Taylor, Woolf, Abul Fazal's Ain-i-Akbari etc. However, nothing is known about his activities for the next twelve years. But we find him again travelling in West Indies, Mexico, New Orleans and New York in the years 1852-1853. in Nicaragua, he encountered the filibusters, and made the acquaintance of General Walker of whom he gives a vivid sketch.[58]

Vigne died at Oaks Voodford Essex, on 12th July, 1863 at the age of sixty two. At that time he was preparing an account of is recent travels for the press. This appeared in the same year under the title: *Travels in Mexico and South American*, London, 1863.[59]

Vigne was not 'a professional author nor a commissioned tourist'. He travelled for amusement, saw much, and was assisted in his observations by the possession of some knowledge of science.[60] This is true, to some extent, for it is clear that he was not in the service of the East India Company', and for 'amusement' too. Yet, it is also true that he did not travel without the encouragement of C.M. Wade, the then political Agent of Ludhiana. In fact, his travels were of reconnaissance nature, and bares the British designs in North-West India in the early 19th century. It becomes very much clear from his activities in Iskardu and Ladakh, and from the statement of Baren Charles Hugel. He writes : "Vigne an Englishman... had extended his Asiatic travels as far as Kashmir to certify that he was an agent of the East India Company".[61]

V

Victor Jacquemont (1801–1832)

Born in 1901, Victor Jacquemont was a son of a Philosopher, who was associated with Destutt de Tracy. Along with his two brothers, Jacquemont received an excellent education, as was being given in public institutions of France in those days, where ancient classics were combined with practical and scientific information, to enable the schooler to be a useful member of society.[62]

Jacquemont intimacy with victor de Tracy, a distinguished legislator made him an ideologist, whereas his acquaintance with Baron Cuvier, strengthened his attachment with natural history, which he had evinced at a very early age. However, after his schooling, he became a member of one of those political societies, so numerous in France, where metaphysical politics was debated. According to these societies, the art of Government was an 'exact science' based on principles unchangeable to the notions of the universe, that is to say that 'one coat to fit hundred individuals'.[63] However, the theories of visionary republicanism did not overshadow his good sense to separate the practical from the absurd, which is clearly discernible from his remarks about the ruler of Asiatic empire.[64]

In his twenties, Jacquemont visited Hayti and United States where his brothers were settled, in both these countries, he displayed his talent for scientific observations in remarkable degree. He was founder member of Paris Natural History Society. Perhaps this reputation helped him in securing an appointment in the museum of Natural History at Paris, on his return to France. However, through the influence of Baron Cuvier, a great naturalist, he was selected by the council of the Museum to fulfill the scientific mission to the East.[65]

With a letter of introduction from Baron Cuvier to Right Hon. Sir Alexander Johnston, Jacquemont arrived at London in 1828. He was given a flattering reception from the Royal Asiatic Society and was allowed to attend the meetings of the Asiatic Society and those of its committee of correspondence. He was at liberty to use its library and museum too, and was unanimously elected one of their foreign members.[66] However, the kind assistance of Sir Alexander Johnston enabled Jacquemont to surmount all the difficulties with which he found himself at the very start of his mission. Sir A. Johnston personally recommended him to the attention and kindness of William Bentinck, the then Governor-General of India (1828–1835), and to the Governors of Madras and Bombay, and the Commander of British Naval Force in India. The President of the Board of Control and the President of the Asiatic Society gave him letters of introduction to all the principal personages in the service of the East India Company.[67]

Jacquemont left Europe with high hopes, unconquerable spirits and a love of adventure almost quixotic, but with an affectionate heart that clung fondly to his family circle. He reached Pondicherry on 11th April 1829, and left for Calcutta on 27th April, 1829.[68] At Calcutta, he spent his time in reading almost all the existing literature, to fix his starting point for research. Combining literary with botanical studies, he read languages, maps, books, engravings too. In any case, he was confident of doing something new in India. He entered upon his project with the satisfaction that of 'all possible, if there should happen to be another possible, this is the best'.[69]

Travelling through different parts of India, Jacquemont reached Punjab in March 1831 with a view to pay visit to the capital of the Punjab where his fellow countrymen were in the service of the *Maharaja*. However, Maharaja Ranjit Singh appointed Shah Din to receive him at Phillaur with military honours. At Lahore, he was received with due honours, and a hearty reception was given by his countrymen, Messrs. Allard, Ventura and Court. After being lavishly entertained for several days, he took his leave on the 18th, and was honoured with a *Khillat* valued at 5,000 rupees in addition to a purse of Rs. 1,100. The services of horse and foot soldiers were placed at his disposal. Raja Gulab Singh was made responsible for his safe passage to Kashmir and the region beyond.[70] He formally quitted Lahore on 25th March, 1831. He travelled in the Alpine Punjab, the valley of Kashmir, and reached Gomber in higher Himalaya, and almost in Tibet. In all he spent about six months in this region, for we find him back to Amritsar around the middle of the same year. From Amritsar he returned to Shimla by way of Mandi and Bilaspur. From Shimla he returned to Delhi via Sabathu, Bassi and Ambala. On December 16th he arrived in Delhi, and stayed there for two months before undertaking the trip to the south which had so fatal a termination. He was attacked with liver complaint, while pursuing his researches in the Ilsand of Salsette. He died on 7th December, 1832 at Bombay, after lingering more than one month in intense agony.[71]

Jacquemont was a voluminous writer, and after his death seven volumes of letters and diaries were published. His letters had for some years formed a regular text-book in French schools. However, their interest for the English reader in the 1830s induced Sir Alexander Jonston to translate them into English to be published in two volumes from London in 1834, entitled : *Letters from India : Describing A Journey In the British Dominions of India, Tibet, Lahore, And Kashmir, during the year 1828, 1829, 1830, 1831, undertaken by the order of the French Government.* In the present century M. Alfred Martineau published a series of extracts from the Journal which Jacquemont kept during his travels, under the title, *The Political and Social State of Northern India in 1830.* This Journal is divided into four parts. The first three parts deals with his travels in India and Tibet. However, his travels in the dominions of Ranjit Singh are dealt with in the fourth part. The relevant portions of this part of the Journal were translated and edited by H.L.O. Garret and published in 1934 as *The Punjab A Hundred Years Ago As Described by V. Jacquemont (1831) & A. Solty Koff* (1842).[72]

Jacquemont's admirable manners, his strength and simplicity of mind, his great power of intellect and above all his warmth and sincerity of heart made him beloved by all who knew him. As a writer he was a careful observer with a trained scientific mind, and while he is on occasions clearly inaccurate, he may in the main be taken as fairly correct.[73]

VI

Baron Charles Hugel (1796)

Very little is known about the early career of Baron Charles Hugel. He was a native of Vienna, born in 1796. Use of the epithet 'Baron' may be indicative of his aristocratic social background. He joined the Austrian Army and rose to be a colonel in the horse regiment, drawing the equivalent of Rs. 2,000 a month.[74] He left the army around 1826, and five year latter in 1831, he thought of travelling through different parts of the world. Towards the end of 1834, he was on his voyage from Manila to Canton. The year following, he visited China,

Singapore, Muluccas, and the island of Penag. Travelling through different parts of the Indian sub-continent and visiting Madras, Calcutta, Benaras, Allahabad, Oudh, Agra, Delhi, he reached Massouri in June 1835.[75] From here he forwarded an application to Maharaja Ranjit Singh for his permission to travel into Kashmir. After spending nearly three months at Massouri, and waiting the requisite permission of the *Maharaja*, he moved to Shimla. At Shimla he was informed by Captain C.M. Wade, about the much waited permission in the beginning of October, 1835.[76]

He left Shimla for Kashmir on 13th October, 1835. Entering the domination of the *Maharaja* from Bilaspur, and traversing the hill principalities, then under the vassalage of the *Maharaja*, he arrived in Kashmir on 18th November, 1835.[77] Spending little over a month in the valley, he left for Lahore around 9th or 10th December 1835. On his way to the capital of the *Maharaja* he visited Baramulla, Muzaffrabad, Naushera, Hassanabdal, Atock, Rawalpindi, Mankiayala, Rohtas, Wazirabad etc. On 11th January 1836, he was at Shahdera, and the day following in the house of Ventura. He presented himself before the Maharaja in the court on 13th January 1836. On 25th January, 1836, after spending nearly a fortnight at Lahore, he left for Ludhiana. On the 26th January, we find him at Amritsar visiting the Golden Temple, and on 27th January at Kapurthala, whence he went to Phagwara and crossed the Satluj at Phillaur.[78] Altogether, he spent in the territories of the *Maharaja* about one hundred and five days.[79]

An account of his travels was published in German at Stuttgart in four parts at 'distant intervals'. It was rather highly priced : 21 16s unbound. The first and third parts comprise the entire journal of his travels in the dominions of Maharaja Ranjit Singh. The part second contains a summary account of the ancient and modern history of Kashmir abridge from Professor H.H. Wilson's paper published in the transactions of the Asiatic society; with sundry miscellaneous particulars, geographical and physical; also an account of the productions, resources and inhabitants of the mountain regions. The fourth part is a sort of glossary and gazetteer, including miscellaneous matters relating to the political, civil and military affairs of the East India Company's Government, from all of which much useful information may be gleaned. Perhaps, all the four parts were published by 1840.[80]

Imperialistic interests of the British Indian Government in 1840s, made it necessary to translate the entire journal containing information about the dominions of Maharaja Ranjit Singh. Thus by 1844, the first and third parts of his journal were ready for the press, translated and edited by T.B. Jervis, to be published in 1845 entitled, *Travels in Kashmir and the Punjab containing a particular accounts of the Government and Character of the Siksh,* from the German of Baron Charles Hugel.[81]

VII

These travellers were born were born and grew to manhood in a particular socio-political and intellectual milieu. The history of early 19th century France was marked by political unrest and popular revolts. The French Revolution set in motion a whole tide of new forces and ideas which had a great bearing on the socio-political and even the economic order of the early 19th century Europe. On the other hand, Great Britain worked hard to suppress revolutionary ideas preached by the French philosophers Montesquieu (1638–1755), Voltaire (1694–1778), Rousseau (1712–1778) etc. She sided with the traditional forces and waged a long war with France, ultimately routing them on the sea and land alike. However, a great victory, which England had achieved against the French at Waterloo, enabled her to be an international power. It had become possible largely due to her superiority in industrial and commercial techniques and a degree of national unity. Europe was still mostly agricultural and ruled by reactionary dynastic monarches.[82] At the same time Germany was a mere 'geographical expression' consisting of a thirty-nine small states. It was ruled through a 'Grand Diet', a loose sort of confederation, and its chancellor was Prince Metternich. Metternich had checked all political developments through the declaration of the Carlsbad Decrees. Nevertheless nationalism was blooming in the realm of ideas. Rather it became a part of every liberal man's outlook, tinged with the romanticism, which coloured the intellectual revival of the time.[83]

Early 19th century, European society was in flux, due to the changed socio-economic set up. The change was marked by the industrial revolution which boosted productions. For instance, in England cotton import, amongst the textile industries around 1820s, amounted to 82 million pounds. Besides textile, industries like iron, coal and engineering showed a boom after Waterloo. England had 15,000 steam engines in 1826. The great age of railway which began in 1830s turned them into one of the chief source of national wealth. Thus, Britain was a country that was fast changing its appearance. The new methods of manufacture and transport rapidly increased its wealth and power.[84]

In France the period of popular revolts was also a period of industrial revolution, though it came into its own only during the post-Napoleonic years. From 1816 to 1829, the French cotton industry tripled its production. The production of pig-iron doubled from 1818–1828. In 1818 there were 200 steam engines which touched the figures 525 by 1832.[85] However, Germany was lagging behind France and England in socio-economic sphere. Though manufacturing, mining and shipping grew fairly rapidly in the post-Napoleonic period and increased national wealth, yet the middle classes, fragmented as they were within the boundaries of thirty-nine German states, were preoccupied with parochial concerns and were unwilling, by and large, to think in terms of national interests. Thus the bulk of production was still centered in the shops of the artisans rather than in factories. The traditional guild system of master, journeyman and apprentice continued to prevail. It prevented mobility of labour and enterprise.[86]

However, industrialism conferred new wealth and power upon the growing middle class of enterprising traders, manufacturers and financiers. Also it created a new industrial working class–the proletariat. Just as the landowners were in general a bulwark of conservatism, so the middle classes were the prime mover of the societal change. Within this economic community, transcending the frontiers of politics, grew both interdependence an common impulses. Restrictions imposed on trade or manufacture by conservative governments in the interests of agriculture were resented and attacked. The new class of the wealthy demanded greater political representation and power, removal of petty restrictions and out-of-date laws, and social recognition for men whose energies and enterprise brought employment to millions. The result was a tide of liberal opinion hostile to the existing order.[87]

At this stage, the interests of the wage-earning classes coincided, to some extent, with the interests of their employers. Both wanted food to be cheap, trade unimpaired, business to prosper. On the other hand, meager wages and bad working conditions compelled them to look towards the state for the protection of their interests. In due course, this class started feeling that without political power their interests were not safe. The state, fearing them more than the middle classes, often contrived to win middle class support by timely concessions, so as to resist effectively the more far-reaching and radical demands of the workers. However, to save their interests, the working classes demanded right to vote and right of free Associations. Thus, the forces of conservatism faced a double demand, from the middle classes and of the working classes. The total effect was to revolutionize the whole meaning and function of government and politics.[88]

The leaven, however, was provided by the intellectuals. Intellectually it was the age of enlightenment. Its advocates edeavoured 'to secularize every department of human life and thought'.[89] The philosophers of the enlightenment not only provided revolutionary ideas to the people, but also gave a new sense and direction to the study of past civilizations. In Germany, for instance, while the school of romantic nationalism was still in the ascendant, a new spirit was introduced into the theory and practice of history by a great German thinker Ranke.[90] Ranke was a contemporary of Baron Charles Hugel. He was the first to make use of archives for the study of the past. Ranke divorced the study of the past as much as humanly possible from the passion of the present and wanted to describe the past simply "as it actually happened". Also, the necessity of founding historical construction on strictly contemporary sources founded the 'science of evidence' by the analysis of authorities.[91] Hugel's narrative of his travels appears to be carrying the traditions of Ranke. For instance, before giving account of his journey, Hugel started with the analysis of all the sources on Kashmir from the times of *Raj Tarangini* to the travel account of Joseph Wolff. He concluded that all the authorities on Kashmir 'are very defective before the times of the Mohammedan's'.[92]

Montesquieu, a French philosopher, preached that man was 'a part of nature and explanation of the historical events was sought in facts of the natural world'. He conceived human life as 'a reflection of geographical and climatic condition, not otherwise than the life of plants'. Thus history was to him 'a kind of natural history of man or anthropology', where institution appeared not 'as free inventions of human reasons in the course of its development, but as the necessary effects of natural causes'. Therefore, he saw 'an intimate relation between any culture and its natural environments'. Also, he laid emphasis that 'economic elements' played a vital role in the rise and fall of the nations'.[93] It is, perhaps, for this reason that Jacquemont came to the East to study 'the natural history of India in all its branches'.[94] Also we find that while commenting upon the Anglo-Sikh relations, Jacquemont was rather curious to note the relative resources of both the powers. By doing so he appears to be following the intellectual traditions set by Montesquieu.[95]

In Great Britain, English 'Radicalism' or Benthanism, as it was called after the name of its founder Jeremy Bentham (1748–1832), was making great influence on the people and politics alike. It advocated 'the greatest happiness of the greatest number'. This slogan became a touch stone of all the governmental policies in Great Britain. It was under the influence of 'utilitarianism' that Moorcroft took his long journey to central Asia, to explore new markets for British manufactures and raw material for her industrial establishment.[96] When Alexander Burnes was exploring

Central Asian markets and ascertaining the feasibility of the navigability of the river Indus, to use it as a channel of British commerce, he too appears to be expressing the philosophy of utilitarianism.[97] Charles Masson's interest in the antiquity and coins of Afghanistan appears to be influenced by the thinkers of the 'Renaissance', who made an extensive use of archaeology, paleography and numismatics for the study of past societies.[98] However, the interests of an individual traveller should not be confused with the interests of the East India Company. For all of them visited the Kingdom of Lahore in a particular historical context with varied socio-political and intellectual background. It is not to deny their connection with the East India Company directly or indirectly.

REFERENCES

1. Garry Alder, *Beyond Bokhara : The Life of William Moorcroft Asian Explorer and Pioneer Veterinary Surgeon 1767–1825,* Century Publishing, London, 1985, 3 (hereafter Beyond Bokhara); Sir Leslie Stephen and Sir Sidney Lee (eds.), *Dictionary of National Biography,* Oxford University Press, London, 1917, Vol. xiii, 784 (hereafter *Dictionary of National Biography*).
2. William Moorcroft, *Travels in the Himalyan Provinces of Hindustan and the Punjab : In Ladakh and Kashmir, In Peshawar, Kabul, Kunduz and Bokhara from 1819 to 1825,* Language Department Punjab, Patiala, 1970 (reprint-first published 1837), xviii, (hereafter *Travels*).
3. *Dictionary of National Biography,* Vol. xii, 784; Moorcroft, *Travels*, xix; Syed Muhammad Latif, *History of the Punjab,* Eurasia Publishing House, Delhi, 1964, 421.
4. Moorcroft, ' A Journey to Lake Mansarovara in Undes' *Asiatic Research,* Vol. xii, Calcutta, 1816, 380–540, *Travels*, xix-xx; *Dictionary of National Biography, 784;* Latif, *History of the Punjab*, 421–22.
5. Moorcroft, *Travels,* xxi-xxii, xxviii, 1-2; *Catalogue of Manuscripts in European Languages,* London, 1937, Vol. II, p. 890.
6. Moorcroft visited Lahore twice : first time he entered Lahore on 6th May 1820 and left it on 15th May 1820; second time, he

reached Lahore on 30th May and left it on 8th June 1820 to recommence his journey towards the hills. Moorcroft, *Travels,* 55–70; and *Catalogue of Manuscripts in European Languages,* 891.

7. Moorcroft, *Travels*, 56–64; *Dictionary of National Biography,* 784; Latif, *History of the Punjab,* 422.
8. Moorcroft, *Travels,* xxiii, xxxiii, 136–37, 150, 152, 215, 249–50,168, 270, 320; *Dictionary of National Biography,* 784; *Catalogue of Manuscripts in European Languages,* 891.
9. Moorcroft, *op.cit.*, xxxviii, 320, 331, 336–385.
10. Moorcroft, *op.cit.,* xxiii, xxiv, xxxiii, xl, xli, 489, 785.
11. Moorcroft, *op.cit.*, p. 881–883.
12. *Ibid.*
13. Moorcroft, *Travels,* xxiii-xxix.
14. In the beginning of March, 1820, Mr. Moorcroft was on his way to Lahore. He entered into the Punjab plains towards the end of August, 1820, and stepped into the territory of the ruler of Ladakh. After two year's sojourn in Ladakh, he again entered into the province of Kashmir in the month of October, 1822. After his stay at Kashmir about ten and a half months, he proceeded towards Bokhara and finally quitted the Sikh territory towards the end of May, 1824; Moorcroft, *Travels,* 23–121, 328–470; *Catalogue of Manuscripts in European Languages,* pp. 889–91.
15. Moorcroft, *op.cit.*, xli.
16. "If I fall or fail, the company will receive for my salary only the compensation of such local knowledge as I may have acquired in countries wholly new Europeans, and which will be found in my journals, deposited for transfer, in case of my death with captain Murray": Moorcroft, *ibid.*, xxiii, xli, xliii.
17. Moorcroft, *ibid.*, xliii.
18. Moorcroft, *Travels,* xlv-xlvi.
19. Moorcroft, *Travels*, xxiii.
20. *Ibid.*, xxii.
21. *Dictionary of National Biography*, III, 389; Alexander Burnes, *Travels into Bokhara; being the account of a journey from India to Kabul, Tartony and Persia; also Narrative of Voyage on the*

Indus from Sea to Lahore, Vol. III, Oxford University Press, Karachi 1973, (4th ed.), I, v-vi, (Hereafter, *Travels).*

22. Burnes, *Travels,* I, vii-viii.
23. *Dictionary of National Biography*, III, 389; Burnes, *Travels,* vii-viii; Henry T. Prinsep, *Origin of the Sikh Power in the Punjab and Political Life of Maharaja Ranjit Singh,* Language Department Punjab, Patiala 1970, 121 (Hereafter *Origin of the Sikh Power).*
24. Burnes, *Travels*, I, x, iii, 6 & 183, Prinsep, *Origin of the Sikh Power,* 125; *Dictionary of National Biography,* iii, 389–90.
25. Prinsep, *op.cit.*, 125; Burnes, *op. cit.*, I, xi-xii, 1-2.
26. Burnes, *op.cit.*, I, xii.
27. Burnes was furnished with passports as a Captain in the British army, returning to Europe, drawn out in French, English, and Persian; and in such terms as would satisfy the people of his real character; and show at the same time, that Government was interested in his good treatment : Burnes, *ibid.*, I, xxviii-xxix.
28. Burnes, *op.cit.*, I, xii.
29. *Dictionary of National Biography*, III, 390; Burnes, Burnes, *op.cit.*, I, xi-xiii.
30. Fauja Singh, *Some Aspects of State and Society under Ranjit Singh,* Master Publisher, New Delhi 1981 (hereafter *State and Society*), 235–26; Narendra Krishna Sinha, *Ranjit Singh*, A Mukherjee & Co., Calcutta, 87–88.
31. Burnes, *op.cit.*, I, xv.
32. Burnes, *op.cit.*, I, xv-xviii; *Dictionary of National Biography,* III, 390.
33. *Ibid.*
34. Burnes, *op.cit.*, I, xviii; *Dictionary of National Biography,* III, 391.
35. Burnes, *op.cit.*, I, xviii, xix, xxxi-xxxii; *Dictionary of National Biography,* III, 390-91.
36. *Catalogue of European Manuscripts,* India Office Library and Records, Vol. II, Pt. II, 1273.
37. Charles Masson, *Narrative of Various Journeys in Balochistan, Afghanistan and the Punjab*, Vol. III, Karachi, 1974, I, x-xi;

(hereafter as *Journeys*). *Catalogue of European MSS*, II, 1273.

38. Masson, *Journeys*, I, xii-xiv; Grey and Garrett, H.L.O., *European Adventures of Northern India (1785–1849)*, Language Department Punjab, Patiala, 1970 (reprint-first published 1929) 187, (hereafter *European Adventures*), *Catalogue of European MSS*, II, 1274.
39. Grey, *European Adventures*, 188; Masson, *Journeys*, xv-xvi; *Catalogue of European MSS*, II, 1275.
40. Grey, *op.cit.*, 192-193; Masson, *op.cit.*, I, viii-ix, xviii-xx; *Catalogue of European MSS*, II, 1276, 1277.
41. Wade to Masson, 5th March, 1835, quoted in Mohan Lal, *Travels in the Punjab, Afghanistan and Turkistan to Balkh, Bokhara, and Herat*, Language Department Punjab, Patiala, 1971, 374; Grey, *op.cit.*, 194-95; Masson, *op.cit.*, I, xxiii-xxiv; *Catalogue of European MSS*, 1276-77.
42. Grey, *op.cit.*, 196; Masson, *op.cit.*, I, xxiv; *Catalogue of European MSS*, 1281.
43. J.A. Norris, *The first Afghan War 1838-1842*, Cambridge University Press, 1967, 188; Grey, *op.cit.*, 199–202; Masson, *op.cit.*, I, xxiv-xxv; *Catalogue of European MSS*, II, 1277.
44. Grey, *op.cit.*, 200-02; Masson, *op.cit.*, I, xxv-xxvi; *Catalogue of European MSS*, II, 1278.
45. Grey, *op.cit.*, 202-209; Masson, *op.cit.*, I, xxvi-xxvii; *Catalogue of European MSS*, II, 1278.
46. *Catalogue of European MSS*, II, 1278-79.
47. T.H. Holdich, *The Gates of India*, 345 quoted in Grey, *op.cit.*, 178.
48. *Dictionary of National Biography*, Vol. XX, 309.
49. G.T. Vigne, *Travels in Kashmir, Ladakh, Iskardo, the countries Adjoining the Mountain Course of the Indus and the Himalayas, North of the Punjab*, Vol. II., Henry Colburn, London, 1842, I, 3 (hereafter *Travels*).
50. *Ibid.*, 19, 22.
51. Vigne, *Travels*, I, 28, 40, 46.
52. *Ibid.*, II, 195.
53. Vigne, *A Personal Narrative of a Visit to Ghazni, Kabul and Afghanistan*,

54. Vigne, *op.cit.*, II, 107-08.

55. *Ibid.*, *Narrative*, 7; *Travels*, I, 235-36; B.C. Hugel, *Travels in Kashmir and the Punjab, containing a particular Account of the Character and Government of the Sikhs* (tr. & ed. T.B. Javris), Language Department Punjab, Patiala, 1970 (reprint-first published 1845), 98 (hereafter *Travels*); Sohan Lal Suri, *Umdat-ut-Tawarikh*, 267-68, 269, 270.

56. Vigne, *op.cit.*, I, 64, II, 95, 108, 403; Sohan Lal Suri, *Umdat-ut-Tawarikh*, 552, 613, 649-50.

57. Vigne, *op.cit.*, II, 403, 410, 415, 418, 427-28.

58. *Dictionary of National Biography*, XX, 309.

59. *Dictionary of National Biography, op.cit.*

60. *Dictionary of National Biography, op.cit.*

61. Hugel, *Travels*, 98; Vigne, *Travels*, I, 19, 71; II, 195; *Dictionary of National Biography*, xx, 309.

62. Victor Jacquemont, *Letters from India : Describing a Journey in the British Dominions of India, Tibet, Lahore and Kashmir During the years 1829, 1830, 1831, under the Order of the French Government*, Vol. II, Edward Churton, London, 1834, I, i-ii (hereafter *Letters*).

63. Jacquemont, *Letters*, I, ii-iv.

64. *Ibid.*, I, iv.

65. *Ibid.*, I, iv-v, 33.

66. Jacquemont, *Letters*, I, vi, vii, xxxvi.

67. *Ibid.*, I, vi-vii, xxxvii.

68. *Ibid.*, I, xx-xxi, 89.

69. *Ibid.*, xxxvi, xxxvii, 11, 31, 47, 88-89, 104-05, 107, 111, 120, 127.

70. Suri, *Umdat-ut-Tawarikh*, Daftar III, 9, 10, 14-18, 23, 81, 83; M.F.O. Dwyer, 'Jacquemont's Letters from India', 'Review', *Journal of the Royal Central Asian Society*, Vol. 23, 234–25.

71. Jacquemont, *Letters*, I, xxxii; Victor Jacquemont & Solty Koff, *The Punjab A Hundred Years Ago* (tr & ed. H.L.O. Garret Punjab Government Record Office, Monograph No. 18, Lahore, 1831), Language Department Punjab, Patiala, 1971, 1, 60–87 (hereafter *Journal*).

72. Jacquemont, *Journal,* I; M.F.O. Dwyer, 'Review' *JRCAS,* 23, 322.
73. Jacquemont, *Letters,* I, xxxii, xxxiii; *Journal,* I.
74. Hugel, *Travels,* 234; Suri, *Umdat-ut-Tawarikh,* Daftar III, 267.
75. Hugel, *Travels,* 16-17, 234.
76. *Ibid.*, 16, 19.
77. *Ibid.*, 19, 98, 104, 144.
78. Hugel, *Travels,* 171-72, 257, 283, 285, 389, 397–400.
79. He entered into territory of Maharaja Ranjit Singh around the middle of October, 1835 and crossed the Satluj for Ludhiana towards the end of January, 1836; *Ibid.,* 21-22, 400,402.
80. Hugel, *Travels,* ii.
81. *Ibid.*, i.
82. David Thomson, *England in the Nineteenth Century (1815–1914),* Penguin, 1973, p. 25–27, 33.
83. C.D.M. Ketelbey, *A History of Modern Times from 1789,* George C. Harrap & Co., London 1964, 179–181; Lewis A Coser, *Masters of Sociological Thoughts : Ideas in Historical and Social Context,* Harcourt Brace Jovanovich, London, 1977, 30.
84. Thomson, *England in the Nineteenth Century,* 13-14.
85. Coser, *Masters of Sociological Thoughts,* 30.
86. *Ibid.,* 77.
87. Thomson, *Europe Since Napoleon,* Penguin, 1966, 117.
88. Thomson, *Europe Since Napoleon,* 118-19.
89. R.G. Collingwood, *The Idea of History,* Oxford University Press, London 1976, 76–81.
90. In Germany, Fichte, Hegel and his Successor Stein, all extolled the German ideas through their works to recreate Germany's historical greatness : Ketelbey, *A History of Modern Times,* 180-81.
91. G.P. Gooch, *History and Historian in the Nineteenth Century, Longmans,* London, 1967, 87, 97.
92. Hugel, *Travels,* 1–12.
93. Collongwood, *The Idea of History,* 78-79; Also see, Gooch, *History and Historians,* 4, 10.

94. Jacquemont, *Letters*, I, v.

95. *Ibid.*, II, 118.

96. Jeremy Bentham and his followers, James Mill and his son John Stuart Mill, dominated English radical thought throughout the 19th Century : Thomson, *England in the Nineteenth Century,* 30.

97. Cunningham, *History of the Sikhs,* 174.

98. Gooch, *History and Historian,* 5; See also, Coolingwood, *The Idea of History, 62.*

2
Historical Context

European travellers to the Punjab remained active for about two decades. William Moorcroft started his travel in the year 1819 and the travels of Charles Masson and G.T. Vigne ended in the year 1840. The period of travel activities more or less co-incides with the period of consolidation as well as expansion of the domain in the west by Maharaja Ranjit Singh. Hence, the travels become all the more significant. In order to understand in their right perspective, a look into the historical context this period is essential.

I

At the end of eighteenth century, Ranjit Singh was a rising power in the Punjab. He was a son of Sardar Mahan Singh, a sardar of Sukerchakya Misl. Sardar Mahan Singh left him a patrimony of "a well administered, large, almost contiguous territory expanding from the middle of Rachna through the middle Chaj to the middle of Sindh Sagar Doab" on his death in 1790.[1] Besides a number of scattered vassals who were expected to pay an annual tribute, over 5,000 horsemen armed with matchlocks and legacy of conflict with the ruler of Gujarat and his allies was also inherited.[2]

Before the close of the eighteenth century two significant events took place in the life of Ranjit Singh, that went a long way in increasing and consolidating his position. His marriage with Mehtab Kaur in 1795 cemented the implied political alliance between the house of Sukrachakya and the house of the Kanhiyas. In 1798, he forged another important link by marrying the daughter of a Nakkai Chief. These three houses now formed a formidable alliance. Precisely because of this, a number of Sikh chiefs accepted Ranjit Singh a common leader in the face of a common threat to the Punjab from Zamah Shah. Consequently, he emerged as the most powerful single Sikh leader among the Sikh chiefs of the late eighteenth century.[3]

The way Ranjit Singh showed gallantry and courage during Zaman Shah's occupation of Lahore in 1798, convinced citizens that he was more promising protector to the people of Lahore than the then Bhangi ruler; Sahib Singh, Chait Singh and Mohar Singh.[4] Consequently, the leading citizens of Lahore requested Ranjit Singh, assuring their full cooperation, to come and take over the city.[5] The offer was too good to be missed. Without experiencing much resistance Ranjit Singh became the master of Lahore on 7th July, 1799.[6]

Ranjit Singh's occupation of Lahore, however, did not go uncontested. The Challenge came from Nizamuddin of Kasur, Gulab Singh Bhangi, Sahib Singh of Gujarat and Jassa Singh Ramgarhia. Nevertheless, no battle was fought due to the death of Gulab Singh Bhangi. This Latter's death demoralized the other allies, who decided to decamp rather than fight. After this the Sikh chieftains never had "a second chance of uniting and far less of overthrowing him."[7] Thus Ranjit Singh's control over Lahore became an established fact which symbolized his political hold over the Punjab.[8]

Ranjit Singh went on liquidating the Sikhs and non-Sikh chiefs alike in a very systematic way. At first he paid attention to those who had dared to challenge him at Bhasin. Sahib Singh Bhangi and Dal Singh of Akalgarh were routed individually at Gujarat and Akalgarh. The territory of Dal Singh was occupied soon after his death while Sahib Singh could only save himself through the intercession of Baba Sahib Singh Bedi. Nizamuddin of Qasur was made to accept Ranjit Singh's over lordship. He had to buy peace by sending his younger brother Kutubuddin as hostage and a promise of yearly tribute. These impressive successes were followed by holding of a grand *darbar* at Lahore in 1801, at which Ranjit Singh proclaimed himself the Maharaja of the Punjab, and struk the first Nanakshahi coin.[9]

In 1802, Ranjit Singh met Fateh Singh Ahluwalia at Taran Taran and exchanged turbans as a token of friendship. The resources of four misls : the Sukerchakya, the Kanhiya, the Nakkai and the Ahluwalia were now united. N.K. Sinha calls these alliances 'as the ladder by which Ranjit Singh climbed to supermacy'.[10] However the initiative always rested with the Lahore chief. Now Ranjit Singh turned his troops toward Sansar Chand. The latter was forced to raise the siege of Lakhanpur. The fort of Naushera was taken from the chief. Jamke was taken from Sahib Singh and his ally Nizamaddin of Qasur was chastised. In 1803, the city of Multan was taken, but it was evacutated after Muzaffar Khan agreed to pay yearly tribute. The chiefs of Jang, Sahiwal and Sujanpur too were subdued. Phagwara was taken to be given to Fateh Singh Ahluwalia. In 1805, the widow of Gulab Singh Bhangi, Mai Sukhan was forced to yield Amritsar. Thus, the most important religious centre of the Sikhs too passed under the sway of Ranjit Singh.[11]

At the end of 1805, the Maharaja had established his supremacy over the six misls in the north of the river Satluj. His ardent desire to subdue the southern misls so as to unite them into 'a single powerful Khalsa state, led him to cross the river Satluj thrice.[12] He led his first expedition into the cis-Satluj region in 1806. The opportunity was provided by a dispute between the Patiala and Nabha States over a village called Dalaudi. Both the parties accepted his verdict and over lordship too. On the way back from Patiala, a number of chiefs were obliged to pay tribute to the *Maharaja* which extended his influence considerably. Next year, Ranjit Singh again invited to settle a dispute between the *Raja* of Partiala and his wife Rani Aas Kaur. He crossed the river Satluj at Harike, and forced a number of chiefs to pay tribute. Besides territories of several chiefs were annexed. This frightened the Malwa chiefs and they decided to send a deputation to see the British Resident at Delhi and implore for British protection against the *Maharaja*.[13] However, at this stage the British did not give an encouraging reply to the Malwa chiefs.[14]

But soon the situation changed and the very next year British envoy Charles Metcalfe waited upon the Maharaja to plead for a defensive alliance against a possible Russo-French invasion from the north-west. While the negotiation was going on, Ranjit Singh again crossed the river Satluj in 1808 alongwith the British envoy. The chiefs of Malerkotla, Shahbad and Thanesar paid tribute to the *Maharaja*. Faridkot and territory of Rani Daya Kaur of Ambala were taken over, and the *Raja* of Patiala felt proud in exchanging his turban with the *Maharaja*. However, in due course the British took the decision that Ranjit Singh could not be allowed to have his political supremacy south of the river Satluj. Even they were determined to execute their plan with force. Consequently, Ranjit Singh had two options: to fight or to yield to the British. He decided in favour of the second alternative. Hence a treaty of friendship was signed at Amritsar on April 25, 1809, fixing the river Satluj as the boundary between the two states. All the cis-Satluj misls thus came under British protectorate.[15]

Thus checked in the east by the British, Ranjit Singh looked towards north-west. From the year 1809 to 1831 the process of conquests and consolidation went on simultaneously. The *Maharaja* was prone to push his frontier up to the natural line of defence. His arms did not stop even at the river Indus. He continued his marches up to the Sulaiman mountains. Dr. Fauja Singh is apt to remark : "the same considerations of security which had pushed the borders of the Sikh kingdom to the left bank of the Indus egged on the *Maharaja* to proceed further in search of a more dependable frontier line."[16] For, unless firm control was established over the whole territorial belt between the river Indus and the Sulaimans mountains, Afghan hordes could easily make their way through the passage in the mountains and concentrate on the right bank of the river Indus thereby threatening the peace of the Sikh dominions.[17]

In the process of acquisition of political power and maintaining it, Maharaja Ranjit Singh made an effective use of several institutions such as : vassalage, *jagirdari*, military and civil administration etc. In principal, the overlord asserted his political control over the subordinate chiefs while leaving the actual administration of a territory in his hand. The subordinate chief could not enter into political alliance with any other power, whether sovereign or subordinate. As a token of his submission, the subordinate chief had to pay annual tribute and to supply contingents whenever he was required to do so. To ensure to continuity of his submission he was generally asked to send hostage. In order to impose these terms on his successor, the suzerain reserved the right to acknowledge or not to acknowledge his succession. While imposing these terms, no difference between the Sikh and non-Sikh chiefs.[18]

In Many instances vassalage was used as prelude to the eventual annexation of the territories of a subordinate chief. The number of autonomous chieftaincy which Ranjit Singh subverted during his reign was in scores, and nearly half of them were first made subordinate.[19] For example, Dear Ghazi Khan, Dera Ismail Khan, Bannu, Kohat, Tank etc. were subdued in the 1820s but remained tributary till these were formally annexed to the Kingdom of Lahore in 1831. Peshawar remained tributary from 1818 till 1834 when it was placed under direct control of the Lahore *Durbar*. So was the case of Multan. It was tributary from 1802 till 1818.[20] Even the Nakkai, Kanhiya, Ramgarhya and Ahluwalia chiefs too were reduced to vassalage in due course. However, all the contemporary accounts confirm that *Maharaja's* hold over his vassals was quite strong.[21]

The most important instrument for the acquision of power was, of course, the army. Ranjit Singh had inherited from his father 5,000 horsemen mostly armed with matchlocks. In 1810, he could muster 15,000 horsemen. He had three regiments of cavalry regularly trained on European line, consisting of about 850 horsemen in 1820. In the early 1830s, the number of regular cavalry was more than 4,000 and the strength of the irregular cavalry was about 10,000. The *Jagirdari* troops were in addition to this cavalry.[22] Two new wings were introduced in army of infantry and artillery. Metcalf noticed that Ranjit

Singh had about 1,500 infantry men, mostly deserters from East India company's army in 1808. Around 1820, the number of trained infantrymen was 10,000 besides 8,000 piadas ment for guard and garrison duties. The total number of guns was now 200. Horse artillery had been introduced. Arms and ammunition were manufactured at Lahore, Amritsar and some other places, with increasing improvement in their quality and effect.[23]

In the beginning of the third decade of the nineteenth century European officers were employed to raise the efficiency as well as the strength of the army which by now consisted largely of the Punjabis. By 1831, there were 21 battalions of about 20,000 men while the number of irregular infantry rose to 24,000. The artillery included about 300 guns at this time. Altogether the number of men in his army touched the figures of 90,000.[24]

To perpetuate his power, the *Maharaja* made an effective use of the *Jagirdari* system. Cash payments were generally made to the men and officers of the regular army and to some *kardars.*[25] Most of the higher functionaries in the civil government, both in the centre and the province, were remunerated through *jagirs*. Not only the fallen chiefs and their important *jagirdars* but also some of the vassal chiefs were employed by the *Maharaja* in his service. Non-*Punjabis* even foreigners came to serve him. However, his hold over his *jagirdars* was quite tight. A word from the *Maharaja's* lips could reduce a noble to a beggar.[26] Besides, controlling succession transfer of *jagirs* too was practiced. The 'fiefs' granted by Ranjit Singh were worth of revenue of 1,09,2800 rupees and could be "withdrawn at any time by his arbitrary will or command".[27]

Furthermore, patronage was extended to the members of various communities. Revenue free grants given by the Mughals and early Sikh rulers to the Muslim, Hindu and Sikh establishments were confirmed invariably. Besides, fresh *dharmaarth* grants were given to the Sikh, Hindu and Muslim establishments and men of know piety.[28] In short, by bestowing *jagirs* on individuals and families from all important castes and communities of the Punjab, the *Maharaja* created and maintained their interests in various region of his kingdom. Their influence among the common people made them useful allies of the state.[29]

Yet another measure which Ranjit Singh adopted for the maintenance of his power was the introduction of large number of institutionalization. With the expansion of territories the secretariat called *daftar-i-'alla'* was also expanded.[30] For administrative purpose the entire territory was divided into primary units called suba, placed under the *nazim*. Every primary division consisted of a number of small units known as *parganas* or *taulluqas*, placed under the *kardar* assisted by *qanungos*, *chaudharis*, and *muqqadams*. However, the smallest unit of administration was a village where *patwari* and *chaudhari* were generally the important functionaries. They were aided by the village *panchayat*. Without any doubt, these institutions were working before the *Maharaja* came into power. The significance lies in the fact that by the standard of the times the arrangements made by Ranjit Singh were both 'elaborate and efficient'.[31]

Thus in 1831, the kingdom of Lahore was at the zenith of its glory. The work of consolidation was almost complete. All the civil and military institutions were functioning well. The might of the *Maharaja* was felt all around. Now Sindh received his attention. For having control to the sea, and through this channel he could have established relations with other powers.[32]

II

A brief look into the Anglo-Sikh relations and the developments in Central Asia, may give us an idea of the interests of the East India Company in the Punjab, Sind and Afghanistan. From the year 1809, when the Amritsar agreement was signed till 1818, we notice no serious problem coming up between the two powers. The reason being that both were busy in their own problems.[33] The *Maharaja* was busy in conquest and consolidation in the north and west. While the British were involved in their campaigns against the *Pindaris, Marathas* and *Gurkahs*. The *Pindaris* and *Marathas* acting in concert presented the most formidable challenge to the British. To make matter worst, while this trouble was brewing and causing concern to the British, the war with the *Gurkhas* of Nepal came upon them. What they needed most at this time was perfect peace on their frontier and they were happy to see that the Maharaja was involved in his own problems and was in no position to exploit their difficulties.[34] The British were hardly free from their entanglements in central and north India when war broke out with Burma in 1824 which dragged on for two year. However, the British came out victorious. About the same time, the famous fort of Bharatpur too fell.[35]

Thus, by the middle of the twenties the British had become undisputed masters of India. The only parts of the country lying outside their jurisdiction were Sindh and Punjab.[36] The great success they had achieved and the absence of any more serious challenge to their sway brought about a marked change become noticeable from 1826 onwards in their policy towards Ranjit Singh even though outwardly every respect continued to be shown to the Treaty of Amritsar. For instance, when Sayid Ahmed (1826–1831) launched a religious war against the Sikhs in 1826, the collections of funds and volunteers in Delhi, Agra and in other *Wahahbi* centre in north India were within the knowledge of the British authorities who did not move even their tiny little finger to stop or discourage them.[37] What is more, when Ranjit Singh's troops were busy in quelling the activities of Sayid Ahmed, the British were trying to assert their protectorate over the territories in the cis-Satluj region which belonged to the *Maharaja*.[38]

A more crucial factor which changed British attitude towards the Punjab was the increased Russian influence in the Persian court. The Russian advance towards Persia had started in the opening decades of the nineteenth century. Gradually its influence in the Persian territory of the Caucasus became considerable and the Persian provinces of Georgia and Armenia passed under its sway.[39] The Treaty of Gulistan (1813) Virtually turned the Caspian see into a Russian Lake by depriving Persia of 'the right to maintain any war ships' in the sea.[40] As a counterpoise to this, Persia concluded a treaty with Great Britain in 1814 at Tehran. Accordingly the British Pledged to go to the aid of Persia if she was attacked by a European power, either by sending arms or by providing a subsidy.[41]

Undeterred by this pledge the Russian troops occupied Gokcha. The British did not help the Shah. The Russians utterly routed the Persians at Tabriz and imposed a humiliating treaty of Turkomanchi in February 1828 on the Shah of Persia. Besides, consenting to pay a huge indemnity, the Persians ceded Azarbijan and some other fertile provinces to Russia. Henceforth, Persia became subservient to Russia.[42]

Consequently, Russian military officers in large numbers descended upon Tehran and assumed the functions of instructors and commanders. In order to prevent Persia to brood over her losses to Russia, a deliberate attempt was made to coax and encourage the Shah of Persia to entertain ideas of expansion towards Afghanistan, Khiva, Khorasan and Bokhara. Soon a plan was crystallized into a campaign against Heart, the Afghan town standing on the western flank of the Hindu Kush and guarding the road to Kandhar and India.[43] Heart was the key to Kabul and a combined Russo-Persian campaign for its possession was considered a big possibility. Though India was much more remote yet it was thought that if Heart was occupied by Persia, her ally Russia may poise a serious threat to British India.[44]

Thus in 1830s the British's fear of Russian was at its peak. On third September, 1829, Lord Ellenborough noted in his political diary : "The Director are much afraid of the Russians. So am I, and the Russians begin to threaten us. They hint that they have open to them the route to Baghdad, and they announce the presence in Petersburg of an Afghan Chief, and of ambassadors from Ranjeet Singh. I feel confident we shall have to fight the Russians on the Indus, and I have long had a presentiment that I should meet them there, and gain a great battle, All dreams, but I have had them a long time".[45] Elsewhere, he noted : "upon the subject of the invasion of

India my idea is that the thing is not only practical but easy, unless we determined to act as an Asiatic power. On the acquisition of Khiva by the Russians we should occupy Lahore and Kabul. It is not on the Indus that an enemy is to be met. If we do not meet him in Kabul, at the foot of the Hindu Koosh, or its passes, we had better remain on the Satluj. If the Russian once occupy Kabul they may remain on the Satluj. If the Russian once occupy Kabul they may remain there with the Indus in their front, till they have organized insurrection in our rear, and completely equipped their army..."[46] As a result a great fear called 'Russo-Phobia' came to grip the minds of the British who in all seriousness engaged themselves in devising counter-measure in self-defence. One such measure was to know about the peoples, the politics, the state of commerce, the mutal relations of different chiefs and above all, the geographical as well as topographical information about the countries lying between the British frontier and the Caspian sea.

This was the era of long and dangerous journeys among the Khanates of Central Asia, by both the Russian and the British travellers to probe the local political combinations and material resources. Nikolai Nikolaievich Muraviev a Russian envoy visited Khiva in 1819-20 and asserted that the possession of Khiva could give Russia a command of all the riches of Asia. He commented : "it would become the point of reunion for all the commerce for all the commerce of Asia, and would shake to the centre of India the enormous commercial superiority of the dominators of the sea."[47] But the Russians were not alone in expecting great advantage from the development of trade with states of Central Asia. When Nikalai was visiting Khiva, William Moorcroft was trying his best to survey the Ladakh end of the route beyond the Himalayas which he hoped that the Tibetian would one day allow him to open up from Niti and Joshimath as the main British commercial high road to Central Asia. Also he wished to examine the mysterious and secret short-cut to Yarkand, by which he believed Ladakh had been invaded by armies in the past, and hoped Central Asia would be invaded by British goods in future.[48]

William Moorcroft was the first to inform his masters about the Russian penetration across the Karakoram into Ladakh and Kashmir as back as in 1808. This job was performed by a mysterious Aga Mehdi on the instructions from the Russian Foreign Ministry and in the guise of merchant from Yarkand. Along this route subsequently came Russian and European goods which were exchanged mainly for Kashmir shawls. Agha Mehdi himself returned several times, narrowly missing an encounter with William Moorcroft in 1812. However, during his residence at Ladakh, Moorcroft came across a letter from the Tsar to the *Raja* of Ladakh which Agha Mehdi had brought some six years before. He was also bearer of a letter to Maharaja Ranjit Singh, the ruler of the Punjab.[49]

However, the missions of both of them were not dissimilar in purpose. The Russians were trying as hard as the British to gain access to the secrets of the Kashmiri shawl weavers. One can see the mixture of rivalry and respect which was such a typical feature of many of the later encounters of the British and the Russian emissaries on the border lands of the empires in Asia.[50] In fact there lay policies of utmost seriousness. Why should the Cabinet of Imperial Russia be devoting so much treasure and efforts to the cultivation of political and trading connections with kingdom so remote from its own frontiers? It could hardly be trade alone. The underlying aim of the Russians seemed to be to open up an entirely new and unexpected approach to Hindustan from the north by way of to Leh, and onwards from there into Kashmir and the Punjab. It was believed where caravans and pack-animals could go, armies could follow, especially the armies of irregular horsemen of the kind Central Asia had known since the days of the Huns and Chenghiz Khan.[51] It was confirmed by Moorcroft that armies of this kind had, in past, reached Ladakh from the north. In one case they had come by a mysterious but apparently much easier route from Khoten further east, which halved the journey from Yarkand to Leh and opened up an easy, direct approach, not only to the plateau of western Tibet but to the plains opposite Delhi. During his stay at Ladakh Moorcroft made it his concern to explore Ladakh end of it near the Pangong Lake. He was convinced that the omniscient

Agha Mehdi had already discovered this short cut and reported it in detail to his paymasters at St. Petersburg.[52]

It was further feared that if the Chinese Turkestan became a Russian province, several dire consequences might follow. For Russia, it was 'by no means impossible'. The consequences, if China's trade became Russia' or if European technology became China's, would be immeasurable. The annihilation of Britain's tea trade alone could be catastrophic. Its loss was summarized as "the cost as two millions of pounds annually to the Exchequer, the comforts of the whole population of Great Britain to whom tea is now become a necessity of life, the employment of an immense capital and the subsistence of thousand's."[53]

Though around 1822, Russia was still as important British ally in Europe as Ranjit Singh was in India yet thin military presence in northern India was dependent on the Sikh good will. In 1822, just at the end of a long period of war and territorial expansion, the Calcutta authorities simply could not contemplate the fresh risk of expansion and commitment in unheard of lands beyond the Himalaya. Even if, they had, London would have overruled them.[54]

By the end of the second decade of the 19th century, the genesis of Anglo-Russian rivalry in the Greek War of Independence became visible from 1821 onwards, the Russians, making use of the vague rights accorded to them in the treaty of Kutehuk Kainardji in 1774, kept up a constant pressure on the Ottoman Porte, on behalf of the Sultan's Christian subjects. The British Government hoped by diplomatic means to keep the peace between Russia and Turkey. Both Castlereagh and Canning aimed at reaching a settlement of the quarrel between the Sultan and his Greek subjects. Canning was of the opinion that peace between Russia and Turkey was essential, for the preservation of the balance of power in Europe and to maintain the Ottoman Empire. At the same time, it was essential to maintain the larger interest of Britain's position in Asia. Canning laboured hard till his death to prevent Russia from intervening alone and to construct a Greek settlement which the Sultan might be brought to accept after the minimum of coercion.[55] The situation became more complex around 1828. Turkey and Russia had gone at war in the beginning of 1828. Britain was still bound by the treaty of London to prevent hostility between Turkey and Greece, and, with some reluctance Duke of Wellington allowed the French to Flush the remaining Turkish/Egyptian troops out of Morea in the summer and autumn of 1828. But Britain remained neutral in the dispute between Russia and Turkey. Wellington viewed the Russian proceedings with extreme distaste, never deluding himself that the Turks might win.[56] In any case, how the British responded to the Russian move toward central Asia, becomes clear from the purpose and nature of information which these travellers collected while visiting the dominions of Maharaja Ranjit Singh.

REFERENCES

1. J.S. Grewal, *The Reign of Maharaja Ranjit Singh : Structure of Power, Economy and Society,* Punjabi University, Patiala, 1981, 3, (hereafter *The Reign of Maharaja Ranjit Singh*).
2. Grewal, *The Reign of Maharaja Ranjit Singh,* 22.
3. Fauja Singh, *State and Society*, 7-9; Grewal, *The Reign of Maharaja Ranjit Singh,* 3; and also, *Maharaja Ranjit Singh, Guru Nanak Dev University,* Amritsar, 1982, 24–28.
4. Shah's supply lines were cut off and Ranjit Singh personally went close to the fort of Lahore to challenge Shah Zaman to a duel. He shouted aloud : 'O grandson of Ahmad Shah, the grandson of Sardar Charhat Singh is here, come out and measure swords with him', Grewal, *Maharaja Ranjit Singh,* 28; See also, Sinha, *Ranjit Singh,* 10-11.
5. The Most prominent among the people extending the invitation to Ranjit Singh were Mian Ashiq Muhammad, Mufti Muhammad Mukarram, Mian Mohkam Din, Mir Shadi, Hakim Rai and Gurbaksh Singh; Fauja Singh, *State and Society,* 9; Also see, Grewal, *Maharaja Ranjit Singh*, 29.
6. Fauja Singh, *State and Society,* 9; Sinha, *Ranjit Singh,* 7-13; Grewal *Maharaja Ranjit Singh*, See also, J.D. Cunningham, *History of the Sikhs*, Low Price Publications, Delhi, 1990, 107-08 (reprint-first published 1849).

7. Fauja Singh, *op.cit.*, p.9-10; Sinha, *op.cit.*, 13; Prinsep, *Origin of the Sikh Power,* 42; J.D. Cunningham, *op.cit.*, 118; Also see, Grewal, *op.cit.*, 30.
8. Fauja Singh, *op.cit.*, 10; See also, Grewal, *op.cit.*, 29.
9. Fauja Singh, *op.cit.*, 10; Grewal, *op.cit.*, 30–32; See also , Sinha, *op.cit.*, 14-15.
10. Sinha, *op.cit.*, 14-15; Fauja Singh, *op.cit.*, 10-11; See also, Grewal, *op.cit.*, 31.
11. Sinha, *op.cit.*, 14-15; Grewal, *op.cit.*, 30, 31, 32; Fauja Singh, *op.cit.*, 10-11.
12. Fauja Singh, *op.cit.*, 11.
13. *Ibid.*, Sinha, *op.cit.*, 21-22, 23, 25–35; 39; See also, Grewal, *op.cit.*, 36-38.
14. Fauja Singh, *op.cit.*, 12; Sinha, *op.cit.*, 23.
15. Sinha, *op.cit.*, 26; Grewal, *op.cit.*, 39; and also, Cunningham, *op.cit.*, 122.
16. Fauja Singh, *op.cit.*, 294–328.
17. *Ibid.*, 304.
18. Grewal, *The Reign of Maharaja Ranjit Singh,* 4; See also, Indu Banga, *Agrarian System of the Sikhs : Late Eighteenth and Early Nineteenth Century,* Manohar Publication, New Delhi, 1978, 39,46,49,50-51 (hereafter *Agrarian System*).
19. In the hills areas under the vassals considerably increased because of the bestowal of new territories on the Dogra chiefs before or after conquest : Grewal, *The Reign of Maharaja Ranjit Singh,* 4, 7.
20. Fauja Singh, *State and Society,* 302-09, 318; Also see, *Sinha, Ranjit Singh,* 4-5; Moorcroft, *Travels,* 27-28, 76, 78, 107; Also see, Jacquemont, *Letters,* II, 63, 74, 104–41, 397.
21. Grewal, *op.cit.*, 4-5; Moorcroft, *op.cit.*, 27-28, 76, 78, 107; Also see, Jacquemont, *op.cit.*, II, 63, 74, 140-41, 397.
22. Grewal, *op.cit.*, 5; F.S. Bajwa, *Military System of the Sikhs,* Motilal Banarsidass, Delhi, 1964, 37–61.
23. Grewal, *op.cit.*, 5-6.
24. *Ibid.*, 6; Also, *Maharaja Ranjit Singh,* 70; F.S. Bajwa, *op.cit.*, 61-75.

25. Grewal, *op.cit.*, 8.
26. Hugel, *Travels,* 158,230.
27. *Ibid.*, 193, 369, 404.
28. Indu Banga, *Agrarian System,* 148–167.
29. Grewal, *op.cit.*, 8-9; See also, Indu Banga, *op.cit.*, 8.
30. Grewal, *op.cit.*, 8.
31. Indu Banga, *op.cit.*, 63-87.
32. Cunningham, *op.cit.*, 172-73; Also see, Sinha, *Ranjit Singh,* 117–23.
33. Fauja Singh, *State and Society*, 239-343; See also, Sinha, *op.cit.*, 71–77.
34. Grewal, *op.cit.*, 44–53; Sinha, *op.cit.*,41–49; Fauja Singh, *op.cit.*, 342–43; Bisheshwar Prashad, *Bondange and Freedom : A History of Modern India 1707–1947,* Vol. II, Rajesh Publications, New Delhi, 1981, I, 150, 178, 218-19, 221, 234–42; Percival Spear, *The Oxford History of Modern India 1740–1975,* Oxford University Press, Delhi, 1971, 121-28.
35. Bisheswar Prashad, *op.cit.*, 242–53; Spear, *op.cit.*, 151–54.
36. Bisheswar Prashad, *op.cit.*, I, 256-57; See also, Spear, *op.cit.*, 163–75.
37. *Foreign Political Proceedings*, 17 June 1831, No.41, quoted by Sinha, *Ranjit Singh,* 80; See also, Fauja Singh, *State and Society,* 346.
38. Fauja Singh, *op.cit.*, 345-46; Sinha, *op.cit.*, 74–77.
39. Bikramjit Hasrat, *Anglo-Sikh Relations, 1799–1849,* V.V.I., Hoshiarpur, 1968, 148; Also see, Fauja Singh, *op.cit.*, 348.
40. Bisheswar Prashad, *op.cit.*, I, 258; Also see, Norris, *The First Afghan War,* 21-22.
41. Fauja Singh, *op.cit.*, 348; See also, Norris, *op.cit.*, 21.
42. Bisheswar Prashad, *op.cit.*, 258; Norris, *op.cit.*, 21–23; Also see, Fauja Singh, *op.cit.*, 348.
43. Fauja Singh, *op.cit.*, 348; Also see, Bisheswar Prashad, *op.cit.*, I, 259-260.
44. Hasrat, *Anglo-Sikh Relations*, 149.
45. Ellenborough's *Political Diary*, quoted in J.A. Norris, *The First Afghan War,* 18.

46. *Ibid.*, 30.
47. Nikolai Nidolaievich Muraviev, *Journey in turkmenia*...1822, quoted in Norris, *The First Afghan War*, 19, 458.
48. Garry Alder, *Beyond Bokhara*, 274; Moorcroft, *Travels*, 153, 215, 222-233.
49. Agha Mehdi is known to the Russian Historians as Mekh Rajailov; Alder, *Beyond Bokhara*, 264-65; Also see, Moorcroft, *Travels*, 228–30.
50. Alder, *Beyond Bokhara*, 265; Also see, Moorcroft, *op.cit.*, 366–85.
51. For the ancient Silk Route see, Andra Gunder Frank, "The Centrality of Central Asia", *Studies in History*, Vol. VIII, No. I, 1992; 43–113.
52. Garry Alder, *op.cit.*, 265-66; Moorcroft, *op.cit.*, 206-08, 215, 217-18, 222.
53. Garry Alder, *op.cit.*, 267.
54. *Ibid.*, 283.
55. Norris, *op.cit.*, 19-20.
56. *Ibid.*

3

The Purpose and Nature of Travel Literature

The European travellers who visited the Punjab in early nineteenth century had diverse socio-cultural background and varied motives and interest. The travel literature covers different areas and also reflects the diversity in the treatment. These accounts are significant to understand the history of the Punjab under Maharaja Ranjit Singh and expansionist designs of British imperialism in India. Information on society, economy and policy is of much value. However, in order to understand these historical works in their proper perspective, their nature and purpose need to be examined.

I

The composition of the party of Mr. William Moorcroft which accompanied him, raises doubt about the nature of the mission. Right from the very start, there was an ambiguity about the whole project. The official purpose of the mission, as defined in Moorcroft's leave of absence was entirely confined to horses and his substantial salary as stud superintendent continued to be paid through the military department as usual. Also, he was said to have given no formal political functions whatsoever and was roundly rebuked when he began to exercise them. However, permission for the journey, and correspondence about its details, was entirely kept in the hands of the political department that the board claimed that they had no official information of it at all.[1]

Moorcroft says that his ulterior motive was to penetrate into Turkistan to get 'best horses in Asia' and to domesticate them in India for cavalry.[2] For the special purpose of their own cavalry, the East India Company had instituted a stud for the purposes of improving breeds of horses indigenous in Hindustan. However, the necessity of obtaining a scientific superintendent from England suggests that the purpose had not been sufficiently served.[3]

The Court of Directors used to send a few stallions from England, every year. Remaining were furnished either by the stud or by purchase. But these were unequal to the demand of the cavalry. The authorities at India were anxious to meet the deficiency by purchasing horses from Calcutta market. But the horses purchased were, sometime, discarded as unfit for the cavalry purpose at the stud.[4] This kind of situation was quite awkward and embarrassing for Moorcroft. In a letter to his friend, he stated about the stud affair; "If I expressed not my disapprobation of horses I considered unsuitable, I should obviously neglect my duty, and when I represent such unsuitableness after purchase, the opinion cannot fail to give umbrage to the party so purchasing. Whilst I remain at the stud, my opportunities of purchasing suitable horses are, of course, very limited. What is to be done"?[5]

In order to improve the situation, Moorcroft strongly recommended 'an infusion of the bone and blood' of Turkman or English horse, in preference to the Arab horse. His recommendations were, at one time, so favourably considered by the authorities in India, that he was asked to select 'a batch of suitable stallions' from England. However, the plan was left in between.[6] He was left with but one alternative; that was to get the Turkman steed. Explicitly, for this purpose in view, he undertook his journey to Balkh and Bokhara.[7] Even the official letter signed by Charles Metcalf, then incharge of the political department at Calcutta, states that he was granted leave "to proceed towards the North-Western parts of Asia, for the purpose there procuring by commercial intercourse horses to improve the bread within the British provinces for military use'.[8]

But it appears to be only a part of a wider dream and enterprise which Moorcroft and his associates code-named 'the Himalaya concern'. This was no less than to test the feasibility of capturing the trade of inner Asia for British woolen, cotton and industrial goods. He was deeply concerned about post-war depression at home and was anxious to boost its economy by opening up Asian markets for British goods.[9] Besides, Moorcroft was also interested in the shawl trade. He believed that the failure in Scotland to rear and breed from the goats, he brought from Tibet in 1812, was the result of careless management; but even if the goats themselves were not available to British industry, there fine wool could be. Since 1812, one Moorcroft's abiding ambitions had been to unravel the secret of the ancient craft of shawl weaving and by harnessing British technology to that ancient craft, capture for Britain the incrative shawl markets of Europe.[10] But Moorcroft did not declare such an aim too openly in his official correspondence at first. More prudently, he argued that the best and the safest way of paying for the horses, would be not by bills or bullion but by barter.[11]

A little commerce hitherto carried on from British India across the Himalaya to the Tartary, from Lhasa up to Yarkand, was almost wholly in the hands of the Kashmiris. They were pursuing their trade with a regular routine, undisturbed by foreign competition or by influx of new articles of merchandise. Favoured by local and political peculiarities, they were successfully keeping a closed barrier against the extension of commerce except by their own channel. Thus effecting a monopoly, they drew their profits from high prices upon a very limited import of manufactures, and from comparatively low prices of grain and raw maertials.[12] having this end in view, Moorcroft, while asking the government to permit him to secure horses from Turkistan, obtained permission to carry with him such articles of merchandise which the thought were likely to be most in demand. Equipped with this favour, he induced two of the mercantile firms of Calcutta, to entrust to his care a supply of goods to the value of about three thousands pounds. Some of the goods were sold or exchanged in Kashmir for shawls. Subsequently, he added to his stock about two thousands pounds worth of coral and pearls. The profit from these articles was, ultimately, intended to be spent in the purchase of horses. At the first instance, these were to be offered to the government for sale, if disapproved of, were to be disposed off through other channels.[13]

For these reasons, Moorcroft intended to reach Leh, the capital of Ladakh, situated beyond the Himalaya on the upper reaches of the Indus. Leh seemed to him to be not only the best place to tap the shawl wool coming down from Tibet and divest it into British territory, but also the best springboard from which to launch an assault on the markets of Central Asia to the North and West. By appearing on the summit of the Niti Pass and by a judicious mixture of bluff, bribery and bloody mindedness, push his way into Tibet to follow the Lhasa-Leh caravan trail to Ladakh.[14] Ladakh itself would offer only a limited market for British manufactured goods, but its role as emporium and depot was important. It stood at the heart of a network of traditional caravan trails radiating outward to every part of Central Asia, from the Caspian to the Pascific.[15] Once the British trade was securely established at Leh, there were three alternatives. He could follow the ancient caravan trail across the Karakoram North-Eastwards to Chinese Turkistan before approaching Bokhara from the East across the Pamirs as Izzat-ullah had done. That was his preferred plan. Alternatively, he could turn North-Westwards and penetrate to Bokhara by way of Gilgit, Chitral and the Upper Oxus. Both routes were totally unexplored by Europeans. Only as a very third best would he risk Sikh opposition and Muslim fanaticism by descending from Ladakh via Kashmir into the Punjab, and then penetrating to Bokhara across Afghanistan, by way of Peshawar and Kabul.[16]

For this, Moorcroft went direct to Leh. He stayed for full two years in the region and applied much of his time in gathering valuable information about every aspect of the region.[17] During this period, he did his best to establish his contact with the Chinese authorities. To further his commercial designs, he suggested "a free intercourse between

British India and Chinese Tartary. Also, he proposed the appointment of 'a British Agent with an assortment of British merchandise, and attempting to effect so good an understanding with the ruling authorities, as to render it available as an enterpot".[18] However, he failed in his mission largely due to the evasive attitude of the Chinese authorities, as also of the opposition of the Kashmiri merchants. For the Kashmiri merchants had have a monopoly over the shawl wool trade and feared the interposition of the European.[19]

Moorcroft hoped to turn the ruler of the kingdom of Lahore, Maharaja Ranjit Singh into an active partner of 'the Himalayan concern' too. "Mixing blarney and commercial blackmail in more or less equal portions, he intended to remind the *Maharaja* that British now had direct access to the shawl wool of Tibet from its own territories. Since British powerlooms would soon compete with Ranjit Singh's own expensive Kashmir product, his best chance of offsetting the consequent and inevitable decline in his revenue would be to benefit from the opening of Central Asia to British merchandise".[20] He proposed to *Maharaja* 'to establish a fixed scale of duties' for the admission of British merchandise into the Kingdom of Lahore.[21]

In Tibet, Moorcroft had become convinced that the Russian were already embarked on their own bid for commercial hegemony in Asia. Behind commerce, he feared, lay vast political and military designs which, if not met and checked, could threaten Britain's strategic position in Asia.[22] The threat could only be met if Ladakh would become a British dependency. Strategically, Ladakh was placed at the cross-roads of Asia. With Ladakh under its protection, Britain could end at a stroke all the developing dangers of a Russian flanking movement, whether into India from behind the Himalaya or into China from the west. Above all the evils that threaten Europe through the conquest of China may be averted by the Company accepting the allegiance of Ladakh.[23]

With these intentions, he induced the Ladakhi authorities to announce their dependence on the Company. He suggested to *Khalum* (*wazir*) of Ladakh that "Ladakh was not dependent either upon Lassa or Lahore". He became the medium of tendering allegiance of Ladakh to British authority. At the same time he wrote to Maharaja Ranjit Singh to expostulate with him on his unjustifiable demand of tribute from Leh. This was not all, he repeatedly requested to his superiors to occupy Ladakh. All these activities are of ambiguous nature. However, the British Indian Government wholly disapproved of his conduct and informed the *Maharaja* that he was acting without the sanction of the British Government. At this Moorcroft was much perturbed and condemned the Government's decision.[24]

Not only Ladakh but Punjab too became a focus of his attention for its rich resources and of its strategic position. Moorcroft was the first British traveller to suggest to the British Indian Government the necessity of annexing the Punjab. He realized that the Punjab with its abundant water resources and fine climate could be one of the richest corners of Asia. He hoped that it would be a great highway for the British commerce passing up the broad rivers and into the heart of Asia. Moorcroft shared his observation with Ranjit Singh himself but not his belief that one day these rich resources would be in the hands of the British. In a letter to Edward Parry, a Director of the Company he wrote "this idea may be censured as ambitious, extravagant and improbable but however, it may be scouted at present, to this conclusion you must come at last".[25] Even he wrote to Calcutta about the suitability of Izzat Ullah, as British Agent at Lahore, once the Bokhara journey was over.[26]

Fearing the Russian advance to India from the extreme North by way of Ladakh and then into Kashmir, Moorcroft coveted it too for British. He advocated that 'its mountain walls made it a natural fortress and its fecundity was such that up to half a million men could be fed and provided with every war material".[27] It was not only a vital defensive bastion but a political and commercial emporium on the road to Asia too. Perhaps for these reasons, he devoted much space to Kashmir and discussed its polity, economy and society in detail.[28] However, he asserted that with 'liberal and wise government' the *Kashmiris* could become the most lively and ingenious people of Asia. If in his assessment the Sikh rule was not 'liberal and wise', then perhaps the only substitute in Moorcroft's mind was the British Government itself.[29] However, the possession of Ladakh, Kashmir and the Punjab was not enough for Moorcroft to check the Russians. It needed an active role of Afghanistan too. In one of his dispatch to Political Department, he urged Calcutta to take much more effective steps to defeat Russian intrigues in Afghanistan and encourage, by influence and support, a pro-British ruler on the throne of Kabul.[30] Apparently, the Peshawar chiefs made an explicit request to be taken under British protection, but after his experiences in Ladakh, Moorcroft wisely did, not more than report in general terms that there seemed to be "a strong desire of a large mass of the population to be placed directly under the protection of the British Government".[31]

Besides, Moorcroft was a man of restless nature. His experiences at the stud since 1812 had diminished his pleasure in the job and he soon made up his mind to never return to it once the great journey was over. There was always the deeper need for challenge, for novelty and for diversion from numbing/ routine. His early life in Britain and his activities at Pusa are clear proof of this instinct. The privation and hardship of the journey were accepted as the price for doing what he most longed to do. He was content with the Bokhara journey. He said that "it was by far the best act of my life and the only time with passing of which I am well satisfied not withstanding the privations and inconvenience and anxieties it constantly presents".[32]

Above all, Moorcroft himself was always adamant that the journey was undertaken strictly for public purposes and the findings were the property of the governments.[33] He was, after all, a senior government servant on full salary. His mountains caravan was carried on to the limit of British territory by commissariat transport animals at public expense and free of custom duties. His medicines and surgical equipment were supplied from public stores, and many of the presents which had originally been purchased at public expense for the 1812 journey, were now formerly released to him once again. Guthire, Izzat-ullah and Hafiz were all public servants on full pay, as indeed were the fourteen Gurkha soldiers who made the escort. Moreover, carefully stewed somewhere in his baggage, Moorcroft carried documents in English, Russian, Persian and Chinese, travelling in search of horses. In all these ways, the mission was an official one. Yet the official element in it was strictly and deliberately limited. For, when he tried to get Lord Hastings to write an official letter of introduction to the ruler of Bokhara, his request was turned down. Moorcroft's position seemed to be somewhat analogous to that of a government secret agent in the garb of a globetrotter in search of fine horses.[34]

II

Alexander Burnes was sent on a complementary mission to Lahore by Lord William Bentinck in 1830. He was to take from the King of England to Maharaja Ranjit Singh, five dray horses of 'a size never before seen in India'.[35] The following year, he travelled from the British frontiers to the confines of the river Oxus, professing that he was going home through land route, for he had a great desire to see 'new countries' and 'the conquests of Alexander.'[36] In November, 1836, Lord Auckland asked him to proceed to Kabul through Sindh. Explicitly, he was going to give a final shape to the policy of British Government, to open the Indus for commerce. This superiors 'commercial mission' was to be carried out with the instruction that "he should establish on the banks of the Indus, and the countries beyond it, such relations as should contribute to the desired end."[37] Was this 'desired end' in 1836 was really a commercial, and in 1831 to horses to the King of Lahore, and in 1832-33, to go to England through land route, for the desire to see new countries, are few but important questions which demands little attention to understand the hidden motives for undertaking these travels.

Lahore *Durbar's* relations with Sindh goes back to the year 1803, when Multan was first invaded. The conquest of Multan in 1818, and the subsequent subjugation of the Daudpotas of Bhawalpur had virtually extended the Sikh influence to the borders of Sindh. As the Sikh armies were busy in quelling the activities of Sayyid Ahmed, Sindh did not receive much attention, except a constant reminder to the Agents of Sindh ot pay tribute to the *Maharaja*. However, with the death of Sayyid Ahmed, the whole country from Peshawar to the borders of Sindh along the left bank of the Indus became secure and the *Maharaja* was free to turn his attention towards Sindh. An open conversation about Sindh with his generals as also with Victor Jacquemont, is an added proof of Maharaja's eagerness with which he was looking forward to conquer this region.[38] As a prelude to the conquest of Sindh, the Maharaja fixed his target at Shikarpur.[39] Hence, having control over this region, the Sikh ruler could have an outlet to the sea, and through this channel he could have established relations with other powers. The British considered it an effort to make a power-block against them. However, the expansionist design of the *Maharaja* was an apparent danger to the British design as well.

For much of the nineteenth century the British Government was obsessed by fear of Russian designs over India. The Russo-Persian threat to Khorasan and Heart was viewed by British statesmen both in London and India as dangerous to the security of British India. However, by 1830, the Russian were actually preparing to swallow up Khiva and Bokhara. Thus, British interests in the Indus and countries beyond sprang out from the exigency of counteracting the Russian move.[40]

Coupled with this was the British interest to sell for the British manufactures in the Central Asian countries. For the bazaars of Bokhara, a central mart between Asia and Europe, were being supplied by over land routes from Russia. Numerous fairs were annually held on the Southern frontiers of Russia, on the banks of Volga, lasting for forty days. The Central Asian merchants made most of their sales and purchases at these fairs. However, there was no party to encounter the Russian exports to Bokhara. Likewise Russia was carrying on an extensive trade with China through Kashgar and Yarkand. Even Russian goods find their markets as far as Kabul and the Punjab.[41]

Russian had the advantage of using Volga, the greatest of the European rivers, for commercial purposes. Therefore, to compete with Russia, it was necessary that the British goods should have been cheaper and in plenty in the Central Asian markets. "If Russia navigates the Volga", "British can (could) command like facilities, by two more grand and equally navigable streams, the Ganges and the Indus".[42] For this exigency the revival of the ancient channel of commerce—the Indus was thought expedient.[43] An inquiry into the condition and manufactures of every region which adjoins the Indus, as well as those situated between it and the Caspean sea, was thought necessity.[44]

The British were also interested in the military resources of the Punjab, Sindh, Afghanistan and other countries lying between it and the Caspin sea. They were interested to know the feasibility of any threat to their Indian possession, which these power could have formed together with Russia from the North-West. Therefore, they were driven to know 'the then state and condition of these tribes who, at different period of history, had sent forth successive hordes to overrun and occupy the fairest regions of Asia'.[45]

Thus, to check the Sikh move towards Sindh, to arrest the growth of Russian empire, to open Central Asian marts for British commerce, to immunes Persia and Afghanistan against Russian influence and thereby avert an opportunity to Russo-Persian invasion on British Indian possession, some of the basic motives of the British expansionists in the 1830s. To meet successfully to these problems, it was thought by the statesmen, both in England and India alike, to enhance the British influence beyond Indus.[46] This needed much information of 'political and geographical nature', which the British lacked at that time.[47]

"The horses", intended for Ranjit Singh, wrote Jacquemont, "was only a pretext and excuse for his journey. In reality, he was to determine the potentialities of the rivers Indus, Satluj and Ravi for navigation and commerce".[48] In the 1820s William Moorcroft had suggested the advantages that might be derived from Indus, by using it as a channel of

British commerce. However, Lord Amhrest did not encourage the idea. But since the publication of James Burne's account of the Sindh in 1829, the idea of using the Indus and its tributaries was being eagerly adopted by the British Indian Government, and by the advocates of utilitarianism.[49]

However, the knowledge of the Indus which the British possessed in 1830s was very 'vague and unsatisfactory'. Sir John Malcolm wrote to the Governor-General in August 1830, that, "the navigation of the Indus is important in every point of view, yet we have no information that can be depended on this subject, except about sevently miles from Thatta to Hyderabad".[50] On the eve of his departure to Lahore, Alexander Burnes was being instructed through a secret letter from the Chief Secretary at Bombay that "the depth of the water in Indus, the direction and breadth of the stream,[51] its facilities for steam navigation, the supply of fuel on its banks, and the condition of the Princes and people, who possess the country bordering on it, are all points of highest interests to the Government". Hence, he was asked to produce 'a comprehensive report on his journey'.[52]

Likewise, the knowledge of the countries lying between the Indus and the Caspin sea was not adequate. Before the departure of his journey to Central/Asia, Burnes wrote to his sister in 1831, that "the Home Government is frightened at the designs of Russia and desired that some intelligent officer should be sent to acquire information in the countries bordering on the Oxus and Caspin".[53] The statement finds support with the instructions which Lord William Bentinck gave to Alexander Burnes in 1832, that "a knowledge of the general condition of the countries through which he was to travel, would be useful to the British Government, independent of other advantages which might be expected from such a journey".[54] Thus in 1831-32, "the authorities, both in England and India, contemplated that much information of political and geographical nature might be acquired in such a journey".[55]

Under such a specific scheme of the British Government for conducting a survey of political and geographical nature, the Kingdom of Lahore received Burnes' attention because of its power and strategic importance. To know the power of the kingdom of Ranjit Singh, Burnes discussed with due interest, the military force and administrative institutions, the revenues, the productions, the natural resources and manufactures, items of export and import. Besides, the composition of the ruling class, its influence on the actions of the *Maharaja*, the Sikh church and its influence on the *Maharaja* were also taken into consideration. Burnes was perhaps the first English traveller to fore see the anarchy that could prevail after the demise of the *Maharaja*. He asserted that the succession would be disputed between Prince Kharak Singh and Sher Singh. However, he was of the view that : "if Sher Singh does not secure a supremacy, this kingdom will probably relapse into the former state of anarchy and small republics; or be reduced to subjection by some neighbouring power."[56]

After surveying carefully all the aforementioned aspects, Burnes conclude that, the Punjab of the 1830s was a most vigorous and well consolidated state. Its military resources were immense. It could produce everything which was sufficient not only for its own inhabitants and army but also it could export things to other countries. The road from one extremity of the country to the other could admit of wheeled carriages, except in the mountains. All the river of the Punjab, including the Indus, were navigable.[57] If the royal house was not enough competent to defend its possession, after the demise of the *Maharaja*, the Sikh masses were strong enough to do so. They formed 'a healthy and vigorous body'. No other race was 'equal to their power'. Hence, Burnes admitted that the Sikhs were 'certainly powerful people' and better constituted to uphold their government.[58]

In brief, the purpose of Alexander Burnes' journeys was to enrich the stock of knowledge about geography, topography, the military resources of the states lying between the British frontier and the river Oxus, the state of commerce in these countries, the state of relations between the rulers of these countries and that of different chiefs and tribes.[59] In fact,

William Bentinck jealously applied the policy framed by Wellington and his colleague to counter the Russian in Central Asia. He sent Burnes in conformity with the Home Government, to collect information of the aforementioned nature. However, his period was of 'reconnaissance and planning'. Bentinck's ground or in other words, information provided by Burnes was essential for the attempt to project British power into Central Asia.[60]

III

Contrary to Moorcroft and Burnes, Charles Masson's initial purpose for his wanderings was not specific. But soon after his residence in Kabul, we find him enthusiastically busy in archaeological and antiquarian researchs.[61] Around 1834, British Indian Government was looking for 'a reliable news writer' in Kabul. In one of his letters to his superiors Captain Wade, Political Agent at Ludhaina, wrote that "it is not merely from the nature of his scientific researches that Mr. Masson's services will be likely to advantageous to the government, but from the observations he has made, and the information he has collected upon the government and resources of the country which of daily increasing interest to the Government of India. His long stay in Afghanistan had not only enabled him to acquire a complete geographical and statistical knowledge of the country, but living like he had done, like a nature of it, on terms of intimacy and familiarity with its inhabitants, he had enjoyed opportunities of making observations which no European has yet possessed".[62] However, it is obvious that one the recommendation of Captain Wade and due to the urgency of the Government to know about the country and its resources Masson was appointed 'as Agent for communicating intelligence' in Kabul on a salary of Rs. 250 per month in 1834.[63]

Charles Massons sole duty was to inform the British Indian Government about the Afghans and Afghanistan. In his printed works of about 1431 pages, only a chapter of about 37 pages have been devoted to the kingdom of Lahore and to the Sikhs.[64] Here again 8 pages are given to the antiquity and geography of the city of Lahore.[65] About 16 pages are given to

Ranjit Singh, his army his nobility, revenue, police and judicial administration etc.[66] His treatment of the subject is not much different from that of Prinsep. However, the Sikhs as people received Masson's special attention. He has devoted about 13 pages to them.[67] But it was not his job to tell to the readers about the religion of the Sikhs. He says that "it may be deemed superfluous to allude to the religious beliefs and opinions of the Sikhs, as those subjects have received the attention of Sir John Malcolm, and others who had access to the best sources of information."[68] His main concern was their present state. He asserted that the Sikhs had widely deviated from the system of its founder. They had become "a nation of infuriated fanatics', in place of 'harmless free thinkers' of the days of Guru Nanak.[69] They were exclusively 'a military and agricultural people'. Their fondness for rearing horses was such, that there was hardly a Sikh in the Punjab who did not have one or more brood mares.[70] Perhaps for their peculiar character and military disposition, the Akalis, amongst the Sikhs, too received Masson's due attention.[71] Brahmanical influence on the Sikhs and their general attitude towards the Hindus and the Muslims are also discussed. The practices and customs of the Sikh were of great interest to Masson.[72]

Since Masson's official duty was to inform the British about the Afghan and Afghanistan, he has devoted a sizeable portion of his printed works to the Sikh-Afghan problem. His narrative of the Sikh-Afghan problem opens with the invasion of Zamah Shah on the Punjab, and closes it with the unsuccessful attempt of Dost Mohammad Khan to take the fort of Jamrud from the Sikhs.[73] It emerges from his treatment issue in the Sikh-Afghan relations, since its conquest by the Sikhs. In his account, the Sikhs appear to be all powerful throughout the period under discussion. The ascendancy of the Sikhs over the Afghans has been attributed to; the meager resources of the Afghans, factionalism amongst the Barakzais, power and shrewdness of Maharaja Ranjit Singh.[74]

His account of the events prior to 1820 is extremely sketchy and factually inaccurate. However, after the death of Fateh Khan in 1818 till 1837, when the final action was fought out at Jamrud, Masson's account of the Sikh-Afghan problem is very regular, vivid and graphic. But he is habitually inaccurate about dates, and gives very few in the printed accounts of his travels.[75] In any case, these short-comings does not diminish the importance of his work as he was an eye-witness to the Sikh-Afghan problem. Most of the events from 1830s onward happened during his stay at Kabul. In the *Catalogue of European Manuscripts*, lying in the India office library, Masson has been acknowledged as the best authority for the politics of Afghanistan and of Sikh-Afghan relation, then year prior to the First Afghan War.[76] His information was considered valuable at the India House, as 'corroborating the accuracy of Captain Burnes' statements'.[77]

Thus, we finds that the work of reconnaissance along the Indus and in Central Asian countries, initiated by Moorcroft in the garb of a merchant traveller was expanded and perpetuated by a diplomat traveller, Alexander Burnes, and it was nearly completed by Charles Masson to the satisfaction of his superiors.[78]

IV

Godfrey Thomas Vigne, wrote his biographer, "was neither professional author nor a commissioned tourist. He travelled for amusement, saw much and was assisted in his observations by the possession of some knowledge of science."[79] Vigne himself says in his works that he was travelling independent of the Company and for his own 'pleasure'.[80] Similar views are expressed by the author of *Umdat-ut-Tawarikh*. But his purpose to travel in the dominions of Ranjit Singh and in the adjoining territories, *e.g.* Iskardo, Ladakh and Afghanistan was much more than that.[81] A letter written by Alexander Burnes on 16th September, 1841, from Kabul to Vigne, creates doubts about his real purpose. Burnes wrote that he was looking with 'great anxiety' for his map and book relating to Kashmir and Giligit, which to him was 'by for the most interesting part' of his wanderings. Also, it was expected 'to fill up the great blank.'[82] Furthermore, in his reply to Alexander Burnes, Vigne wrote that he had done "his best in furtherance of this objects he alludes to."[83]

One of Vigne's motives of visiting Little Tibet (Iskardo) was to ascertain the degree of anxiety which its ruler had have for the friendship of the British.[84] The conquest of Kashmir by Maharaja Ranjit Singh in 1819 had alarmed the ruler of Ladakh as to that of the Little Tibet. He was convinced that his country would be the next target of Ranjit Singh's policy of aggrandizement. In order to save himself from any such eventuality, the Balti ruler tried to cultivate friendship with the British in order to seek protection from them. When William Moorcroft was residing in Ladakh in 1820–22, Ahmad Shah, the Balti chief, sent him a present of gold-dust and proffered his services. Moorcroft did not encourage the offers, as these would have given unmrage to the ruler of Ladakh who at that time was at war with Baltistan.[85] But he wrote an ambiguous letter to Ahmad Shah holding out promises of British support. Therefore, the Balti ruler continued to expect British help. In 1835, Ahmad Shah wrote to C.M. Wade, the Governor-General's Agent at Ludhiana : "It must not be concealed that from the beginning I have been moved by an anxiety beyond bounds to connect myself with the well-wishers and faithful servants of your government by ties of friendship and to identity myself with reserves with their interests."[86] When C.M. Wade read this letter to Vigne, he made up his mind visit at once this place, which 'no European had visited earlier.'[87]

When Vigne met Ahmad Shah, he gave him 'exceedingly kind and flattering hospitality', with the belief that he was an officer of the Company "to investigate the pretension to friendship and provide protection against the Sikhs".[88] He told Vigne that "he had all his life prayed that he might set eyes on a Feringhi before he died, and that now his wish was granted."[89] But Vigne told him that he was not in a position "to enter into any arrangements, either with or for him." However, he promised to give a favourable report of him to C.M. Wade on his meeting with him.[90] Not only this, Vigne picked up Nasim Khan with him to Ludhiana, "where he could pick up intelligence for his master and render assistance to him, by merely remaining in a British cantonment, as the Sikhs would be sure to think of him an ambassador, and should not dare to invade a country whose king they imagined to be in treaty with the English."[91]

However, Vigne appears to be much concerned with the security of British Indian possessions from the North-West. He opened that "our North-West frontier was not like any other; it was the only one on which there was a chance of serious invasion, and we ought long ago to have known more of it. In this particular, Lord Auckland's predecessors are more to blame than he is."[92] He advocated the policy to be pursued by the British Government in regard to the Alpine Punjab and Kashmir. Referring to the activities and intentions of Jamwal brothers; Dhiyan Singh, Gulab Singh and Suchet Singh, he asserted that "these three brothers have long been masters of the Alpine Punjab, with the exception of the valley of Kashmir; for the seizure of which they have long been preparing."[93] Raja Gulab Singh having taken Ladakh in 1835, had since been intent on the occupation of Little Tibet; "for the purpose of completing a military circle around Kashmir, and of being able to pour his troops into the valley from every side, immediately upon the death of Ranjit Singh."[94] Vigne thought that "the best line of action that the East India Company can adopt, "to follow up that display of its love of legitimacy which it has so lately evinced at Kabul, by reinstating the rightful *Rajahs* upon their Ghuddis."[95] Thus, he hoped of dividing the power of the chiefs. It would be "the surest way of gaining the affection of the people."[96]

This conviction of Vigne made him interested in the Himalayan region, and he strongly recommended the conquest of Kashmir a necessity for the protection of British empire in Asia, as also of weaking and encircling the kingdom of Lahore.[97] Perhaps for this purpose, Vigne examined all the passage to the valley from all the directions. He had learnt from Abul Fazal that there were twenty-six roads to Kashmir, but an active mountaineer could enter the valley in many places besides regular passages. He could trace out only twenty-three passages from which a man could approach the valley.[98]

The defensive capacity of the valley was also examined by Vigne. He found that "Kashmir enjoys the singular advantage of being at the same time both a fortress and a magazine; and although the battle for the valley would be fought on the outside of it, yet the progress of an invading power might be opposed step by step, as it often has been, from the mountain summits around each of its passes."[99]

Vigne was convinced that the occupation of Kashmir would be useful to solve the problem of defence of British India from the North-West. He advocated that, "when a road is made through the pass from Baramula to Dhrumtawur, an army of any strength, and most perfectly appointed, may be marched, in from four to six days, from the healthy atmosphere of Kashmir, to defend the passage of Attock or Torbela; and with such protection on the North, Bombay as the capital of India on the South and the Indus between them, the British possessions in Hindustan ought to as safe from foreign invasion from the Westward, as such an extended line of frontier can possibly be made to render them."[100]

He viewed the occupation of Kashmir as "the accomplishment of the one thing needful for the consolidation of British power in Northern India."[101] He regretted for the delay which the East India Company had made for its conquest. However, he asserts that had the government done so, "it might have long since been in possession of the Punjab, and friendly relations have been established with the court of Kabul, is an assertion based perhaps, upon no unreasonable conjecture."[102]

Kashmir appeared to Vigne a rich land where Christian missionaries could pursue their work with due success. He asserted that "the Mohammedans will not fail to attribute to the finger of God, and consider it as a step towards the fulfillment of their belief, that the whole world will become subject to the power of the Christians. The missionary may here pursue his labours with some visible hopes of success, when the prevalence of English associations shall have weakened the effects of caste, and the prejudice of Islam; and the magnificent valley, hitherto the theater of a hundred faiths, will become the Alma Master of our Eastern conquests, and the great and central temple of a religion as pure as the eternal snows around it."[103]

In brief, Vigne's travels bare British designs in the North-West of India in the 19th century. They unveiled the countries that Gulab Singh soon welded into compact Jammu and Kashmir state. Hugel appears to be right when he asserts that "Vigne and Englishman, who had extended his Asiatic travels as far as Kashmir to certify that he was an Agent of the East India Company. I am surprised that Captain Wade should neither have spoken nor written to me about them."[104] Thus, if Moorcroft, Burnes and Masson were active in Afghanistan and Central Asia, to enrich the stock of knowledge about people, princes and politics of these lands, Vigne was equally active for similar purpose in the North-Western India.

V

Victory Jacquemont's visit to India was aimed at to investigate the Natural History of India in all its branches, to enrich to Royal Museum of Natural History at Paris, and to promote the progress of science.[105] However, he was given "liberty to conduct any other investigation that he might deem of importance."[106] Using this discretion, Jacquemont combined his scientific investigations with due interest in the polity, economy and society of the dominions of Maharaja Ranjit Singh in the context of his relations with the British as a colonial power, Also background of political rivalry between France and England and the presence of French officers in the army of Ranjit Singh led Jacquemont to know about the kingdom of Lahore, for it had maintained its sovereignty against expanding British imperialism.[107]

Jacquemont wanted to know the possible danger to the British power in Asia. This obliged him to compare the resources of the *Maharaja* as also of the Company. He opined that "Ranjeet Singh's is the only power which had stood with that of the British. But the respective revenues of the two states will give you their relative resources that of the company amounts to twenty-six millions sterling; that of Runjeet to three; and he can only come up to this amount by excessive taxes, which tempt his subject to throw themselves in the hands of the British."[108] Besides revenues, the military potentialities of the *Maharaja* appears to be a major concern of Jacquemont. He asserted that the *Maharaja* had "only 25,000 well disciplined troops, and with so small a force, he makes his Northern neighbours tremble."[109] He noted that such was the taste among the Sikhs that Ranjit Singh could expand his army to 80,000 if he wished so.[110] However, in his view, the *Maharaja* was obliged to grind his country with imposts in order to maintain his on the European footing. But this very army could become a threat to the dominions of the *Maharaja*. For Jacquemont felt sure that 'one day he company would extend its frontier from the Satluj to the Indus, and his army would not offer any vigorous resistance; it would be easily pursuaded to change its allegiance, for it had no guarantee of pay or promotion and no system of pensions.'[111]

Jacquemont also commented upon the administrative machinery of the kingdom of Lahore. He observed that the revenue was being collected by 'farmers' with the help of the *kardars* and a number of clerks employed by the farmer for this purpose. The rates of assessment was more than half of the gross produce, and the cultivators were left with "what was barely necessary for their susbistance."[112] These *kardars* and tax collectors were corrupt and rapacious. The country, Jacquemont thought, was groaning under the burden of taxation and welcome British rule.[113] The administration of justice too was not liked by Jacquemont.[114] However, the police and spy system of the kingdom of Lahore was an excellent as compared to the Paris police. He found that governor of Kashmir better informed than the Prefect of Police in Paris.[115]

Jacquemont was of the view that the Sikh rule in Kashmir was oppressive and incompetent. Sikh governors had practically ruined the province. Each year more land was left uncultivated, and more villages were abondoned by their inhabitants who fled towards Kabul or the Punjab in search of less oppressive masters.[116] Kashmir appeared to Jacquemont a deserted and miserable province, and the people cared very little for Ranjit Singh's order. There was a total insubordination of the petty hill chiefs to the *Maharaja*, and the habitual rebellions of the subject against their chiefs. In the hills he asserted, "each village was at war with the next."[117] On the other hand, the conditions in British India were better. He sincerely wished the English to extend their frontiers from the Satluj to the Indus.[118]

Jacquemont was the first non-English traveller to speculate the probable termination of the kingdom of Lahore. On this assumption he turned to the person of the *Maharaja*. After weighing all the pros and cons of his personality, he found in the *Maharaja*, 'a Bonaparte in miniature' with excellent 'intellectual curiosity' whose conversation was like a 'nightmare'. He was the 'first inquisitive Indian', who asked Jacquemont about India, England, Europe and Bonaparte, made enquiries about the military and revenue resources of France, discussed hell, paradise, soul, devil and God.[119] Also, the *Maharaja* appeared to Jacquemont 'a successful sovereign'. He was an absolutely independent monarch, and possessed the greatest power in Asia after the British. He was better obeyed by his subjects than the Mughal emperors at the zenith of their power.[120] As a statesman Jacquemont found him 'most suspicious, false, and deceitful of Asiatic princes', but a 'skilful diplomat and a very politician'. Compared to him the most skilful French diplomat was a simpleton.[121] Above all, he was 'a perfect old fox', and 'a despot in the true sense of the word.'[122] Jacquemont asserts that Ranjit Singh never bothered about the thought that "what would happen after his death. He took no measures to ensure a continuance of his dominions. He subscribe to the principle of 'after me the delquqe.'[123]

With these views, Jacquemont turned to the royal family and found that 'Kharak Singh, the eldest and legitimate son of the *Maharaja* was feeble minded', and without any talents. Sher Singh, another son of the *Maharaja*, was 'very intelligent'. However, Jacquemont felt quiet sure that "the Sikh monarchy will end with the death of Runjeet."[124] The two princes would fight for the throne, and the great chiefs would rise to assert their independence. In such a state of affairs, the British would invade the Punjab to occupy it on the slightest pretext.[125]

Another area of interest to Jacquemont was Anglo-Sikh relations. For the *Maharaja* had told Jacquemont that "the

British and I have one heart between us."[126] However, Jacquemont does not make any secret of British intentions. It is clear from his observations that the British Government wanted to extend its frontiers from the Satluj to the Indus. The idea was to check the expansion of Ranjit Singh's kingdom towards Sindh.[127] In accordance with the instruction from the Court of Directors, the Amirs of Sindh were pressed to sign a treaty "affording every facility and protection to the commercial and military navigation of the British on the Indus."[128] This was done without any reference to the *Maharaja*. In this view the meeting of the Governor-General with the *Maharaja* at Ropar was meant to frighten him, with the show of the superiority of British arms rather than to solicit his willing consent to the British proposals: "what Lord William want with Runjeet Singh, I am unable to guess, to frighten him, perhaps, and show him how easy it would be to annihilate him. The colonel of one of the two regiments of English cavalry in the Calcutta presidency writes to me from Semla that he has been appointed to command, not the escort, but the army, which is to accompany the Governor General to his interview with Ranjeet, if it takes place; or the embassy to Lahore, in the reverse case. He will take his regiment of lancers, regiment of native cavalry, one English infantry, two of seapoys, and a battery of light artillery–all picked for the occasion. I do not know how for the *Maharaja* will relish so may honours."[129] Above all, Jacquemont asserted that the British might crush Ranjit Singh in a couple of months, if they wished it.[130]

Thus, we finds that the contents of Jacquemonts *Letters* and *Journal* were connected with his general purpose of informing his contemporaries on the polity and economy of the kingdom of an Asian ruler in close contact with the expanding European colonialism.

VI

Baron Charles Hugel says that his chief motive was to know "the greatness and power of the East India Company, the Maharaja's ally and more recently the kingdom founded by Ranjit Singh, who like a skilful architect, has formed so many insignificant unpromising fragments, one majestic fabrice, seemed to me the most wonderful objects in the world."[131] This suggests that his sole purpose to visit the kingdom of Lahore was to know the power and then state of the *Maharaja's* resources, for it was the only part of the Indian sub-continent bordering on the vast empire of the East India Company to escape from its encroachment.[132]

Both for his specific and general purpose of gratifying his own curiosity, and that of his countrymen, Hugel goes into the historical background of Maharaja Ranjit Singh. He covers the history of the Sikhs from Guru Nanak to the proclamation of the British Government, protecting the Cis-Satluj States in 1809, in about 23 pages. Equal number of pages have been devoted to the history of Ranjit Singh from his predecessors to his own times.[133] Since contemporary kingdom of Lahore was his primary interest, he turned to the causes which facilitated the smooth rise of the *Maharaja*. In his estimation, the causes which favoured the expansion of the dominions of the East India Company, favoured Ranjit Singh too. Furthermore, he attributes *Maharaja's* rise largely to the political situation of the Punjab and the help rendered by Sada Kaur at that political juncture.[134]

Hugel was deeply interested in the army of the *Maharaja* which had enabled him to conquer and maintain such an empire. He traces the evolution of the Sikh army from the year 1809, the year in which it was supposed that the *Maharaja* started re-organizing his army on western lines. Hugel gives a detailed and vivid description of the dress, movement, equipment, pay, the words of command, and above all the fighting strength of the different components of the war machine. However, he found the army of the *Maharaja* to withstand any force likely to appear from the west of the Indus.[135] The expenditure incurred to maintain such a powerful army was not an easy matter. Therefore, Hugel turned to the resources of the kingdom of Lahore : its products, manufactures, trade and commerces revenue and natural resources, all are taken care of in his account.

To know, how the *Maharaja* escaped the encroachment of the British, Hugel got interested in the Anglo-Sikh relations.

He has discussed it in detail from the year 1809 to his own times. He found the *Maharaja* a subordinate partner who could never impose his will on the British. He felt certain that the integrity of the kingdom of Lahore rested on its relation with the British. For this he suggested that, "a treaty offensive and defensive with the British Government, having a guarantee for the integrity of his possessions, was the only thing that could ensure the dominion of Ranjit Singh."[136] However, he was equally certain that the British would not offer such a document which would have prevented them from 'taking immediate advantage of any sudden occurrence which might fall out."[137]

Future of the kingdom of Lahore depended on the capability of the successors of the *Maharaja* too. For this Hugel became interested in the heirs of Ranjit Singh. He found that according to the Sikh law of succession Kharak Singh's right to the throne was unquestionable but he was in utter destitution of the qualities of 'his ever ruling of over the scarcely united empire of the Sikhs.'[138] Hugel Visualized the anarchy that would prevail after the demise of the *Maharaja* and the role that the Jamwal brothers and Sher Singh would play in preserving the integrity of the dominion of the deceased *Maharaja*. He found Jamwal brother powerful enough and shrewd too to "avail them selves of the first opportunity to throw of the yoke. They would seize Kashmir which was most accessible from their lands. Sher Singh, on the other hand, could most probably take possessions of the portions of the kingdom, where he may happen to be in the command of the army, when Ranjit Singh's death took place. Disorder and anarchy was bound to prevail until the whole empire became a portion of the vast dominions of the British."[139] On this assumption, Hugel discussed the boundary question, and his conviction was that the British should keep the Indus as its western boundary.[140]

The nature and purpose of the travel literature helps us to understand it on broader perspective of British imperial designs. It indicates that there was a dichotomy between the real purpose and the purpose explicitly expressed. For example, the East India Company maintained that the sole purpose of Moorcroft's travel was to procure horses to improve the breed for the cavalry of British military. But the real purpose was other than that and was kept secret. Even Moorcroft had little doubt that the entire mission was of political nature. Similarly, Alexander Burnes' mission was claimed to be a commercial one whose sole aim was to open the Indus for commerce. But the political motive of the East India Company was not limited to commerce. It appears that the dichotomy was purposely maintained for precise diplomatic reasons. For example, Moorcroft, at time took some decisions of political nature out of enthusiasm, whereas the Government not only disapproved his conduct but also informed the *Maharaja* that he was acting without the sanction of the British Government. Also, when Moorcroft tried to obtain an official letter of introduction to the ruler of Bukhara written by Lord Hastings, he was flatly refused.

The dichotomy served a device to keep the real purpose secret. It also helped to form a precise, broad-based and far-sighted complex diplomatic policy under constantly changing situations. On the other hand, the travel literature contains a wide variety of observations on diverse areas. This rich information helped them to review the policy in a changed situation. Hence, there is a dichotomy between the diplomatic policy of the Government and the popular impression in the form of travel literature. For example, Vigne was of the opinion that the occupation of Kashmir would be great value to solve the problem of defence of British India from North-West. But the British policy was quite different. The policy of neutrality adopted by the company was regretted by Vigne. The complexity of the policy was such that even Jacquemont failed to understand. Writing about the meeting of Lord William Bentinck and Maharaja Ranjit Singh, Jacquemont comments, "what Lord William wants with Ranjit Singh, I am unable to gues, to frighten him, perhaps, and show him how easy it would be to annihilate him".

The travel literature suggests us the diplomatic subtaties policy of the East India Company towards Lahore Durbar. Its

Policy was not a direct confrontation, but neutrality. But at the same time the East India Company continued to achieve its desired ends. It did not remain static. The earlier impression of friendship, cooperation and neutrality underwent a change in the latter phase. When Moorcroft wrote a letter to the *Maharaja* for unjust demands from the chief of Ladakh as the considered that Ladakh was not dependent on Lahore, the Company condemned his conduct and informed the *Maharaja* that Moorcroft had no authority. But when Ahmad Shah, the Balti chief, wished to seek protection against the Sikhs from the Company, Vigne promised him to give a favourable report to C.M.Wade. He also took Nasim Khan with him to stay at Ludhiana with Wade to give the Sikhs the impression that the Chief was under their protection. It appears that the British policy was aimed at exerting psychological pressure on Lahore without explicit change in their earlier stand.

The East India Company, through these travellers, collected informations on a wide variety of subjects. The information comprised of socio-economic condition and the military power of the Punjab. The people of Punjab and their culture as well as the geography of the country are discussed in the literature. Besides, various political factors and the seeds of dissension are also looked into. But the policy toward Lahore had a much wider perspective. It had a far-sighted planning. The diverse coverage by these travellers and their information on a number of subject is an indication of purpose and nature of information of this form of literature. It is misleading to deduce that the intention of the British policy was encircling the Punjab by frustrating the expansionist designs of the *Maharaja*. At the same time, the Company also kept its eyes on the Russian threat and tried to explore the commercial possibilities in Central Asia.

The travel literature is rich in information on a variety of subjects The observations about the life and conditions of the Punjab and politics and society are also commented upon. Major political issues are discussed in the form of personal observations. But it does not propound the policy of the Company explicitly. So its evidences in general and on polity in particular are not the view of the Company but that of the travellers. As the travellers were entrusted with a specific mission by the Company their evidence echo official policy. Hence, the significance of the literature lies in the fact that it contains useful informations on major issues and conditions of the early nineteenth century Punjab. They are the document, based on personal observation, of contemporary life and history of the land. They should not be confused with the Company's officials policy, but indicate the process to frame a precise diplomatic policy to achieve desired ends.

REFERENCES

1. Moorcroft, *Travels,* xxi, xxii, xxiii, xxvi, xliii, 2; Also see, Alder, *Beyond Bokhara,* 214.
2. Moorcroft, *Travels,* xvi, xl.
3. *Ibid.*, xix.
4. *Ibid.*, xxvi.
5. *Ibid.*, xxvi-xxvii.
6. *Ibid.*, xx, xl.
7. *Ibid.*, xxii, xl.
8. Alder, *Beyond Bokhara*, 209.
9. Moorcroft, *op.cit.*, xx, xxv-xxvi, xxix, xxx; Alder, *op.cit.*, 210, 250, 255, 263.
10. Moorcroft, *op.cit.*, 206-08, 212; Also see, Alder, *op.cit.*, 210.
11. Alder, *op.cit.*, 210.
12. Moorcroft, *op.cit.*, xxix-xxx.
13. *Ibid.*, xxi.
14. Alder, *op.cit.*, 216-88; Also see, Moorcroft, *op.cit.*, 3–5.
15. Moorcroft, *op.cit.*, 153, 206–213, 222; See also, Alder, *op.cit.*, 216.
16. Moorcroft, *op.cit.*, 206, 222, 227; See also, Alder, *op.cit.*, 216.
17. *Ibid.*, 137–139.
18. Moorcroft, *op.cit.*, xxx.
19. *Ibid.*, 150, 152, 215, 233, 268, 269, 270, 320; See also *Dictionary of National Biography*, XIII, 784.

20. Alder, *op.cit.*, 233.
21. Moorcroft, *op.cit.*, 62, 233; See also *Dictionary of National Biography*, XIII, 784.
22. Alder, *op.cit.*, 211.
23. *Ibid.*, 270.
24. Moorcroft, *Travels,* xxxiii, 152, 250; See also, Alder, *op.cit.*, 270; *Dictionary of National Biography*, XII, 784.
25. Alder, *Beyond Bokhara*, 50, 239, 301.
26. *Ibid.*, 315.
27. *Ibid.*, 295, 304.
28. Moorcroft, *Travels,* 320-451.
29. *Ibid.*, 345–46; Also see, Alder, *op.cit.*, 295.
30. Alder, *op.cit.*, 311.
31. Moorcroft. *op.cit.*, 470-71; Also see, Vigne, *Travels,* I, vi; Alder, *op.cit.*, 311.
32. Alder, *op.cit.*, 211-12; Also see, Moorcroft, *op.cit.*, xviii-xx.
33. Moorcroft, *op.cit.*, xliii; See also, Alder, *op.cit.*, 215.
34. Alder, *op.cit.*, 295; Moorcroft, *op.cit.*, xxii-xxiii.
35. Burens, *Travels,* I, viii, ix, xxvii; See also, *Dictionary of National Biography*, III, 389.
36. Burnes, *op.cit.*, preface, 16.
37. Alexander Burnes, *A Kabul: A Personal Narrative of a Journey to, And Residence in that City in the Years 1836,* 7, & 8. John Murray, London, 1843 (2nd ed.) 1-2, (hereafter *A Kabul*).
38. Jacquemont, *Journal,* 39; Sinha, *Ranjit Singh*, 117-23; Bikrama Jit Hasrat, *Life and Times of Ranjit Singh,* V.V. Research Institute, Hoshiarpur 1977, 141–44.
39. Shikarpur was only 30 *kos* from the dominions of the Sikhs, Commercially as well as politically, it was an important town. It had commercial connections with many remote marts. Its possession would lay Afghanistan and Baluchistan under tangible control. What was most interesting, was that more than half the population were Sikhs and only one-tenth were Mohammedans, with a revenue over three lakhs: Sinha, *Ranjit Singh*, 119.
40. Burnes, *Travels*, I, ix; B.J. Hasrat, *Life and Times of Ranjit*

Singh, 144-146; Bisheswar Prashad; *Bondage And Freedom,* 257-58; For details on Russian advance towards central Asia. See, ch. II infra.

41. Burnes, *op.cit.,* 423-24, 429, 430–36.
42. *Ibid.*, II, 444.
43. Burnes hold the view that, 'the navigation of the Indus and its tributaries rivers, when laid open to the merchant, must advance the interests of commerce, In the revival of an ancient channel to exchange the goods of distant nations, we behold with equal pleasure the advantage of British supremacy in India, and an increased outlet for the commodities of our commercial country; *Travels*, II, 395-96.
44. Burnes, *op.cit.,* II, 396.
45. *Ibid.*, II, 262.
46. In the 1830s, a powerful body of opinions both in London and Calcutta hold that if disaster was to be prevented, Afghanistan : Burnes, *Travels,* I, xi.
47. *Ibid.*, III, ix.
48. Jacquemont, *Journal*, 40.
49. Percival Spear, *The Oxford History of Modern India,* 163; Cunningham, *A History of the Sikhs*, 174; Burnes, *op.cit.*, I, xiv.
50. Burnes, *op.cit.*, I, ix, III, 1 & 2.
51. Burnes, *op.cit.*, I, ix.
52. *Ibid.*, III, 4-6.
53. Manazir Ahmad, *Lord William Bentinck,* Chugh Publication, Allahabad 1970, III, Norris, *The First Afghan War,* 50.
54. Burnes, *op.cit.*, I, xxviii.
55. *Ibid.*, III, I.
56. Burnes, *op.cit.*, II, 233, 285-86, 296, 297-98.
57. *Ibid.*, II, 288-89; III, 288, 299.
58. *Ibid.*, II, 285-86.
59. Burnes, *A Kabul*, 207, 225, 234.
60. Norris, *The First Afghan War,* 50-51.
61. Masson, *Journeys*, I, vii, viii, 3; Grey, *European Adventures,* 176-77, 193-94; Norris, *op.cit.*, 70.

62. Grey, *op.cit.*, 194.
63. *Ibid.*, 193-95; Norris, *The First Afghan War*, 70.
64. Masson, *Journeys*, I, 401–44.
65. *Ibid.*, 408–16.
66. *Ibid.*, 425–34, and 436–44.
67. *Ibid.*, 417-25, 433–36.
68. *Ibid.*, 417.
69. *Ibid.*, 417-18.
70. Masson, *Journeys,* I, 433–34, 438.
71. *Ibid.*, 436-37.
72. *Ibid.*, 424, 433, 435-36, 437-38, 451.
73. *Ibid.*, 397, 427-28.
74. Masson, *Journey,* I, 14, 143, 165, 397, 427-28; III, 34–60.
75. *Catalogue of European MSS*, II, 1281.
76. *Ibid.*
77. Masson, *op.cit.*, I, xxxiv.
78. Grey, *European Adventures*, 193–96.
79. *Dictionary of National Biography*, XX, 309.
80. Vigne, *Travels*, I, 19, 113-14; II, 71, 236.
81. Suri, *Umdat-ut-Tawarikh*, Daftar III, 237, 242, 267, 270, 348, 376, 434-35, 452, 552, 613, 459-60.
82. Vigne, *Travels*,I, iii.
83. *Ibid.*, IV.
84. *Ibid.*, II, 195.
85. Moorcroft, *Travels*, 271-72.
86. C.L. Datta, 'Zorawar Singh's conquest of Baltistan', *Proceedings Punjab History Conference,* 1966, 144.
87. Vigne, *op.cit.*, II, 95.
88. In all his excursions in this region, Vigne was attended by Ahmad Shah, his son Achmet Ali Khan, and sometimes by Nasim Khan, the *Vazir* : Vigne, *op.cit.*, II, 217, 223, 227, 236, 319.
89. *Ibid.*, 225.

90. Vigne, *Travels*, II, 236-37.
91. *Ibid.*, 202.
92. *Ibid.*, I, xviii.
93. *Ibid.*, Narrative, 252-53.
94. Vigne, *Narrative,* 248–252; *Travels*, II, 196.
95. Vigne, *op.cit.*, 253.
96. *Ibid.*
97. *Ibid., Travels,* II, 67.
98. For instance; Baramulla Pass, Punch (Pukhil) Gul Murg, Tos Mydan, Sung-i-Sufyd (Chunz), Pir Panjal, Nadaun Sar, Sedan, Kuri (to Rihursi), Col-Narwana (Kuligam), Bnihal, Sir-i-Bul to Kishtwar, MirBul by Tarn Kasam bridge to Kishtwar, Nabug-Nyh (to Ladakh), Pahalgam (Amar Nath), Duras, Koh-i-Hamon, Bunderpur by Gurys and Deotsh to Iskardo, Labab to Gurys, Kurnawar to Muzaffarabad and three passage over the snow in Kamraj: Kurnau, Bangus (Vehamu) and from the village of Huresh under Setasar. He found that sixe of these: Col-Narawa (Kuligam), Bnihal, Duras, Lolab to Gurys Kunawar to Muzaffarabad and Kuri remained open for whole of the year cannon on wheels into Kashmir, Vigne, *Travels*, I, 148-49, 164, 197, 199, 208, 215, 217-18.
99. *Ibid.*, II, 67.
100. Vigne, *Travels*, II, 67.
101. *Ibid.*, 66.
102. *Ibid.*, 66-67.
103. *Ibid.*, II, 68–690.
104. Hugel, *Travels,* 98.
105. Jacquemont, *Letters*, I, v.
106. *Ibid., Journal*, 1.
107. *Ibid., Letters*, II, 118.
108. Jacquemont, *op.cit.*, II, 118.
109. *Ibid.*, 217.
110. *Ibid.*, I, 221-22, 329, 342, 385, 395, 397, 401; II, 142, 183, 217, 194; *Journal*, 24, 51,52, 53, 56.
111. *Ibid.*, I, 232-33; *Journal*, 59.
112. Jacquemont, *Letters*, I, 82.

113. *Ibid.*, *Journal*, 59,67,70,78–82.
114. *Ibid.*, *Letters*, I, 398-99; II, 156; *Journal*, 50,65,70-71.
115. *Ibid.*, 73; II, 170.
116. *Ibid.*, *Journal*, 49,70.
117. Jacquemont, *Journal,* 63-64 , *Letters,* II, 23-24, 53.
118. Jacquemont was the first non-English traveller to speculator the probable.
119. *Ibid.*, *Letters*, I, 396, 400; II, 248; *Journal*, 36-37, 40-41, 45, 49–51, 54–55, 58.
120. Jacquemont, *op.cit.*, I, 399; II, 140-41, 244.
121. *Ibid.*, I, 383.
122. *Ibid.*, I, 342; II, 168, 236, 376, 399.
123. *Ibid.*, II, 329; *Journal*, 55.
124. Jacquemont, *Journal*, 55.
125. *Ibid.*, *Letters*, II, 118-19, 290, 328.
126. *Ibid.*, *Journal,* 40.
127. *Ibid.*, 39; *Letters*, I, 231.
128. *Ibid.*, II, 221.
129. Jacquemont, *Letters,* II, 112.
130. *Ibid.*, 118-19.
131. Hugel, *Travels*, 293-94.
132. *Ibid.*, xiv.
133. Hugel, *op.cit.*, xiv, 261–283, 356–381.
134. *Ibid.*, 369, 388.
135. Hugel, *Travels*, 284, 289, 328–36, 325.
136. *Ibid.*, 409.
137. *Ibid.*, 277, 335-36, 409.
138. Hugel, *Travels*, 287-88, 385, 405.
139. *Ibid.*, 405–07.
140. *Ibid.*, 410–14.

4

Evidence on Polity

Most of the travellers do not provide a systematic account of the political career of Maharaja Ranjit Singh except Baron Charles Hugel.[1] But his account is based on the work of Henry T. Prinsep.[2] However, the information on the functionaries like *subedar, kardar, kiladar, qanungo, kotwal* etc. and the province, pargana and village as a unit of administration lack details and systematic presentation. But their observations on the early nineteenth century Punjabi polity should not be treated as insignificant. In fact the interests of the travellers lie more in the working of certain institutions such as revenue, military, justice and above all the nobility of the kingdom of Lahore. Also, their prime interest was to observe carefully the Anglo-Sikh and Sikh-Afghan relations. In the chapter an attempt is being made to study the evidence provided by the travel literature on polity.

All the travellers agree that the factionalism which existed among the chiefs of the Punjab provided an opportunity to the rapid increase of *Maharaja's* power. Disunited as they were they could not withstand before the superior power of Ranjit Singh, who had 'unshaken confidence in his own resources' and submitted them to him.[3] By this time, all those chiefs who carried the battle-axe of the people against the Mughal and the Afghans had ceased to exist.[4] The rapid fall of the Durrani power, subjection of the Kabul court to factional intrigues and counter intrigues also contributed to the rise of the *Maharaja*.[5] Hugel observes that "the same causes which operated in favour of the extension of the East India Company's dominion contributed also to give Ranjit Singh unlimited power in the Punjab."[6]

The conquests and consolidation of the kingdom of Lahore is broadly marked by three phases : from the occupation of Lahore to the year 1809; from this date to the year 1818; and from the death of Fateh Khan in 1818 onward until Maharaja's advance towards Sindh and Chinese territory was checked by the British. Occupation of Lahore in 1799 signalized the downfall of the independent Sikh chiefs and the consequent superior authority of the conqueror.[7] Henceforward, unchallenged by both Muslim and Sikh Chiefs alike, Maharaja Ranjit Singh extended his domain as far as the river Jamuna. His field of activities was limited to the river Satluj by a treaty with the British in 1809.[8] However, his expansionist policy was directed to other directions. The hill states drew his attention where Sansar Chand was very powerful. But with his subjugation, all the Hindu principalities in the hills tendered their submission. Ever *sardar*, no matter what his faith might be, had to pay him tribute. If hencefused to obey he was summoned to the camp, was deprived of his territories and sent in chains to Lahore.[9] Death of Fateh Khan, the powerful Kabul *wazir*, in 1818 made Ranjit Singh free from the West. The year following he conquered Kashmir. He succeeded in extending his dominion across the Indus to Jallabad, half way between Attock and Kabul. Hugel strongly believed that "nothing but death or some change in the policy of the East India Company would deter him from attempting the conquest of Kabul itself."[10] However, in the North, general Jorawar Singh extended the frontier up to the border of China.[11]

Thus, when Burnes visited the kingdom of Lahore in the 1830s, he found that the Punjab was 'one of the few countries on the globe', which had both, 'political and natural limits defined'. On the North it was bounded by the Himalaya; Westward by the Indus, and on the South and East by the river Satluj.[12] Watered by the five rivers, the territory of the Maharaja was 'compact and his hold over it was strong'. His government was 'most vigorous and well consolidated'. But this vigour was sufficient only 'for a native state.'[13]

Number of administrative institutions have drawn the attention of these travellers. Revenue of the kingdom of Lahore is one of them. According to their estimation, the net revenue of the kingdom of Lahore amounted to about two and a half *crores* of rupees per annum.[14] It includes all the revenue appropriated by the *jagirdars* and religious personnel.[15] Jacquemont observed that the *Maharaja* received a great deal in kind, contribution of horses, camels, cloths, grain and lastly of soldiers from his vassals in addition to net revenue. It was estimated about three crore of rupees.[16] Both Masson and Jacquemont affirms that after defraying all the expenses of the state the Maharaja's net saving was rupees one crore annually.[17] However, the bulk of the receipts came from the land revenue.[18]

Batai (sharing) was the predominant mode of assessment of the land revenue, though all the other methods did exist side by side.[19] The share of the state was fixed according to the productivity of the soil as of the capacity of the cultivators to pay. For example Moorcroft tells us that in the province of Kashmir the state demand was one half of the total produce. One fourth of the remaining half was taken extra as *abwab* and *kharch* and *takavi*. In all, it amounted to 7/8 in the case of *sarkishit* and 3/4 in the case of *pahikishti* land.[20] In Multan for instance, the cultivators paid 1/3 of the gross produce.[21]

The revenue was farmed to the highest bidder. These travellers describe the farmers of the kingdom of Lahore as the most 'rapicious' and 'oppressive'.[22] Being independent of the provincial governors, they collected the exactions arbitrarily. At the outset, they were presumed to be dishonest and aware of the fact that, "rifle the peasant and are prepared to the rifled in return".[23] However, the exactions as regulated by the state were 'mild'.[24] Both Burnes and Masson are of the view that peasantry was in 'a most prosperous condition' and did not have any complain about the state exactions.[25] Hugel writing towards the end of the reign of the *Maharaja* describe the state policy as, "the exactions are carried to a certain point, and if they exceed this, the people emigrate and the land is left uncultivated. Hence, the inhabitants, although never meeting with indulgent forbearance, have their capabilities of endurance estimated by the selfish economy of their masters as a driver takes care not lay a heavier burden on his beast than he thinks it able to carry".[26]

The army of the *Maharaja* was a special interest to these travellers, yet none of them, have given a systematic account of its evolution. All of them made observations about the state of the army which they saw or which were paraded before them on particular occasion. Hugel, however, have traced the evolution of the army on the western model from the year 1809 onward. In his assessment, the *Maharaja* did not achieve much success until the appointment of generals. Allard and Ventura in 1822. With their appointment, an all out attempt was made to discipline the *Punjabi* troops in Western techniques.[27] Since his account prior to the year of his visit to the kingdom of Lahore is mostly based on Prinsep's work, the significant part of his account is that of his own observations made during 1835-36 when he was in the dominions of the *Maharaja*.[28]

On the basis of the observation of these travellers, the army of the *Maharaja* could broadly be divided into three parts : the model brigade; regular troops-infantry, cavalry and artillery; and irregular troops. Burnes, Hugel and Masson agree, with minor differences, that the army commanded by the *Maharaja* was around 80,000 in number. The disciplined or regular troops amounted to 25,000 infantry, 5,000 cavalry and 150 guns.[29] The irregular troops which were all cavalry or *gorcharas*, amounted to 50,000.[30] Both Hugel and Masson writing towards the end of the *Maharaja's* reign have given a detailed list of different wings of the army. However, Hugel's estimate is based on Captain Murray's paper. Therefore, we are left with only Masson's account. According to him, the total army of the *Maharaja* was 73, 400 detail of which is as under :

In Kashmir	10,000	Under the orders of Suparsad, the Brahman Governor.

With the King	3,000	
Kharak Singh	2,000	
Sher Singh	3,000	Song of the king
Tara Singh	1,500	
Raja Daiyan Singh	5,000	Prime Minister
Hari Singh	10,000	In command of the frontier on the Indus
Khushadal Singh	3,000	Gurcheris, generally near the king
Sham Singh	800	One of the old chiefs
Fati Singh	500	In authority towards the Satluj
Ganda Singh	800	Garrison of Multan
Officer Commanding at Mankirah	500	In garrison
Najib Regiment	1,000	Ranjit's first raised Battalion
M. Allard's Cavalry	3,000	1. Regt. Lancers 2. Reft. Dagrs
M. Ventura's Infantry	4,000	2 Battal. Regt. I Regt. Light Infantry and I Regt, of Gurkas
M. Caurt's Infantry	1,000	Battalion Regt.
M. Avitable's Infantry	1,000	Battalion Regt.
M. Mevius's Infantry	1,500	Battalion Regt.
M.Campbell's Cavalry Mr. Garror's Cavalry	1,200 600	These officers were dismissed when I was at Lahore; the Regt. Light Cavalry
Dowkal Singh Paltan	1,000	Battalion Regt.
Newly raised Battalion	1,000	Under drill
Camp of the late Mr. Amise. Infantry Cavalry	 4,000 2,000	 Battalion Regt. Light Cavalry at present without commander or European chief
Artillery, reckoning Broadly ten men to Gun, and supposing 200 guns	2, 000	Principally horse artillery and now in course of training by M. Allard

Allownaces for the troops of Raja Gulab Singh of Jammu and the several petty Sikh chiefs dispersed over the country, and not otherwise included.	10,000	
Total	73,400[31]	Battalion Regt.

Five regiments of infantry were paraded before Burnes, who found them 'neatly dressed in white, with black cross belts, and bore muskets'. There was a mixture of Hindustani, Sikhs and Gorkhas in every corps. The brigade manoeuvered under a native general officer, and through its evolution with 'an exactness and precision', fully equal to the British troops. It was commanded by General Ventura.[32]

Moorcroft formed a very favourable opinion of the cavalry of the *Maharaja*. He observed that, "not a single horse neighed, or was restive or vicious in the slightest degree, or was uneasy at mounting, or diverged from the path, though the *Maharaja* affirmed that they had not been ridden sometime past."[33] However, Jacquemont and Burnes were not satisfied with the royal stud. For instance, Burnes found the horses 'caparisoned in the richest and most superb manner', but 'under limbed.'[34] Jacquemont described the cavalry of the *Maharaja* 'very inferior to the Company's.[35]

Burnes formed a very high opinion of Maharaja's artillery. Fifty one pieces which were paraded before him were six pounder drawn by six-horses. He observed that, "the evolution were not rapidly performed; but the celerity was considerable; and no accident in overturning or firing occurred throughout the morning."[36] The guns were 'well cast' and 'carriages in good repair.'[37] However, Jacquemont and Hugel finds many faults in this branch of the army as the guns were of different calibers, not well casted, and likely to be worn out after few discharges, and no uniformity in balls.[38] In any case, the *Maharaja* told Burnes that , each gun charged rupees 5,000 annually in the pay of the officers and men and in keeping up the horses. He had 100 pieces of field artillery, exclusive of battering guns and mortars.[39]

The pay of the troops was higher than the Company's regular troops. For instance, an infantry man got Rs. 7 a month, one rupee higher than the British. Out of these Rs. 7 deduction for clothing, arms and food were made. Regular cavalry man got Rs. 28, which were Rs. 8 more than the cavalry man in British India.[40] However, the pay and promotions were not subject to any set rules. Jacquemont noted that "one Captain may get only Rs. 28 or Rs. 30 a month, another Rs. 40, some as much as Rs. 50 or 60. The *Raja* gives some colonels as much as Rs. 50 a day while, other get only Rs. 10 or Rs. 12".[41] Masson observed that the officers made by the *Maharaja* himself received extravagant allowances, while those promoted by the commanding officers received only the regulated stipend.[42] Besides cash salaries, the regular troops were also paid in the form of Kashmiri Shawls. The *Maharaja* told Burnes, "I gave a chief, who may entitled to a balance of 300 rupees, shawl to the value of 500, he is well pleased, and the state is benefited."[43] Jacquemont noted the *Kardar* of Kotli paying his troops both in cash and kind.[44] The irregular or *Jagirdari* troops were paid through assignment of land revenue in lieu of their services to the state.[45] Promotions were generally made on the recommendations of their supervisor. However, *Maharaja* could appoint, promote, demote and even dismiss any soldier or commander alike. Jacquemont noted in the 1830s that, "so far military ranks has not been a matter of purchase; but there is such a demand for services and promotion that the buyers would be plentiful."[46]

All the travellers are unanimous in condemning the *Maharaja* for his irregularities in the payments of his troops. The whole army was kept sometimes from 12 to 14 months in arrears.[47] The reasons assigned for this are varied. For instance, Burnes asserted that the *Maharaja's* 'growing friendship with the British Government' and the 'increasing avarice of age' were the main cause of his inattention towards the army.[48] Similar views have been expressed by Jacquemont who observed that the irregularity in payment was not due to any financial restrain but of the 'increased avarice' of the ruler.[49] Hugel found it a good means of securing the fidelity of the troops. In any case, the system of keeping the army in arrears was a serious drawback for it generated 'indiscipline' rather than securing fidelity. However, Masson observed that though the army was paid with unpunctualities the soldiers were certain of receiving all arrears once during the years.'[50]

The dress, drill and equipments of the troops of the kingdom of Lahore received a general applaud of these travellers.[51] Both Hugel and Masson gives a detailed information about the dress and equipments of the soldiers. Hugel, who was present on the parade, on the festival of Basant in 1836 says that all the soldiers were clad in yellow uniforms on this particular occasion. Otherwise, "the uniform consisted of a velvet coat or gabardine, over which most of them wore a shirt of mail. Others had this shirt made to form a part of the tunic. A belt round the waist, richly embroidered in gold, supported the powder horn, covered with cloth of gold, as well as the Persian Katar and the pistols which many of them carried in addition to those weapons. Some wore a steel helmet, inlaid with gold, and surmounted with the kalga or black heron's plume; others wore a cap of steel, worked like the cuirass in rings; the cap lies firmly on the turban, and covers the whole head, having openings for the eyes. The left arm is often covered from the hand to the elbow with a steel cuff inlaid with gold. The round Sikh shield hangs at the back, fastened with straps across the chest, a quiver at the right side and bow slung at the back being carried as part of the equipment' a bag made in the belt holds the balls, and a tall bayonet, frequently ornamented with gold, held in the right hand when the man is on foot, and carried over the shoulder when in the saddle, completes the dress."[52] However, both the Sikhs and the Muslims wore for head-dress *pagri*, each regiment adopting a distinguished colour, as red, blue, green etc. In other respects they were clothed similarly to the native troops in the British Indian services, sometimes presenting 'a strange medley of European customs with those of the Punjab.'[53]

All the troops, regular and irregular excepting the irregular cavalry had the French words of command. The French Legion or model brigade had the eagle and the tri-coloured flag, with the inscription Gobind Singh.[54] However, the band of the army was found in agreeable to appearance as to sounds by Hugel who noted that, 'no two sounded together in tune.'[55] Sword, spear, musket, matchlock, flintlock with a bayonet, shield, bow and arrow, pistol etc. were the usual weapons of an infantry and cavalry man.[56] Generally, the soldiers were allowed two to three months leave every year; but all were to be expected to return at the festival of Dushehra, when the *Maharaja* reviewed the assembled forces of his kingdom, which was usually held at Amritsar.[57] The mass system introduced by the *Maharaja* for his soldiers was quite 'an unusual thing' for Jacquemont. Each company of hundred men had four cooks, who prepared the meals. Each soldier received his ration in a bowl and ate separately. It was provided at a deduction of two rupees a month for each soldier.[58]

Jacquemont found Maharaja's troops better than to his expectations in every respect.[59] Burnes found them as "drilled as European, fully equal to the troops of the Indian army, but destitute of the most essential quality of a soldier-discipline".[60] However, proficiency of the troops of the kindom of Lahore surprised Hugel, who noted that, "during my stay in Lahore, his Highness the *Maharaja* has honoured me with a review of those regiments which were here by chance, and which, although soldiers only of a years standing, astonished me by their good appearance and their quick fire; they are decidedly more advanced than recruits of the same standing are in Europe. If I had to proffer my opinion upon the service which may be expected from them, I should say that the troops of the *Maharaja* are fully prepared to dispute the palm of victory in the plains of the Punjab with any army crossing the Atock. The Austrians are celebrated for their shooting at the target but there cannot be better short than one of the Gorchelis, who, every time he fired, shot through the vessel placed as the target."[61] However, in his assessment, the army of the *Maharaja* was 'superior' to any coming from across the Indus, but not of coming from the East of his dominion.[62]

Very little information is available about the judicial system of the *Maharaja*. Most of the evidence are about the administration of justice in the province of Kashmir. Only a few observation gives insight into the attitude of the ruler towards justice, forms of cases and punishments awarded.

Jacquemont observes critically that there were no magistrate among the Sikhs, to dispense justice on the basis of equity. In the absence of judicial officers, an accused could appeal directly to the ruler.[63] But Hugel and Vigne are of the opinion that the office of the Qazi or chief judge was functioning during the reign of the *Maharaja*. The institution had been in continuation since the times of the Mughals. According to Hugel, General Ventura was appointed as Qazi of Lahore.[64] Mohammad Afzal was chief judge of Kashmir.[65] Moorcroft, who was the first traveller to visit the valley of Kashmir after its occupation by the *Maharaja*, refers the Kotwal of Srinagar as the chief officer of justice.[66]

According to Jacquemont, robberies were prevalent in the dominions of the Maharaja.[67] But in Hugel's eyes, the Punjab was much safer than Hindustan. The *Maharaja* used to call every village, near which the robbery took place, to a very strict account and made the inhabitants pay the value of the property stolen to the loser.[68] However, the petitioner had to pay to the judge for his decision, often without the slightest prospect of redress.[69]

Capital punishments were given, but rarely, for the *Maharaja* was always unwilling to inflict punishment of death of mutilation.[70] Hanging is heard of only in the case of lawless tribal people. A slayer of bullock or cow too was punished with death.[71] A homicide was rarely put to death. If one man killed another deliberately or accidentally, he was fined rupees one thousand to two thousand and if he could not pay, he lost his ear or nose. However, penalties and strips were the usual punishment, for serious crimes like the slaying of kind was never heard off.[72]

A chain of informers from the ward of a city or from a village or district to the *Maharaja* in person was observed by Jacquemont, For example, in the larger cities, each quarter, each ward had its own informer, who made a daily report to their superiors of all events in their respective districts. This information was transmitted to the Kotwal, who carried it to the Governors. In the office of the Governor, the choicest of these 'delatious or lies', were sorted out again, and then directly sent to the *Maharaja*.[73] As each officer in hierarchy had 'the most tremendous power over his subordinate', the latter were afraid to make reports to their superiors which were not complete or exact. However, says Jacquemont that, "the Governor of Kashmir is thus certainly better informed than the Perfect of Police in Paris."[74]

Jacquemont found Maharaja's police system in an excellent working. For instance, all the post established for collecting the duties of all description were meant also for collecting information of political nature.[75] These customs officers, observed Jacquemont, were 'the first link in an immense chain of intelligence', which conveyed to the Governors of the Province and to Ranjit Singh himself, information on all details which his prudence or his avarice might desire. Further, he comments that, "our Paris police know nothing in comparison with those of Kashmir, the Punjab or even the British India.'[76] We learn from these travellers, that the *Maharaja* used to appoint "a reporter of events in their journeys, to accompany them, but in fact to keep watch on their activities."[77]

Both Moorcroft and Jacquemont does not present a happy picture of the administration of justice, in the province of Kashmir. Moorcroft states : "The Sikhs seem to look upon the Kashmirians as little better than cattle, the murder of a native by a Sikh is punished by a fine to the government, from sixteen to twenty rupees, of which four rupees are paid to the family of the deceased, if a Hindu, and two rupees, if he was a Mohammedan."[78] Jacquemont comments that "throughout the whole viceroyalty of Cashmere, there is no tribunal to settle private disputes upon the basis of equity."[79] However, Hugel, who visited the valley at the close of *Maharaja's* reign, speaks differentially. He observed that, "men are too valuable to the present ruler of Kashmir to be lightly spared : penalties and strips are therefore, the usual punishments. The people seem contented with the justice dealt out to them, and admitted to me that more than one guilty persons in every twenty is ever visited with the reward due to his crimes. The dreadful cruelties perpetrated by their earlier rulers, who, for the smallest offences punished them with the loss of their noses or ears make the poor Indian well satisfied with their present comparatively mild government, and in truth there is very little oppression on the part of the governors and thandars."[80]

The splendour and the composition of the Lahore *Darbar* has drawn much attention of the travellers. Both Jacquemont and Hugel describe it as 'a singular' one, for the *Maharaja* did not have any throne.[81] He used to sit on a plain golden arm chair, while his courtiers, with the exception of Hira Singh, sat upon the carpet.[82] The court colour was yellow or green. All the chiefs and officers, except Hira Singh, used to wear yellow garments.[83] All the nobles and attendants were splendidly clad and displayed a profusion of gold and jewelled ornaments.[84] Hugel who visited the court of the *Maharaja* in 1836, describes five prominent courtiers according to their ranks : Raja Dhyan Singh, Khushal Singh, Raja Suchet Singh, Hakim Azzizuddin and Khalifa Nuruddin. The other grandees of the Sikh court were with the army or in their own territories. The feasts of the Holi and the Dushehra generally brought them to the presence of the *Maharaja*. The most distinguished among them were Fateh Singh Ahluwalia and Hari Singh Nalwa, the latter rose to the highest estimation through his bravery and an intrepid generalship.[85] All travellers talk highly of the faqir brother *i.e.* Azizuddin, Nuruddin and Imamuddin.[86]

Burnes was deeply interested in knowing the extent of influence which the Sikh Sardars could exercise over the actions of the *Maharaja.* He found a complete ascendancy of the Maharaja over his nobles.[87] The *Maharaja* had subverted or neutralized the power of most of the members of the original Sikh confederacy. He filled their places by 'minions of his own'. Burnes appears to have in his mind the newly created *Rajas* like Jamwal brothers. Hugel refers to the elevation of Jamadar Khushal Singh and Ram Singh. For instance, Khushal Singh was a cook before becoming a Deoriwalla (chamberlain). He enjoyed a great confidence of the *Maharaja* for some time. However, these newly created men were not capable of exerting much influence on the Maharaja.[88]

Both Burnes and Hugel sensed a danger to the Sikh monarchy from the power and activities of the Jamwal brothers, after the demise of the *Maharaja*. Hugel observed that, "one of the greatest obstacles to the duration of the empire founded by Ranjit Singh, consists in the imprudence of suffering so much power to accumulate in the persons of his vassals."[89] These brothers, who were powerful "in money, troops, cannon and fortresses, would with great difficulty be brought into subjection by the arm of the feeble successor of Ranjit and several others are similarly circumstanced."[90] Burnes, however, pointed out that, "it may be imagined that such a long line of innovations has not been effected without exciting the jealousy, perhaps envoy of the old Sikh chieftains."[91]

In this connection the Sikh church was capable of exerting influences on the *Maharaja*. Burnes felt certain that the head of the Sikh Church, Baba Sahib Singh Bedi had enough power to "frustrate the designs of any ambitious prince", by advocating crusade in support of the Sikh religion.[92] However, he found that, the *Maharaja* was aware of this fact and had taken care 'to enlist the church in his cause', by constantly receiving its priests with 'distinction and confidence'.[93]

The *Maharaja* appears to be a successful suzerain in the eyes of these travellers. For instance, Moorcroft noticed that Sansar Chand once a powerful ruler, was a vassal of Ranjit Singh and had to go to his court once a year. Though he was never asked to pay tribute, yet he had to render military service whenever required.[94] No foreigner could pass through the territory of a vassal without the prior permission of the *Maharaja*. The *Raja* of Mandi was so frightened of his Sikh master that he did not allow Moorcroft to pass through his territories, unless he secured permission from the Maharaja.[95] The *Raja* of Kullu was fined rupees 80,000 for having facilitated Shah Shuja's retreat to Ludhiana, and rupees 50,000 for giving cooperation to the British against the Gorkhas.[96] The chief of Ladakh requested Jacquemont to use his influence with the Maharaja to get his arrears due to the treasury of Lahore cleared.[97] Between Baramulla and Mazaffarabad, all the petty chiefs, *Rajas* and *Khans*, were tributaries of the *Maharaja*. Each one of them had, at least one family member as hostage in Kashmir. Even, if there happened to be no male child, their wives and daughters were kept as security for their good behaviour.[98] However, non-Muslim chiefs were no exception in this respect.[99]

As a rule the *Maharaja* never approved of strong forts in the territories of his vassals.[100] Even Fateh Singh Ahluwalia, 'a brother of turban to Ranjit Singh', was instantly summoned by the *Maharaja*, when he heard of the erection of a fortress between Lahore and Ludhiana by him.[101] However, the Jamwal brothers seems to have been an exception in this regard. *Maharaja's* fondness for Hira Singh, the son of Raja Dhyan Singh, was exploited by the trio *Rajput Rajas* : Dhyan Singh, Suchet Singh and Gulab Singh. They made every use of their influence, 'to fill their coffers, and nourish the art of corruption.'[102] Gulab Singh was managing the salt mines and holding a large portion of territories in the Jammu region. Dhyan Singh was exercising his art in the court. He was 'fortifying his native vicinity of Bimber', which he had strengthened by guns taken from Lahore, a fact which no one disclosed to the Maharaja.[103] However, they were judiciously preparing themselves for the future. Both Dhyan Singh and Gulab Singh had long intended to make themselves the master of Kashmir after the demise of the *Maharaja* and having this end in view they were constantly increasing their resources.[104] Unlike other travellers, both Moorcroft and Vigne did their utmost to know the feelings of the vassals with regard to the *Maharaja*. Consequently, they suggested that the vassals of the *Maharaja* were so tired of his high handedness, that almost all of them wanted to come under the British protection, whenever, they could find a suitable chance.[105]

The hold of the *Maharaja* over his *jagirdars* was equally strong; a word from his lips could reduce a noble to a beggar.[106] Transfer of *jagirs* was quite usual.[107] Confiscation of property after the demise of a *Sardar* was a common practice.[108] The 'fiefs' granted by the *Maharaja* were worth a revenue of 1,09,28,000 rupee and could be withdrawn at any time by his arbitrary will or command. These grants of lands were given in perpetuity.[109]

Not only the English, but also the French and German travellers observed the contrast between the resources of the Kingdom of Lahore and the British Empire. In Jacquemont's assessment, Ranjit Singh was the only ruler, who could possibly withstand the British, but even his resources were meager as compared to the British Government.[110] Hugel states that "Ranjit Singh is considered altogether independent of the British Indian Government and in truth is as much so as his position as a weaker neighbour can admit of".[111] Similarly, Burnes noted the 'vigour' of the *Maharaja's* government sufficient only 'for a native state'.[112]

Hugel viewed that the treaty of 1809 was a great set-back to Ranjit Singh's cherished desire to command the whole Sikh nation, but he felt bound to sign it. He remarks that "angry as the *Maharaja* was, he was aware of the necessity of coming to terms with the British Government, whose territories actually bordered on his own".[113] Hugel records that, the *Maharaja* resisted the British demands so long as he could afford it. But when he found himself too weak to act against their wishes, he yielded.[114] The treaty, however, obliged him to increase his power towards North and West. But this was not necessarily what the British wanted. If they did not interfere, it was only because they had many 'weighty affairs on their hands'.[115]

Jacquemont does not keep the British intentions in secret.[116] He suggests that the British Government wished to extend its frontiers from the Satluj to the Indus. So they wanted to prevent Ranjit Singh's design of expansion towards Sindh.[117] In accordance with the instructions from the Court of directors, the *Amirs* of Sindh were pressed hard to sign a treaty affording 'every facility and protection to the commercial and military navigation of the British on the Indus".[118] However, fear of the Sikh danger made the Sindhi to comply the British proposals.[119] This was done without and reference to the *Maharaja*. Hugel thought that it was an act of disgrace on the part of power like the East India Company.[120]

The meeting of the Governor-General with the *Maharaja* at Ropar and the treaty was discussed by the travellers. But they appear to give impression that they are unable to understand the precise cause of the meeting. Jacquemont viewed that the meeting was intended to cement the friendship between two powers and to know *Maharaja's* views about the British Scheme of Navigation of the Indus, and above all, perhaps, it was meant to frighten him with a show of the superiority of the British arms rather than to solicit his willing consent to the British propaslas.[121] Besides, the supposed Russian danger was also made a point.[122] However, the *Maharaja* submitted to the proposals though unwillingly and half-heatedly.[123]

Jacquemont believed that "some day or other (but not for some years), the Company will extend its empire from the Sutluj to the Indus".[124] Hugel observed that the friendship between these two powers was "strong, sincere, reciprocal, full of confidence and without reserve, and it is in the interest of both the parties to maintain it".[125] But he felt certain that the integrity of the Sikh empire rested on its relations with the British Government. For this, he suggested that a treaty offensive and defensive with the British government was the only things that could ensure the dominion of the *Maharaja*. But such a treaty would have prevented the British from taking immediate advantage of any sudden occurrence which might fall out.[126]

The Sikh-Afghan relations are discussed in detail by Masson. For instance, Moorcroft simply observed a sharp distrust existing among the Barakzai brothers, and their inclination to attach themselves with the British.[127] Burnes was more interested to know the power of the rulers of Afghanistan and find out possibility of their being able to resist the Russo-Persian threat and the Sikh pressure.[128] Likewise, Vigne was much interested in the British policy being pursued towards Afghanistan.[129] Though Hugel's account of the Sikh Afghan problem is largely based on Prinsep's work, yet its insertion into his account, expresses his concern. Jacquemont casually made references to the activities of Sayid Ahmed, dissension at the Kabul court and the advantages that Ranjit Singh took of it.[130]

But Masson's account is more significant and authentic as he remained very close to the events which happened during this period. For instance, apart from his long stay at the Court of Dost Mohammad, he was at Peshawar, when Sayyaid Ahmad was active against the Sikhs. When Peshawar was annexed to the kingdom of Lahore in 1834 Masson was there. He accompanied the Afghan forces up to Bassowal when Dost Mohammad marched against the Sikhs. From this time till the flight of the Amir from Shekhan, Masson remained at Jalalabad. In fact, his account is based on his personal observations.

Massons's narrative of Sikh-Afghan relations opens with the invasions of Zamah Shah on the Punjab and closes with final encounter between the Sikhs and the Afghans at Jamrud in 1837. His treatment of the subject, prior to the events of 1820, is extremely sketchy and factually inaccurate. But the events after the death of Fateh Khan in 1818 become significant part of his narrative.

With the death of Fateh Khan the frail constitution of the Afghan monarchy began to crumble. There was a heavy pressure from the Persians and the Sikhs. Tacking advantage of the political upheavals at Kabul, Ranjit Singh reduced Peshawar to a tributary state and annexed Kashmir to the kingdom of Lahore.[131]

The Sikh-Afghan relations mainly revolved around Peshawar after its conquest in 1818. Muhammad Azim Khan, who was heading the Barakzais at Kabul could not tolerate the aggressions of the Sikhs and after great preparation, declared war against them. But he was deserted by his brothers who were holding Peshawar at that time. Afraid of fighting alone against the Sikhs, he left the field without combat.[132]

Masson has discussed Sayyid Ahmad's struggle against the Sikhs into two phases. In the first phase, the Durrani chiefs of Peshawar joined the Sayyid against the Sikhs. In the second phase, the Sayyid directed his hostilities towards the chiefs of

Peshawar. Before his attempt against the Sikhs, the Sayyid was in such a high spirit that "he considered himself the master of Peshawar and the Sirdars as his vasslas."[133] He, even, distributed the Sikh towns and villages among his followers. This made the Peshawar chiefs suspicious. As a result, they kept themselves aloof in the action which followed and the Sayyid could barely save his life. But, he continued his attempts on Peshawar and was once successful in occupying it, for a short while. However, he was killed in an encounter with the Sikhs at Balakot in 1831.[134]

After the conquest of Peshawar in 1818 till its annexation to the kingdom of Lahore in 1834, it Afghan chiefs were practically the vassals of the *Maharaja*. They were allowed to retain their territory on payment of tribute and placing their sons as hostages in the court of Lahore. However, Masson found the Peshawar chiefs very impatient under the Sikh yoke, but every manifestation of contumacy only tended to reinforce their subjection.[135]

The way in which Ranjit Singh annexed Peshawar in 1834, seemed quite ridiculours to Masson. No chief of Peshawar dared to resist the Sikh forces. Hari Singh Nalwa occupied the valley of Peshawar with 9,000 men, while some years before, Ranjit Singh coming in person with 25,000 men, did not venture to retain it.[136] Commenting upon this, Masson says, true it is , "since that period the spirit of the Mohammedans had become dejected by repeated defeats and that there was, as universally is, treachery in the Durrani Camps and Councils."[137] Sultan Mohammad Khan, "in place of adopting any means of defence had sent away the better part of his troops, and prohibited the citizens and people of the country from defending the city, as they wished."[138]

Masson has discussed in details, the measures taken by Dost Mohammad Khan, to recover Peshawar from the Sikhs. After declaring crusade against the Sikhs, 'Dost Mohammad Khan secured the help of the Mullas to justify the assumption of the dignity of Padshah', and the means applied to collect funds for the war against the infidels which amounted to five lacs of rupees. In Masson's opinion, the funds raised by the

Amir should be considered 'as compulsory loans', and not 'as absolute extortions.' However, in spite of the great preparations, 'the Amir began to distrust his power for the expulsion of his foes from Peshawar by force of arms and should have been glad, by any fair pretext to have been enabled to withdraw from the contest.' Not only the Amir but also some of his officers were convinced that it was useless to fight against the numerous and disciplined Sikh forces. Sultan Mohammad, at the last moment, went over to the Sikhs. Consequently, the Amir had to retire without combat with the Sikhs.[139]

Masson's account suggests that, the defection which took place in the Afghan camp at Shekhan, and which subsequently resulted in the flight and disgrace of the Amir, was not a sudden development. It had its germs even before the assumption of the title of 'Padshah' by the Amir. The ceremony was not attended by all the chiefs and relatives of the Amir. His brothers were not willing to see him as their superior. Sultan Mohammad Khan left for Bajor, before the ceremony, on the pretext of collecting support in the warfare against the Sikhs.[140]

The last and final encounter between the Sikhs and the Afghans took place in 1837 at Jamrud. The Afghans had to retire without achieving much success against the Sikhs, partly owing to the lukewarm attitude of Hazi Khan, but mainly due to a large and disciplined Sikh force, the position of the Afghans in this action can easily be discerned from the conversation of Masson with some of the leading persons involved in the conflict. For instance, when Masson asked Jabar Khan, whether he should congratulate for the victory, he replied, "for God's sake, do not mention it."[141] Mohammad Akbar told Masson that the victory was not 'owing to the wound of Hari Singh', while Mirza Sami Khan exclaimed that they were obliged to return because they did not have anything to eat.[142]

It emerges from Masson's account that Peshawar remained the most important issue in the Sikh-Afghan relations since its conquest by the *Maharaja*. In Masson's pages, the Sikhs appears to be all powerful throughout the period. The ascendancy of Ranjit Singh over the Afghans has been attributed to the factionalism in the Afghans camp superiority of the Sikh arms and the diplomatic skill of the *Maharaja.*

Since the *Maharaja's* health was not promising, all the travellers visiting in the fourth decade of the early nineteenth century, ventured to discuss the probable termination of the Sikh Kingdom. For instance, Jacquemont alluded in one of his letters to his father in December 1831, that, every one now ask me what will happen in the Punjab and Kashmir at the death of Ranjeet."[143] Burnes observed that "since the demise of such a man is fraught with much political importance, and his infirmities and habits holds out but faint hopes of longevity, we turn, with increased interest to speculate on the probable termination of this kingdom."[144]

Consequently, a question was posed that who would be the probable heir to the throne? To answer this question, they turned to the family of the *Maharaja* and questioned the legitimacy of his male issues, Perhaps, Jacquemont was the first to say that the *Maharaja* had only one son Kharak Singh and that two without talent and without any chance of succeeding to his father.[145] Burnes, Hugel, Vigne and Masson all subscribed to this view, with the difference of words only.[146]

Hugel, who like Burnes and Masson visualized that the succession would be disputed, observed that Naunihal Singh, the grandson of the Maharaja was a promising, clever, and active youth, but "as he was no More than fifteen it depends much on Ranjit Singh's health, whether he will be able to consolidate a party strong enough to enable him to succeed his grandfather, in suppression of his father's right."[147]

Both Burnes and Hugel found Sher Singh the most influential and rising person and consequently the main contender for the throne. In his final analysis Bunres, however, opined that "if Sher Singh does not secure a supremacy, this kingdom will relapse into the farmer state of anarchy and small republics; or be reduced to subjection by some neighbouring power"[148] But, "it is to be remembered that he is a superiors child and with many friends he has some enemies, and will have to contend with the legitimate son, and perhaps, the treasures of his adopted father."[149] However, both suggested that the end of the anarchy would be with the annexation of the Punjab by the British.[150]

The evidence on Punjab polity under Maharaja Ranjit Singh forms a part of the travel literature. It is sketchy in nature and lacks systematic exposition, though it represents a variety of interests and diverse socio-cultural background of the travellers, yet it underlies a uniform, complex and far-sighted diplomatic policy. The persistent dichotomy of apparent and the real purpose in the travel literature also points to the same direction. The evidence provides an idea of the diplomatic policy of great precision and prudence, pursued by the East India Company to check the expansionist designs of the *Maharaja* both in the east and the west, to counter the Russian threat both political as well as commercial, to pursue their commercial activities in the greater parts of Asia and finally to annex the Punjab.

REFERENCES

1. Hugel is the only traveller who goes into the historical background of the *Maharaja*. He covers the history of the Sikhs from Guru Nanak to the proclamation of the British Indian Government, protecting cis-Satluj states in 1809 and the history of Ranjit Singh from his predecessors to his own times.
2. Hugel, *Travels*, 3, 356, 357.
3. Hugel, *op.cit.*, 364-65, 368; Masson, *Journeys*, I, 403, 416-17.
4. Hugel, *op.cit.*, 392.
5. Masson, *op.cit.*, I, 427–73, 438-39; Burnes, *op.cit.*, II, 314.
6. Hugel, *op.cit.*, 369.
7. Masson, *Journeys*, I, 416-17.
8. Hugel, *Travels*, 277–79.
9. *Ibid.*, 369, 379; Moorcroft, *Travels*, 76; Vigne, *Travels*, I, 107.
10. Hugel, *op.cit.*, 212, 379, 403.
11. Vigne, *Travels*, II, 254, 330.
12. Burnes, *Travels*, II, 279, 282, 295; Hugel, *op.cit.*, 403.
13. Burnes, *op.cit.*, II, 294, 295.
14. Burnes, *op.cit.*, II, 288, 316; Masson, *op.cit.*, I, 430-31;

Jacquemont, *op.cit.*, 10; Hugel, *op.cit.*, 403-04.

15. Burnes, *op.cit.*, III, 297.
16. Jacquemont, *op.cit.*, 49.
17. *Ibid.*, Masson, *op.cit.*, I, 431.
18. Vigne, *op.cit.*, I, 310; Hugel, *op.cit.*, 403.
19. Moorcroft, *Travels*, 73, 119, 344, 405.
20. *Ibid.*, 344,405; Vigne, *op.cit.*, I, 310-11; Jacquemont, *op.cit.*, 70.
21. Masson, *op.cit.*, I, 398.
22. Moorcroft, *op.cit.*, 345, 441, 444; Jacquemont, *op.cit.*, 70, 79, 81, 82; Vigne, *op.cit.*, II, 120.
23. Burnes, *op.cit.*, 297-98; Moorcroft, *op.cit.*, 345, 441.
24. Burnes, *op.cit.*, III, 298.
25. Burnes, *op.cit.*; Masson, *op.cit.*, I, 30, 398.
26. Hugel, *op.cit.*, 405; Moorcroft, *op.cit.*, 343.
27. Hugel, *op.cit.*, 366–68.
28. *Ibid.*, 3, 404.
29. Burnes, *Travels*, II, 286, 287; Hugel, *Travels*, 305, 404; Jacquemont, *Letter*, II, 217.
30. Burnes, *op.cit.*, II, 287; Hugel, *op.cit.*, 368.
31. Masson, *Journey*, I, 431-32.
32. Burnes, *Travels*, III, 155-56; Moorcroft, *Travels*, 59; Jacquemont, *Letters*, I 385; *Journal*, 51.
33. Moorcroft, *op.cit.*, 58-59, 60.
34. Burnes, *op.cit.*, I, 16; III, 154.
35. Jacquemont, *op.cit.*, I, 385; *Journal*, 51; also, Moorcroft, *op.cit.*, 55; Hugel, *op.cit.*, 368; Masson, *op.cit.*, I, 436.
36. Burnes, *op.cit.*, III, 165.
37. *Ibid.*, I, 32.
38. Jacquemont, *op.cit.*, 52-53; Hugel, *op.cit.*, 329-30.
39. Burnes, *op.cit.*, III, 166; Hugel, *op.cit.*, 404.
40. Jacquemont, *op.cit.*, 43, 51; Burnes, *op.cit.*, I, 16; II, 287; Masson, *op.cit.*, I, 437.
41. Jacquemont, *Journal*, 52.

42. Masson, *Journeys*, I, 437.
43. Burnes, *Travels*, III, 164.
44. Jacquemont, *op.cit.*, 67.
45. Hugel, *op.cit.*, 330; *Ibid.*, II, 287; Masson, *op.cit.*, I, 433.
46. Jacquemont, *op.cit.*, II, 193; *Journal*, 32, 52.
47. Burnes, *op.cit.*, I, 78; II, 228; Jacquemont, *op.cit.*, I, 222; *Journal*, 31-32, 52; Vigne, *Travels*, II, 119-20; Hugel, *Travels*, 284, 355; Masson, *Journeys*, I, 437.
48. Burnes, *op.cit.*, I, 78; II, 288.
49. Jacquemont, *op.cit.*, 31-32.
50. Hugel, *op.cit.*, 284; Masson, *op.cit.*, I, 437; Jacquemont, *op.cit.*, 51, 52, 68; Vigne, *op.cit.*, II, 19-20; Burnes, *op.cit.*, II, 287-88.
51. Jacquemont, *op.cit.*, 24, 52; Burnes, *op.cit.*, III, 155; Masson, *op.cit.*, I, 432; Hugel, *op.cit.*, 241, 285, 331, 339, 346-47.
52. Hugel, *op.cit.*, 331.
53. Masson, *op.cit.*, I, 432; Hugel, *op.cit.*, 285.
54. Hugel, *op.cit.*, 284, 289; Burnes, *op.cit.*, III, 102, 156; Jacquemont, *op.cit.*, 24.
55. Hugel, *op.cit.*, 305.
56. Moorcroft, *op.cit.*, 27, 48, 329; Jacquemont, *op.cit.*, 28, 52; Burnes, *op.cit.*, III, 155; Hugel, *op.cit.*, 99, 198-99, 284; Vigne, *op.cit.*, I, 70.
57. Masson, *op.cit.*, I, 439; Jacquemont, *op.cit.*, 58-59.
58. Jacquemont, *op.cit.*, 51-52; Burnes, *op.cit.*, II, 287.
59. Jacquemont, *op.cit.*, II, 183, 217.
60. Burnes, *op.cit.*, II, 286; III, 102, 155-56, 296.
61. Hugel, *op.cit.*, 289, 334-35.
62. *Ibid.*, 332.
63. Jacquemont, *op.cit.*, II, 52, 58, 67, 156; *Journal*, 65.
64. Hugel, *op.cit.*, 317.
65. Vigne, *op.cit.*, II, 37-38, 72.
66. Moorcroft, *op.cit.*, 345.
67. Jacquemont, *op.cit.*, II, 156.

68. Hugel, *op.cit.*, 316, 319, 340; Masson, *op.cit.*, I, 426.
69. Vigne, *op.cit.*, II, 120; Moorcroft, *op.cit.*, 345; Hugel, *op.cit.*, 128-129.
70. Hugel, *op.cit.*, 317.
71. Jacquemont, *Letters*, II, 52, 58; *Journal*, 65; II, 73.
72. Hugel, *op.cit.*, 156; Jacquemont, *op.cit.*, 70-71.
73. Jacquemont, *op.cit.*, 73.
74. *Ibid.*
75. *Ibid.*; Vigne, *op.cit.*, I, 247-266.
76. Jacquemont, *op.cit.*
77. Hugel, *op.cit.*, 29, 59-60, 121, 124; Burnes, *op.cit.*, III, 136; Vigne, *op.cit.*, I, 245-46.
78. Moorcroft, *op.cit.*, 442.
79. Jacquemont, *op.cit.*, II, 156.
80. Hugel, *op.cit.*, 156.
81. Jacquemont, *op.cit.*, II, 15; *Journal*, 42; Hugel, *op.cit.*, 288.
82. Hugel, *op.cit.*, 286, 301; Moorcroft, *op.cit.*, 57; Jacquemont, *op.cit.*, 36; Burnes, *op.cit.*, III, 161.
83. Hugel, *op.cit.*, 286, 287, 301; Burnes, *op.cit.*, III, 155.
84. Masson, *Journey*, I, 443.
85. Hugel, *op.cit.*, 387-88; Masson, *op.cit.*, I, 440; Vigne, *op.cit.*, II, 73-74; Burnes, *op.cit.*, III, 144, 148, 150.
86. Moorcroft, *op.cit.*, 56, 57-58, 62; Hugel, *op.cit.*, 292; Jacquemont, *op.cit.*, 42, 50; Burnes, *op.cit.*, III, 144.
87. Burnes, *op.cit.*, II, 283, 284; Hugel, *op.cit.*, 388.
88. Burnes, *op.cit.*, II, 285; Hugel, *op.cit.*, 292, 384; Masson, *op.cit.*, I, 425-26; Jacquemont, *op.cit.*, 49-50.
89. Hugel, *op.cit.*, 288.
90. *Ibid.*; Burnes, *op.cit.*, II, 285.
91. Burnes, *op.cit.*; Masson, *op.cit.*, I, 441.
92. Burnes, *op.cit.*, II, 286.
93. *Ibid.*
94. Moorcroft, *op.cit.*, 76, 78; Vigne, *op.cit.*, I, 107-08.

95. Moorcroft, *op.cit.*, 26-27, 104; Vigne, *op.cit.*, I, 79-80, 85-86; Jacquemont, *op.cit.*, II, 184-85.

96. Moorcroft, *op.cit.*, 107.

97. Jacquemont, *op.cit.*, II, 140-41.

98. Hugel, *op.cit.*, 83-84, 116, 186, 188-89, 196; Vigne, *op.cit.*, I, 182-83, 192-98, 195; II, 181-82; Burnes, *op.cit.*, I, 293-94; II, 292; Jacquemont, *op.cit.*, II, 150; *Journal*, 85.

99. Vigne, *op.cit.*, I, 133, 156-57, 158, 192-93; Moorcroft, *op.cit.*, 9, 18, 41; Hugel, *op.cit.*, 40, 53, 61, 83-84, 174, 384-85.

100. Hugel, *op.cit.*, 74.

101. *Ibid.*, 397.

102. Burnes, *op.cit.*, II, 284; Vigne, *op.cit.*, II, 422.

103. Burnes , *op.cit.*, II, 285; Vigne, *op.cit.*, I, 238-39, 245; Burne's and Vigne's observations does not withstand the facts. By 1831, the *Maharaja* had felt himself strong enough that he relaxed restrictions imposed on his *Jagirdars*. He himself allowed them to keep guns, and demanded a service of artillery as well along with their contingents of horses and footmen: Fauja Singh, *Military System of the Sikh*, 68.

104. Vigne, *op.cit.*, I, 183, 218-19; II, 107-08, 196, 392; Burnes, *op.cit.*, II, 285, 294, 337; Jacquemont, *op.cit.*, II, 166; *Journal*, 61-62; Hugel, *op.cit.*, 288.

105. Moorcroft, *op.cit.*, 79, 104, 107. Vigne, *op.cit.*, I, 85-86, 145-46, 156-57, 158, 179-80, 192-93.

106. Hugel, *op.cit.*, 158, 330.

107. *Ibid.*, 193.

108. Jacquemont, *op.cit.*, 73.

109. Hugel, *op.cit.*, 404.

110. Ranjit Singh's revenue was only three million sterling while the company's was twenty six millions sterling. To cope with the British he had to raise more taxes, which might have excited the inhabitants of the Punjab to throw themselves into the hands of the British : Jacquemont, *op.cit.*, II, 118.

111. Hugel, *op.cit.*, 16.

112. Burnes, *op.cit.*, II, 294-95.

113. Hugel, *op.cit.*, 277.

114. *Ibid.*, Jacquemont, *op.cit.*, 20.

115. Hugel, *op.cit.*, 284.

116. When Ranjit Singh asked Jacquemont about the Governor-General's visit to Shimla. He said that Wade had prepared for me a very diplomatic reply to this question namely that 'the friendship which the Governor-General felt for the Rajah made him desire to be near him. But Jacquemont told the truth that 'it was to avoid the heat of Calcutta': *Journal*, 37.

117. Jacquemont, *op.cit.*, I, 231; *Jounal*, 39.

118. *Ibid.*, II, 221.

119. *Ibid.*, *Journal*, 39.

120. Hugel, *op.cit.*, 234-35.

121. "What Lord William wants with Ranjit Singh, I am unable to guess, -to frighten him perhaps and show him how easy it would be to annihilate him. The colonel of one of the two regiment of English cavalry in the Calcutta Presidency, write to me from Simla that he has been appointed to command, not the escort, but the army which is to accompany/Governor-General to his interview with Ranjit, if it take place' or the embacy to Lahore, in the reverse case. He will take his regiment of lancers, a regiment of native cavalry, one of English infantry, two of Seapoy's and a battery of light artillery-all picked for the occasion. I do not know how far the *Maharaja* will relish so many honours': *Letters, II, 112.*

122. *Ibid.*, 276.

123. *Ibid.*, 290.

124. Jacquemont, *op.cit.*, I, 232; II, 221, 255-56; *Journal,* 39.

125. Hugel, *op.cit.*, 335-36.

126. Hugel, *op.cit.*, 409.

127. Moorcroft, *op.cit.*, 469-70.

128. Burnes have devoted about 50 pages to the Afghan affairs from 1809 to the death of Azim Khan in 1824. Out of these fifty only five pages are given to the Sikhs and the Afghans : *Travels*, II, 299–345.

129. Vigne have given about 37 to the Afghan affairs, but we find only 2½ pages about the Sikh-Afghan problem, and that too is based on Prinsep and Masson's works. Rest of the pages are

devoted to the then current question among the English whether or not the Auchland's decision to support the Shah was right or wrong and on whom to lay the responsibility of British disaster at Kabul: *Travles*, I, v-xxxix, 235.

130. Jacquemont, *Letters*, I, 408; II, 8, 57, 83, 87; *Journal,* 13, 30.

131. Masson, *Journeys*, III, 34, 35, 39-40, 47, 48, 51-52, 64.

132. Masson, *op.cit.*, II, 56, 57–60.

133. Masson, *op.cit.*, I, 133.

134. *Ibid.*, I, 14, 132-35; 137, 142-43, 165; III, 79-80.

135. *Ibid.*, I, 132.

136. Masson, *op.cit.*, III, 229.

137. *Ibid.*, III, 228.

138. *Ibid.*, III, 224-29, 266-67.

139. Masson, *op.cit.*, III, 305-314, 328, 331, 333–48.

140. *Ibid.*, III, 307-08, 310.

141. Masson, *op.cit.*, III, 395.

142. *Ibid.*, 381–97.

143. Jacquemont, *op.cit.*, II, 238-39.

144. Burnes, *op.cit.*, II, 283, 296.

145. Jacquemont, *op.cit.*, II, 328; Before Jacquemont, Prinsep had discussed the question of legitimacy : *Origin of the Sikh Power*, 42, 50.

146. Burnes, *op.cit.*, II, 296; Hugel, *op.cit.*, 287, 288, 356, 406; Masson, *op.cit.*, II, 441-43; Vigne, *op.cit.*, I, 180; II, 425.

147. Hugel, *op.cit.*, 287-288, 406-09; Masson, *op.cit.*, I, 442.

148. Burnes, *op.cit.*, II, 297.

149. *Ibid.*, 298; Hugel, *op.cit.*, 288; Masson, *op.cit.*, I, 442.

150. Burnes, *op.cit.*, 296-98; Hugel, *op.cit.*, 406-07.

5

Evidence on Economy

The European travel literature under consideration contains much information on the economy of the kingdom of Lahore. Although, the mainstay of the people of the kingdom of Lahore was agriculture, yet a considerable portion of its population was engaged in industrial and trading activities. The information that we have in travel literature pertains to agriculture, industry, trade and natural products. In the chapter, the evidence on economy would be looked into in order understand its historical significance.

I

Large productive plains, watered by never failing springs of the Himalaya were the natural assets of the agriculturists of the kingdom of Lahore. Bist Jullundhar *Doab* and the *Majha* tract in the Bari *Doab* were well peopled and richly cultivated, and so was the case of the Rachna *Doab*. The Chaj and Sindh Sagar Doabs had less land under cultivation.[1] However, these were rich in vegetable, mineral and animals.[2] Extensive pastures along the river banks, in the mountains and sub-mountaince regions were not less valuable than the tilled land; as these supported numerous herds of cattle and thereby provided subsistence to a considerable portion of its population.[3]

Agriculturists of the kingdom of Lahore produced food grains, pulses, oil seeds as well as cash crops; vegetables and fruits included. Wheat, barley, maize, millet, rice were the food grains. Grams, *mung, mash, maser, moth, rajmah* were included in the pulses. Amongst the oil seeds, rape, mustard, linseed, sesame etc. were important.[4] Rice was largely raised in the sub-mountain regions, and in the valley of Kashmir it formed the staple crop where three fourth of the cultivated land was under rice cultivation. A superior quality of rice known as '*bara* rice' was produced in Peshawar, around the river Bara.[5] Cane thrived well in all the Doabs.[6] Cotton was raised at many places, but chiefly it was grown in the Bist Jullundhar *Doab*, and on the skirts of the mountains.[7] Tobacco was cultivated in many places in Bist Jullundhar, Bari and Rachna Doabs. But the produce of Multan and Kashmir was of a good quality.[8] Saffron was raised in Kashmir; the town of Pampur was famous for its quality product.[9] Indigo was reared in Multan and eastward of Lahore. Vigne observed wild indigo around Mansabal and the Wular lake in Kashmir.[10] Opium was largely raised in Kullu and Dera Fateh Khan.[11] Hugel noted the cultivation of ginger and turmeric which was exported largely to China.[12]

Vegetable culture too was well known to the farmers. Almost all the eastern varieties of vegetables were produced extensively such as pumpkins, turnips, carrot. Spinach, potatoes, turnip, cucumber, lettuce, melon, water-melon,[13] the floating gardens in the lakes of Kashmir received special attention of Moorcroft and Vigne. These were a good source of income to the peasants as well as to the state as these were heavily taxed.[14] *Sinhara* (waternut) produced in the lakes of Kashmir gave average return, as estimated by Moorcroft in 1823, from 96 to 120,000 ass loads. It yielded Rs. 1,00,000 a year to the state as revenue.[15] The stem of the Nymhea louts supported nearly 5,000 person for eight months in Kashmir alone.[16] Besides, rivers, lakes and ponds provided fish as a food to the wealthy and a source of income to the poorer.[17]

Moorcroft gives us a very detailed account of the management of poultry and bee-farming in the province of Kashmir, but neither he nor any other traveller under discussion gives any information about this profession being pursued in other parts of the kingdom of Lahore. The fact that after the famine of 1833, when poultry perished in the Valley, col. Mian Singh imported it from the Punjab to start this pursuit afresh, suggests that this trade was well known to the *Punjabis* too. In the province of Kashmir, it was the general practice of the farmers to have several hives in a house. Moorcroft was all praise for the Kashmiri method of bee-keeping that he suggested its imitation in Europe. However, the return was less than an ordinary yield of a good swarm in England. Also *Kashmiris* were ignorant of using it as the basis of fermented liquor. It was sold at the price of about three pence a pound but wax was considerably dearer.[18] The valley of Lolab was famous for the best quality of its poultry, and the practice of capon was known. The *Kashmiris* designed their houses in such a way that it could provide shelter to their poultry. Also, it was managed it the boats.[19]

Extensive pastures along the river banks and on the skirts of the mountains supported numerous herds of cattle of the pastoral tribes, such as *gujars*, *chaupanapals* and *gulubans*. Buffaloes, cows, bullock, sheep, goats, camels, horses and mares of superior description were found n abudance.[20] The land of *Majha* (a tract between the rivers *Ravi* and *Beas*), was celebrated for its horses. The Dhani horse was well known as its oxen. Mules reared on the banks of Jhelum were strong and capable of bearing great burden; while the camel on the southern parts of the Punjab were equally serviceable. Moorcroft, observed excellent brood mares in the valley of Jaswal in the hills.[21] Besides, sheep and goats were reared in plenty in the hills as also in the plains. Wild goats too were in abundance in the forest which yielded aslitus or fine shawl wool.[22] The profession of rearing cattle not only provided subsistence to a good number of families by selling milk and ghee, but also to a considerable portion of the population directly or indirectly engaged in the leather industry, as in selling flesh for food.[23] The plantation of orchards was not out of practice in the hills, as in the plains. The horticulturists of the kingdom of Lahore produced: mangoes, oranges, banana, fig, jaman, lemon, guava, jamboo, bair, greengage, dates, apples, pomegranates peaches, apricots, walnuts, quinces, pear, grapes, almond, cherries, plums, mulberries, horse-chestnut, edible pine (jelgoza) etc.[24] about eighteen or twenty varieties of grapes were cultivated in Kashmir; the best were originally brought from Yarkand. The plains of Kamraj in the province of Kashmir produced the best quality of apples.[25] Four varieties of walnuts were grown. Besides eating, its oil was used for cooking and burning in lamps. Oil-cakes prepared from its oil were given to cattle as feed, its husk furnished black and green tints to dyers. Apart from the nuts eaten by men, the oil and oii-cakes yielded Rs. 1,13,000 a year to the province of Kashmir.[26] Sericulture and flowery culture too was practiced.[27]

None of the travellers except Moorcroft have raised the question of proprietary rights in land in the Punjab. But he too raised this question in the case of the province of Kashmir alone. He observed that 'from time out of mind', the land belonged to the rulers of the valley.[28] As a corollary to this system, the status of the cultivators appears to be as those of the 'occupancy tenants'. A cultivator used to pay two share of his produce; one as a rent and the other for the protection, the ruler afforded to him. Vigne says that "out of hundred *Kharwars* fifty were set apart fro the *Maharaja,* twelve and a half more were taken as governor's prerogative; out of the remaining thirty seven and a half, the cultivator had to pay other cesses due to the persons connected with revenue machinery.[29] Nevertheless, some rights were granted to the villagers to get benefits from pastures, forests, pathways, burial and cremation grounds etc.[30]

To ensure the extension of cultivation, several kinds of incentives were provided to the agriculturists. Measures taken in the province of Kashmir after its conquest well illustrate the attitude of the ruler towards the peasantry. Zamindari system was done away with and so was the beggar. A peasant and a headman was treated alike; each one was individually answerable to the state for the expected return.[31] No trukee was charged for the first year in the case of *Paikishti* land from those who brought new land under cultivation. From second year it was charged at the rate of two *tarks* instead of four, the usual rate. After the famine of 1833, the revenue officials were asked to tour the valley at the time of sowing each harvest, and prepare a fresh list of the houses and peasants. The seed for sowing and grain corresponding to the requirement of the peasants till the crops were ready for harvest were distributed. This seasonal help or *takavi* as it was known chargeable at the time of harvest given directly to the cultivators and not through the *muqaddam*.[32] Furthermore, items of extra demands were withdrawn; even the rate of *trukee* was reduced from five to four *tarks*. Incentive was given to the producer of grapes by lifting ban on the making of wine, which had been imposed by the earlier ruler.[33]

In terms of operation and implements, the agriculture of the kingdom of Lahore remained traditional; but it was not primitive. The implements were simple but not crude.[34] Organic fertilizer was used. In Kashmir, besides manuring the rice field, the equality of the soil was improved by the distribution of clod of fresh earth.[35] Besides rain, irrigation was done by streams, springs, canals cut from the rivers, wells, jhalars etc.[36] Two sets of harvest were gathered in a year : the *rabi* crop, sown in October-November and reaped in April-May, and the Kharif, sown in June-July, and reaped in September-October. Rotation of crops and double cropping was practiced. Attempts were made to introduce better varieties by importing seeds from other regions. Similarly, quality of fruits was improved through engrafting.[37]

II

Industries of the Kingdom of Lahore have drawn the attention of almost all the travellers. Textile, a major industry of the period has been discussed at length. It includes woolen, cotton and silk textiles. Other industries discussed by these travellers are metal industry, turnery, boat building, pottery, saddlery, basket making, wine making, sugar industry and perfume making. Besides, the wages and working conditions of the workers engaged in these industries are also discussed.

Textile industry of the kingdom of Lahore produced woolen, cotton, and silk fabrics of numerous descriptions to suit the demands of its inhabitants as of the distant countries. Woolen goods were manufactured at many places in the hills as in the plains. Besides, Amritsar and Srinagar, other places where woolen goods manufactured were Lahore, Pathankot, Gurdaspur, Nurpur, Chamba, Kullu, Badarwah, Kishtwar, Islamabad and Bijbeara.[38] However, Srinagar and Amritsar remained the largest and therefore the most important centres for the production of woolen fabrics. Kashmiri shawls were known for the 'fineness of its texture and brilliancy of its colours', besides being 'light and warm'. Both Hugel and Vigne have attributed the origin of this industry to the renowned Muslim king. Zain-ul-abidin who ruled Kashmir in the 15th century.[39] However, during the reign of the Sikhs, the shawl industry reached at the highest level of its perfection. Even it surpassed the European manufactures.[40] In the 1820s, this industry engaged 1,20,000 Kashmiri.[41] Apart from weaving, several other crafts were allied to this industry.[42] A good number of people were involved in bringing the shawl wool into Kashmir and Amritsar as in other centres.[43] The value of shawls and shawl goods manufactured in Kashmir in 1820s was about 35,00,000 per annum which doubled in 1830s.[44] Vigne noted in the 1840s about 3,000 shawl *dokans* or looms working in Kashmir.[45] Kashmiri settlers at Amritsar produced a considerable quantity of shawls but Amritsar shawls were not a match to the Kashmiri produce.[46] Besides, shawls, Kalin Pashmina too were manufactured in Kashmir.[47]

Besides shawls, blankets of both superior and inferior kinds we produced.[48] *Pattu* was made from second wool known as *phiri,* its texture was very strong.[49] *Asli tus* was worked into tusi which formed a warm, soft cloth of gray colour much worn in the hills. A texture made of *asli tus* mixed with other wools was made for export.[50] Amrisar weaver produced 'thick and warm' woolen stuff known as sege, mainly for the consumption of the army.[51] In addition to these an immense variety of woolen articles were manufactured. For instance, women's veils or square shawls, girdles for the waist, *doshals, patka* or turbans, shawls, carpets, trousers, netted cloth, *gulbadan, lungis,* caps, short and long stockings, canopies, curtains saddle cloths, elephants husing, *palang posh,* coverlet, neckerchief, waistbelts, postin (cloth left long in the line pelisses), leggings, waist-strings, pillow-bier, bags, purses, covers for tomb-stones, hangings in front of recesses or cupboards, dish covers or napkins of various qualities and patterns.[52] Cotton cloth of various texture was manufactured at Multan, Lahore, Amritsar, Hoshiarpur, Srinagar, Peshawar and Bhawalpur. In fact, every village, particularly in the plains, produced some cotton for its consumption and the Punjabis wree not only self-dependent in their needs for cotton cloth, but exported it to distant countries.[53] Generally, the fabric produced was coarse and flimsy, and in appearance it was considered to be much inferior to British manufacture. But it was stronger and durable. Being much cheaper it was liked by the people.[54] However, a finer kind of cotton cloth and muslin of superior description was also produced in large quantity. Hoshiarpuri white cloth was renowned in distant part of the country. Its whiteness was attributed to the remarkable efficacy of its water.[55] Multani chintzs had a good name in Central Asian countries.[56] Multani carpets were inferior to those made in Persia; but those of Kashmir were certainly superior to the Persian manufacture.[57] *Lungis* were made at many places but the Bhawalpuri *lungis* were known for fineness of their texture.[58] Besides, places of blue and white cloth for turbans, *kamarband*, and stockings, cotton tents were also manufactured.[59]

Fabrication of silk cloth of various kinds was famous not only in the kingdom of Lahore but throughout Hindustan and Central Asian countries.[60] *Kais*, a silk manufactures of Multan, had a merited reputation in Hindustani markets due to the strength of its texture and brilliancy of hue. It was available in all colours and valued from Rs. 20 to 120 per piece. Though it was less delicate in texture than the silk *lungis* of Bahawalpur, yet it had an extensive sale, for the Hindustani weavers were unable to rival either in their colour or durability.[61] A considerable manufacture of 'satin' called *atlass* was also done at Multan. The kincob or brocade too was manufactured but it was inferior to the produce of Gujrat and Bengal. Other important items of silk fabric were : *lungis*, *gulbadan* or red silk cloth for ladies' trousers, and *chikun* or flower worked in silk upon cotton ground, scarfs, shashes, pieces for the gowns of women, trouser strings etc.[62]

Allied with the textile industry was the art of dyeing and embroidery, Multan, Lahore, Amritsar, Hoshiarpur and Srinagar were among the important centres of dyers.[63] Both Moorcroft and Vigne refers dying as an important occupation which was invariably hereditary. The Kashmiri dyers were said to be able to give as many as sixty tints to shawls, most of which were permanent.[64] Many sorts of apparels were decorated with embroidery such as caps, shoes, belts, garments, elephant trappling; tent particularly the royal tents, *phulkaris,* shawls etc. It was done at many places, but Srinagar was the most important centre of embroiders after Amritsar. Moorcroft has given a detailed process through which shawls were being embroidered both in the loom and out of it. He counted 400-1500 needless on the loom being employed according to the lightness and heaviness of the embroidery.[65] However, for embroidery silk and gold thread was usually used.[66]

Amongst the metal based industries, iron and brass industry was the most important. Besides making implements for the uses of agriculturists, the blacksmiths and *thathiars* made a number of articles for domestic use from iron as also from brass. Guns, pistols, muskets, matchlocks, flintlocks, poniards, bayonets, cannon-balls, helmets, shields, swords, spears, coats of mail, and breast-plates wre manufactured at Multan, Lahore, Amritsar, Jammu, Srinagar and Kohat.[67] Royal *karkhana* of Lahore produced guns of various calibers. Burnes observed six pounder guns, well cast and of good carriage. It was made at Lahore and costs Rs. 1000.[68] Lehna Singh got manufactured big gun of a metal cast from iron bars, at Amritsar.[69] The Kashmiris were excelled in the art of manufacturing gun and pistol barrels. These were of two kinds; the plain and the damasked or twisted.[70]

The manufacturing of damasked sword blades was no longer in practice in Kashmir. Yet some of the blacksmiths continued the manufacturing of these swords.[71] Masson found rifle barrels of good quality being extensively manufactured at Kohat.[72] A coarse kind of cutlery, swords, scissors, and knives, such as used by sailors, were made at Dera Ghazi Khan in abundance.[73]

There are starry references in this literature to the goldsmiths making gold and silver ornaments to be used by both the sexes.[74] Gold ornaments were used mostly by the royal household, nobility and rich individuals.[75] Ornaments of silver and copper were made for the poor. Jacquemont refer to many small factories at Lahore engaged in making copper ornaments and vases.[76] Silver was largely consumed by the mints, where silver coin, known as Nanak Shahi rupee, was coined.[77]

Turnery in wood appears to be an important occupation in the kingdom of Lahore. Moorcroft found many turners in wood at Hoshiarpur.[78] Vigne noted wood carving a prized trade being run at Srinagar. He got prepared a model of the Kashmirian mosque in deodar to carry it to England.[79] wooden toys, wooden clogs, windows and doors of very elegant lattice work, walking sticks, pike-handles, combs flutes, spinning wheels, and several other articles of furnitures and of domestic use were made of wood. Kashmiri artisans were well known for the art of turnery, ornamental carving in wood, inlaid work of different woods, ivory and mother of pearl.[80] They were equally excelled in making boats, bridges, temples, mosques and houses of imperishable deodar.[81]

Boat building was an important occupation allied with wood industry. Pind Dadan Khan, Attock and Jhelum were the important centres of this industry. At Jhelum, Moorcroft, saw good workmen engaged in boat building, who could 'fit the planks together with great nicety'.[82] These were of different sizes and denomination but generally classed into two oihh: the *zehurq* and the *dunga*. A zohurq could carry provisions from 100 maunds to 100 maunds.[83] Deodar wood used for the construction of these vessels came from the hills in the lower Himalaya, through the river Jhelum. *Tahli* and other wood were found in plenty along the river banks.[84] Alexander Burnes have given us a very detailed account of the construction, repair, uses and abuses of different kinds of boats.[85] According to his estimation a zohurq made of deodar could cost from Rs. 100 to Rs. 800 Nanak Shahi at Pind Dadan Khan.[86]

The literature contains references to the work of pottery and saddlery too. Earthen pots were made in large number for domestic as also for agricultural use. In the hills particularly in the valley of Kashmir, *kangirs* was made in considerable quantity.[87] Both Moorcroft and Masson refers to saddlery as an important occupation. Moorcroft found yirak leather of Kashmir much useful to Great Britain.[88] Ornamental pen cases was an art for which the *Kashmiris* had long been celebrated.[89] Paper was made from old cloths and cotton rags in considerable quantity in the plains as in the hills. The Kashmiri also used wild hemp and a kind of reed found near Shalimar for making paper; it was of five variety and considered superior to the produce of the plains. One quire of best quality paper was sold for two rupees.[90]

Basket making was an important cottage industry. Towards the hills, Moorcroft observed that "each village had a plantation of willows, they were all pollards: the twigs are used for baskets."[91] The utility of basket in the Punjab was immense.[92] Similarly, mats were manufactured in large quantity.[93]

Plumes were made of heron's feather as these were in great demands by the army. It was worn by the soldiers and offices alike. These were of various kinds. However, for the use of royalty and nobility or richly ornamented with pearls emeralds and rubies.[94]

Wine making too was known to the natives of the kingdom of Lahore. Burnes found that the *Punjabis* preferred the 'Pungent fiery drink of the their soil.'[95] Mountaineers made spirituous liquor named *buza*.[96] Hugel gives us a recipe of the brandy which was specially brewed for the *Maharaja*, called the royal wine.[97] Brandy and wine was also made in Kashmir from the indigenous grapes. Moorcroft did not appreciate the Kashmiri method of making and preserving liquor. He wished that with proper treatment and care the wines of Kashmir might be made rival many of those of Europe.[98] However, it was much preferred to the finest wine that Europe could produce, for the latter was less strong than the former.[99]

Sugar was extracted from sugarcane.[100] Oil was extracted from walnut kernels, sesame, linseed, rape, mustard etc.[101] Above twelve thousand ass loads of walnut kernels were annually appropriated to the oil-press in Kashmir. Its gross yield, in the form of oil and oil-cakes, was rupees 1,13,000 a year. It was extensively used in cooking and for burning lamps, besides being an article of export.[102] Moorcroft was much impressed by its qualities, as for extracting perfume, and using it for medicinal purposes, that he strongly recommended its introduction into Europe and British Indian province as well.[103]

Roses of different variety and colour were in abundance in the gardens as in the vales, and rose water was distilled. However, distilled rose water of Kashmir was surpassingly fine, and *attar* made from it was of a good quality.[104] Scent was also made from the Jasmin (Yasmin), the tuberose (Jambak), narcissus (Nerghis), chamomile (Babena), and of the yellow rose (Zeba).[105]

Raisin and vinegar was made from grapes. A very fine cooling beverage was made from the quinces. Besides, confectioners and bakers could be found in almost all the cities and towns in the kindom of Lahore. They well knew the art of preserving fruits of many kinds to be used as sweatmeat as also a tonic medicine.[106]

Organizationally, the industrial activities may be classed into two; the urban industries and the rural crafts. Both private and state ownership existed. The private establishment fulfilled the needs of the public as also produced goods for export and for the royal use too. Royal *karkhanas,* as the state establishments were popularly known, concerned mainly with state requirements. The rural industries generally met the local requirements and provided basis for varying degree of self-sufficient village economy.

There are references in this literature to the general condition of the workers and management of these establishments, particularly the private concerns. For example the shawl weaving industry was, perhaps, the biggest one in the kingdom of Lahore. It employed, 1,20,000 persons of both the sexes in Srinagar alone. Several categories of artisans were alliked to this industry.[107] The weavers were all male commencing to learn the art at the age of ten. In all transactions there were two parties; the master and the schooler, the former being capitalist and the latter the mechanic. They worked under four different conditions; work for wages, on contract base, a sort of partnership and equal division of the profit. Amongst these, the first was, perhaps, the worst one as under this condition the wage labourer was not better than a 'bondslave.'[108] A first rate shawl weaver did not get more than rupee a day, whereas a weaver of ordinary skill drew eight *annas* a day. A beginner in this profession just got two *annas*.[109]

Working conditions were not congenial to health too. One of the shawl factory visited by Hugel was described as "one of the most wretched abodes that my imagination could well picture. They work in winter in a room which is never heated, lest dust or smoke might injure the material"[110]

The plight of the spinners was equally bad. Spinning industry in Kashmir aloe employed 1,00,000 female. Out of these 90,000 were spinning for livelihood while rest of them worked for obtaining shawls either for themselves or for their families.[111] A woman commenced her work at day break extending her labour until very late in the night, using moonlight when available to avoid expenses of oil for lamp.[112] Putting such a hard labour, these spinners could not earn more than three rupees eight *annas* a month. Subtracting the price of wool from it, it left only one rupee eight *annas* a month or about three paises a day. However, in some cases, the earning was nearly double depending upon the demand of the market and fineness of the yarn.[113]

III

Mineral resources of the kingdom of Lahore were immense. The range of hills, extending from Jhelum to Indus had extensive deposits of rock-salt. Salt was also found in Mandi in the foot hills. Eight hundred thousand maunds of salt was annually extracted from the salt Range at Pind Dadan Khan. Being an article of export; it brought considerable profit to the state.[114] Depositaries of coal and iron too were found in the foot hills.[115] Lime-stone, gnesis and mica slates, a silicious girt and gypsum was found in the hills.[116] Lead and copper too was found in the hills.[117] Alu, sulphur and antimony was found in the salt range and other high lands of the Punjab.[118] Gold was found in the sands of Chenab and Indus.[119] The Punjab plains yielded a considerable quantity of nitre. A best quality of charcoal was made from *tooree* or milk-bush; it provided a necessary ingredient for manufacture of gun power.[120] Burnes refers to the existence of wells of naphtha (petroleum) in the province of Peshawar.[121] Saltpetre was manufactured in considerable quantity on both sides of the *Ravi*.[122]

Forests were another useful natural resources. The mountains were coated with rich forests; theses provided many kinds of wild fruits and varieties of wood trees, as also several species of useful animals. Wood of deodar was the most valuable products of these forests, its timber was of the finest quality and articles made of it could last for centuries. Besides, wood for fire and charcoal was found in plenty. A large number of cattle were fed on the leaves of trees, wild grass; dried or green and verdents. Many kinds of herbs too were collected from these forests. For instance, the roots of *kuth* or custus were collected by the inhabitants of the parganas of Lar Kohima, Kamraj, Bankil and Lolab. These were exported to Amritsar in considerable quantity. Moorcroft puts it as one thousand as loads. The drug prepared was sent to Calcutta for export to China. Similarly, morels a sort of mushroom grown on the hills of Kashmir was used as vegetable and medicinal purposes.[123]

IV

The kingdom of Lahore was dotted with several cities and numerous towns of small and large size through which the trade was conducted. These travellers enumerate; Multan, Lahore, Amritsar, Srinagar, Peshawar, Dera Ismail Khan, Dera Ghazi Khan, Pind Dadan Khan, Attock, Hazro, Jhelum, Rawalpindi, Hoshiarpur, Nurpur, Kullu, Chamba etc. The towns or *qasbas* were linked to a varing degree to the villages around and served as a local centre for collecting and distributing goods for bigger towns and received their necessities in return from these towns. Similarly, the bigger towns received the surplus of the smaller towns and supplied it to the bigger commercial marts like Multan, Lahore, Amritsar, Srinagar, Peshawar, receiving in return their necessities. Thus a village or a cluster of villages was linked with the commercial cities at the top, both through roads and water ways.[124]

The goods exported from the kingdom of Lahore included : agricultural, industrial, as also the natural products. Grain, Sugar, indigo, '*Bara* rice', rock salt, roots of Kuth or costus and arms were sent to British India, China, Bokhara, Tartary, Persia and to other Muslim countries.[125] Multani chintz, *atlass* (satin) and *kais* (silk fabric), Dera Ghazi Khan's *gulbadan*, durries or stripped or plain silken cloth were exported to Sindh, Persia, Central Asian countries and British India. Burnes noted the trade of Multan of the same nature as at Bhawalpur but on larger scale. Within a decade, a trade of ten lacs of rupees was driven in chintz alone from Bombay to northern parts of India. However, trade in this article was on the decrease with Persia. The Multani chintz could not compete with the British manufacture and the price of the Multani chintz remained the same in the 1830s, what it was in the 1820s; whereas the British produce could be purchased at one sixteenth of its value, what it was in the 1820s when the British produce first entered into the Persian market. Also, it had ceased to be a rarity. Both coarse and finer sort of cotton cloth, cotton and silk *lungis* and *susis bafta* were supplied to Afghanistan, Central-Asian countries and to the province south of the river Satluj. Burnes noted a transit trade of coarse white cloth from the Punjab, at Dera Ismail Khan, as 3000 camel-loads or 1,800,000 yards annually. Hoshiarpuri fine muslin of white colour was sent to Delhi and white and red to Jaipur and Bikaner.[126] Cotton of the Punjab was 'well fitted for the China market too'.[127] Sugar and indigo were exported to Bokhara and other Muslim countries. Burnes refers to the export of indigo, from Dera Ghazi Khan to the west, as 2000 maunds in the year 1837.[128]

However, the most celebrated article of export was the woolen manufacture of Amritsar and Kashmir, particularly the Kashmiri shawls. Shawls and shawl goods were extensively exported to British India, Tibet, Ladakh, Bokhara, Russia, Central Asian countries and Europe. A store of shawls, worth 50 lakhs of rupees was run at Amritsar by the state. Hugel refers to the shawl merchants of Amritsar who showed him some letters with orders from London and Paris. In the year 1832, shawls worth of two lakhs of rupees were sent to Russia alone; Kashmiri shawls was a craze of its nobility.[129]

Pashm and silk was imported from Bokhara, Tibet, Ladakh, Khotan and Yarkand.[130] Tea came from China and Ladakh, but a finer kind of tea and musk was supplied by Yarkand and Khotan.[131] Copper, gold, borax, drugs, dye stuffs and hardware were imported from Russia, Yarkand, Bokhara, Kohat, Baltistan, Ghazni, Kandhar, England and Hindustan.[132] Fruits fresh as well as dried came from Afghanistan. Horses and sheep came from Kabul, Bokhara, Persia, Turkistan and Ladakh.[133] Felts, camlet, dried sheep-skins, Yambo silver, steel for making *chakmaks*, boots, leather, brocade, nankins and velvet, broad cloth and muslin were imported from Russia and England. However, finer articles, such as watches, cutlery, jewellery, China ware, glass, pearls and precious stones were also imported but the quantity was very small; for these were used by the royalty and rich individuals.[134]

References to the inter-regional trade are not wanting. Jacquemont observed existence of commercial intercourse between the protected Sikh states and the kingdom of Lahore. Ludhiana had many bankers, who had correspondence at Amritsar, Lahore, Kashmir, Attock and Peshawar,[135] Burnes noted a considerable traffic in manjot (maddar) from westward of Indus to Bhawalpur.[136] Silk fabrics and carpets of Multan were destined for Lahore and Amritsar. Hoshiarpur cotton cloth was largely consumed in the plains of the Punjab.[137] Moorcroft found traffic with the plains from the hills, consisting chiefly by the barter of grains for Lahore salt. Hill districts were supplied with coarse chintz, blankets, cotton cloths from the Punjab plains and were paid with opium and musk at Kullu.[138]

Iron, Copper, Sulphur, logwood were exported from the Punjab plains to the valley of Kashmir. Shawls, shawl wool, blankets, dried fish, fruits dried as well as fresh, caraway seed, saffron, *chob-i-kost,* roots of *kuth*, came to Amritsar in large quantity. Timber used to come from the hills in large quantity to the Punjab plains. Vigne, observed that Raja Gulab Singh was used to order the construction of timber rafts which were floated down the *chinab* river to be sold in the plains.[139]

Several communities controlled the trading activities within and without the kingdom of Lahore. There are references to Aroras, Banias, Gosains etc. amongst the Hindus and the Lohanis amongst the Muslims in this literature. However, Shikarpuri Hindu and Lohani were the most important communities; for long distance trade was by and large in the hands of these merchants. Both external and internal trade was conducted at different levels and in different ways. For example, some merchants were directly involved in the trade, while some were operating it through their agents. Burnes, observed that these merchants had their houses of agencies in many countries from Astracan and Meshid to Calcutta. In Kabul, he found that Shikarpuri merchants along had eight houses of agencies. Yet at an other level trade was controlled by lending monetary assistance to the traders operating on lower level.[140] Furthermore, in some cases the merchants controlled the production units by advancing loans to the owners of the factories to purchase raw material, to pay wages to the workers and also for their personal use.[141]

Both coins as well as exchange of goods were the prevalent means of commercial transactions. In the rural areas and in the hill regions like Hazara, Kashmir, Ladakh, Kullu etc. barter system was in vogue. For instance, at Kullu produce of the plains was exchanged for opium and musk, while provinces south of the Himalaya exported various articles of domestic use to the Ladakhis which were paid for salt, tea, dyes, borax, sheep, wool and gold dust.[142] However, in the towns and cities cash system appears to be predominant. Coins of various nomenclatures were in vogue but Nanak Shahi rupee served as a standard.[143] It was of pure silver weighing 11 mashas and 2 rattis. Copper coins, fractions of rupee; *anna, paisa* and *piee* were coined. Besides, gold mohur was also minted. The royal mints at Lahore, Amritsar, Srinagar also figure in the travel literature. The worth of rupee-coin of various denomination used in the kingdom of Lahore was determined according to the exchange rate fixed to their monetary value ranging from ten *annas* to sixteen *annas* and six paisas. However, Nanak Shahi rupee was equal to the Calcutta rupee. The gold mohur was equal to sixteen Nanak Shahi rupees.[144]

Like coins, weights and measures too were not uniform. *Chawal, ratti, masha* and *tols* were used for weighing precious metals like gold and silver. Grain was weighed as *Chatak, pao, ser, batti, dhari, kacha* and *pacca* maund, cloth was measured as *girha*, and *gaz*. Distance was measured in *kohs*, whereas *sarsai, karam, marla* and ghamaon were the usual measures of land.[145] However, there were certain reginal variations in the scale of weighing and measuring. Far instance, in some areas the maund was of forty *sers* while in some forty-two *sers* formed a maund, yet in some areas *kacha* maund of sixteen *sers* was in force. In the province of Kashmir, *Kharwar, tarak, manwata* and *pals* were used as for weighing grains as also other commodities. Horse's load and man's load was also taken as a unit of weight in the valley of Kashmir. *Kharwar* was also a measure of land in this region. Liquid articles were measured as *paji*.[146] Likewise, *kohs* varied from region to region. For example, Vigne, observed Akbar's *kohs* tower near Agra of two miles distance from each other; and in the hills one and a half miles formed a *kohs*, and so was the case in the Punjab proper. In the valley of Kashmir, a mile and three quarters made a *kohs*.[147]

Means of transport were varied but traditional. Horses, ponies, camels, mules, bullocks, elephants, sheep, human carriers (porters), carts and boats were used to carry provisions and passengers. Admitability of roads, quality and quantity of the goods to be conveyed determined the means to be used. For example, in the hills, mules, hill-ponies, sheep and porters were mostly used. Carts driven by oxen, horses, mules, asses, camels were used in plains. The use of elephants was confined to the royal personal and rich individuals.[148] However, the cheapest mode of transport was the boats. As all the five rivers of the Punjab were navigable and could admit boats of considerable size; a notable transaction was done through these rivers. Burnes found fifty boats being used in the salt trade alone at Pind Dadan Khan.[149] Moorcroft observed that grains and other provisions were being carried into the heart of the city of Kashmir through boats. A large kind of boat used by the Kashmiri could carry provisions to the extent of 150 tons.[150]

Encouragement provided by the *Maharaja* to the mercantile communities in different ways went a long way to flourish the commercial activities in the kingdom of Lahore. Besides, making roads and waterways free from the robbers and highway men, the *Maharaja* issued orders to his officials to provide every type of facilities to the carvans of goods passing through their respective jurisdictions, including the safety of life and property of men and material involved.[151] To satisfy the needs of the huge standing army, the nobility and royalty, the state itself was a big buyer of goods produced within its own dominions, as also imported from the outer world. Not only this, towards the end of his reign, the *Maharaja* started directly participating in trading activities with British India.[152] In addition to these, banking facilities were available through *hundi* system, as also the benefits of loans from the rich bankers or *shahukars*, who resided in all the capital marts of the kingdom of Lahore.[153]

To encourage the industrialists, the *Maharaja* made it a regular feature of using native productions at his court and included these, particularly, the shawls of Kashmir and silk of Multan in the *Khilats* to honour the foreign dignitaries as to his nobles.[154] Commenting upon the manufactures of Multan, Alexander Burnes observed that "Ranjeet Singh with much propriety encouraged their manufacture, since he captured the city and by giving no other cloth at his court, has greatly increased their production..."[155] This was also true with other production of the kingdom of Lahore.

Occasional references to the prices of various commodities, which occurs in this literature does not give an adequate idea of the situation. For instance, Moorcroft visiting in the 1820s, gives prices of some of the commodities, which he bought at Budarwah: shawl wool, tea and horses at Kashmir and Amritsar.[156] Burnes visiting in the 1830s gives prices of some provision, as prevailing in the city of Peshawar and Dera Ghazi Khan only.[157] However, these stray references, suggest that the prices were not uniform in the dominions of Ranjit Singh, and there was a general rise in the prices. Take for example, an average rate of 40 sers wheat, allowing for reginal variation, was a rupee in the 1820s. In the 1830s it was weighed as 32½ *sers* a rupee in the city of Peshawar which was five *sers* less than could be had in 1809 for the same amount. Fine rice was weighed as 36 *sers* for a rupee in the hills in the 1820s, but in 1837, Burnes noted in Dera Ghazi Khan, 40 *sers* fine rice being weighed for three rupee.[158]

The information provided by the travellers is descriptive in nature and does not cover the whole aspects of economy. With regard to agrarian economy no specific information on land tenure, revenue administration, proprietary rights in land in the Punjab etc. is available. However, the observations of these travellers suggest that the pattern of agrarian economy remained traditional. There was no shift in cropping pattern from food stuffs to cash crops; therefore, non-monetization of rural economy. Proportion of land given to food grains was larger than the cash crops. For instance, in the province of Kashmir shali occupied ¾ of cultivable land.[159] Similarly, the Punjab produced more grain than it was consumed by its inhabitants. Production of fruits too was increasing. Moorcroft observed that acre-wise yield of walnut was much larger than any portion of Europe.[160]

On industry, very detailed information is available. Almost all the major industries such as textile, metal based industry, tannery, boat building, pottery, basket-making, wine-making etc. are discussed at length. The facts suggest that the productions of shawls and shawl goods doubled during Ranjit Singh's reign, so was the case with other industrial produces.[161] Significant point is that no change or innovation in the sphere of technology or methods of production occurred. Similarly, there occurred no significant change at the organizational level. Merchant's control over the producers and productions was fairly strong. Advances too were made to the workers. But its use was confined to the purchase of raw material and to feed the labourers.[162] The merchants did not invest their capital for the purchase of new implements. Consequently, the forge and bellows of the black-smith, spinning-wheel of the spinner, and handloom of the weaver, all remained as they were. In short, there was a strong element of continuity rather than any change. Both the producer and the merchants maintained the traditional attitude to work.[163] But inadequate information debar us to determine the volume of trade. The travellers do not provide any systematic account of the custom duties and the number of shops run at capital cities. However, from an increased volume of productions one can discern that the trade if the kingdom of Lahore was in a flourishing state. Alexander Burnes, whose one objective was to acquire information about the possibility of advancing British commercial interests, was rather dismayed to find that though commercially the Punjab possessed for greater facilities than any other part of the country, yet there existed, but very limited chances to sell the British productions with due advantage, for the habitants of the kingdom of Lahore were being supplied with native productions in such exuberance that it was relieved from 'any dependence on external resource.'[164] Hence, the information on trade is inadequate to understand the dynamism of economy of the kingdom. The observations of the travellers lack critical approach. To some extent it can be explained in the varied. Interests as reflected in their evidence on economy. Moorcroft, Vigne, Hugel and Jacquemont are more concerned about conditions of the peasants in the province of Kashmir. The wages and working conditions of the workers are also underlined. They are more critical about the oppressive policy of the kingdom of Lahore. On the other hand, Burnes is more concerned about the Punjab. He is critical about the insufficient irrigational facilities prevalent at that time. Vigne and Moorcroft show keen interest in sericulture and flowery culture. Similarly, textile industry is mainly discussed by Moorcroft, Hugel and Vigne and Burnes. Among them, Moorcroft, Hugel and Vigne discuss the textile industry of Kashmir and Amritsar whereas the textile industry of Multan and Peshawar has drawn attention of Burnes. The wooden industry has been discussed by Moorcroft and Vigne. Moorcroft, and Burnes discusses boat industry. Among all the travellers, Moorcroft covers almost all the fields of economy discussed by these travellers. He even discusses the management of poultry and bee farming in Kashmir.

All European travellers are unanimous in condemning the Sikh rule in the valley of Kashmir as oppressive and tyrannous. They feel that too much extortion caused the impoverishment of the peasantry leaving no alternative but flight to the neighbouring states in search of less oppressive master. This resulted in the scarcity of population causing thereby the fall of the cultivable land. Consequently, the land revenue decreased considerably.[165] Similarly, the fiscal policy of the *Maharaja* is the centre of criticism. According to these travellers every articles, indiscriminate of necessities or luxury were taxed. Alexander Burnes goes to the extent of saying that the 'most excessive duties' had ruined the trade of the Punjab, particularly the trade in horses. For, in order to avoid the duties, the merchants from India to Persia were in the habit of avoiding the route of Lahore, Attock, and Peshawar, in preference to the route via Delhi, Hansi, Bahawalpur and Sindh.[166]

But the criticism does not conform to the reality. Even the information provided by these travellers contain contradictions. With regard to the plight of the peasantry in Kashmir as a result of the oppressive state policy, the picture that we have is altogether different. The flight of the peasants was not due to the oppression alone; the exactions wee carried to a certain point. Also the administration of the Sikhs was not so bad as compared to the Afghans. The low return of the revenue appears to be the result of the withdrawal of certain cesses after the famine of 1833. Above all, it was the natural calamity like earthquake, famine and cholera which reduced the population to one fourth of its former number.[167] The average monthly expenses of cultivator's household appears to be satisfactory. In 1835, the average monthly expense of a family was about two Hari Singh rupees (2sh.8d) whereas the household expenditure of the Punjabi counterpart was about three large rupees (6sh.) The daily wages of the agricultural labourer were about 8 *sers* (12 lbs) of paddy. After meeting the daily requirements of the members of his family, he could save the rice worth one *anna* a day or about two rupees (2sh 8d) a month.[168]

The condemnation of *Maharaja's* fiscal policy too, does not stand firm in the light of the information. For example, Burnes himself states that the *Maharaja* was encouraging indigenous manufactures in a variety of ways. To quote one example, Maharaja Ranjit Singh had made it a regular feature to include his own productions in the *Khilats* (robe of honour) to honour the foreign dignitaries as also his courtiers.[169] To improve the breed of horses, he had established his own stud.[170] Above all, we find in other sources that the custom duties prevalent in the kingdom of Lahore were less than those of Afghanistan and British Indian possessions.[171] Also, the production of shawl goods alone was double of what we find in the beginning of Ranjit Singh's reign. It was presumably the case with other trades.[172]

The contradiction indicates that the travellers did not approach the economic conditions of the period critically. Even their emphasis on the traditional aspects of economy and to prove that it was but continuation of earlier economic conditions also suggest the lack of seriousness. The contemporary scholars have suggested that in spite of the dominance of traditional features and lack of any innovation and change of great magnitude, the economy of the period did not remain the same. It had its own distinct features. This also points that the primary purposes of these travellers was not to explore the economy. Their interest in the economy was superfluous and secondary. Moorcroft writes"...I was travelling in a mercantile character alone, without pretending to any political authority, I declared making him this assurance, and, thanking him for his civility and friendly intensions preserved in my determination to appeal in person to Ranjit Singh".[173]

REFERENCES

1. Burnes, *Travels*, I, 14, 43; II, 299; III, 175-76, 181, 307; Hugel, *Travels*, 27-28, 62; Jacquemont, *Letters*, I, 384.
2. Burnes, *op.cit.*, II, 288, 396-97; II, 298-99.
3. Moorcroft, *Travels*, 49, 94, 344, 407; Burnes, *op.cit.*, I, 10-11; II, 289; III, 287, 298-99; Vigne, *Travels*, I, 210, 301; II, 68, 149, 169.
4. Burnes, *op.cit.*, I, 402-403; II, 325-26; III, 298-99, 326; Moorcroft, *Travels*, 53, 45, 328, 348, 357, 360, 471; Vigne, *op.cit.*, I, 68; Ii, 29, 33, 62-64, 114-15, 162, 183, 204, 307-08, 459.
5. Hugel, *Travels*, 33, 34, 86, 98, 179; Vigne, *op.cit.*, I, 308-09; Moorcroft, *op.cit.*, 348, 446; Burnes, *op.cit.*, II, 321–25.
6. Moorcroft, *op.cit.*, 53; Burnes, *op.cit.*, I, 43-44, 402, II, 325; III, 303.
7. Vigne, *op.cit.*, Ii, 187; Burnes, *op.cit.*, II, 400; Moorcroft, of *op.cit.*, 85, 451, 459.
8. Burnes, *op.cit.*, I, 403; III, 130, 304; Moorcroft, *op.cit.*, 53.
9. Vigne, *op.cit.*, 204; II, II, 33-34, 459; Hugel, *op.cit.*, 125; Moorcroft, *op.cit.*, 359, 412.
10. Burnes, *op.cit.*, I, 402; III, 303; Vigne, *op.cit.*, II, 148, 198.
11. Masson, *Journeys.*, I, 37; Moorcroft, *op.cit.*, 85.
12. Hugel, *op.cit.*, 205-06; Vigne, *op.cit.*, II, 187.
13. Burnes, *op.cit.*, I, 402; II, 325-26; II, 122-23; Moorcroft, *op.cit.*, 334–348, 353-54; Vigne, *op.cit.*, II, 91; Masson, *op.cit.*, I, 415; Hugel, *op.cit.*, 144, 347.
14. Moorcroft, *op.cit.*, 338, 353-54; Vigne, *op.cit.*, II, 62, 90-91.
15. Vigne, *op.cit.*, II, 115, 156; Moorcroft, *op.cit.*, 345, 350, 403, 404, 433, 434.
16. Jacquemont, *op.cit.*, II, 77; Moorcroft, *op.cit.*, 351; Vigne, *op.cit.*, II, 89, 114, 115.
17. Jacquemont, *op.cit.*, II, 147; Moorcroft, *op.cit.*, 404; Vigne, *op.cit.*, I, 156, 178, 207, II, 115–117.
18. Moorcroft, *op.cit.*, 361, 362, 363, 364, 404..
19. *Ibid.*, 409.

20. Moorcroft, *op.cit.*, 49, 94, 344, 407; Vigne, *op.cit.*, I, 210, 301; II, 68, 149, 169; Burnes, *op.cit.*, I, 10-11; 289; II, 287, 298-99.

21. Moorcroft, *op.cit.*, 49; Burnes, *op.cit.*, I, 11, II, 289.

22. Hugel, *op.cit.*, 222, 240; Vigne, *op.cit.*, I, 206-07, 209; II, 14-15, 189-90; Moorcroft, *op.cit.*, 49, 100.

23. Vigne, *op.cit.*, II, 141, 149, 169; Moorcroft, *op.cit.*, 359, 395, 405, 407.

24. Burnes, *op.cit.*, I, 41-42; II, 324-25, 403; III, 81, 120, 282, 304, 308; Moorcroft, *op.cit.*, 88, 98, 107-08, 110-11, 177, 305, 358, 406, 409, 410; Jacquemont, *Letters,* II, 41, 60, 146; Vigne, *op.cit.*, I, 151, 204-05; II, 24, 32, 62, 69, 70, 86, 87, 100, 104, 109, 113, 161, 162, 168, 207, 213, 397-98; Hugel, *op.cit.*, 36-37, 81; Masson, *op.cit.*, I, 414-15.

25. Moorcroft, *op.cit.*, 358; Vigne, *op.cit.*, II, 86, 161.

26. Vigne, v II, 168; Moorcroft, *op.cit.*, 355-57.

27. Vigne, *op.cit.*, Ii, 121-22; Moorcroft, *op.cit.*, 357–61.

28. Moorcroft, *op.cit.*, 344, 361.

29. This references to the fifty percent of the produce as a share of the *Maharaja* appears to be an equal division between the owner and the cultivator, and the other one-fourth, as a share of the state in lieu of the protection afforded to the cultivator : *op.cit.*, I, 311.

30. Moorcroft, *op.cit.*, 344; Also on the authority of *Tarikh-i-Kalan.* D.C. Sharma affirms that the sale of residential plots was allowed in the city of Kashmir. A tax known as *Qazia* was levied on land transaction at the rate of one rupee for the state, and two *annas* as a fee of the *patwari*. Did this right exist in other nine *Kasbas* of the valley during the Sikh rule, is not known. But it is certain that proprietary rights were granted by Maharaja Hari Singh in 1933: *Kashmir Under the Sikhs,* Seema Publication, Delhi 1983, 146 fn 257.

31. Vigne, *op.cit.*, I, 30; Moorcroft, *op.cit.*, 344.

32. Paikishti was a land more remote from the city, near the city it was termed as *Sarkishti*, *Trukee* was a sort of interest on the advance of grain which was provided to the farmers to overcome famine conditions during the governorship of Raja Sukhjeevan Mal (1753–62). *Tark* was sort of measure equal to six seer: Hugel, *op.cit.*, 109; Vigne, *op.cit.*, I, 322; Moorcroft, *op.cit.*, 344.

33. Moorcroft, *op.cit.*, 358-59.
34. Vigne, *op.cit.*, I, 309; Hugel, *op.cit.*, 58; Burnes, *op.cit.*, I, 44.
35. Moorcroft, *op.cit.*, 349; Vigne, *op.cit.*, I, 309.
36. Burnes, *op.cit.*, I, 9-10, 70; II, 323, 289; III, 108-09, 120, 121-22, 175-76, 287–306; Vigne, *op.cit.*, 203, 405; Moorcroft, *op.cit.*, 25, 92, 350, 406, 408, 410, 417, 471; Hugel, *op.cit.*, 62, 196, 227.
37. Moorcroft, *op.cit.*, 350, 354.
38. Moorcroft, *op.cit.*, 119, 415; Hugel, *op.cit.*, 62; Vigne, *op.cit.*, I, 144, 197, 205, II, 23.
39. Hugel, *op.cit.*, 118-119; Vigne, *op.cit.*, II, 128. It seems that this industry existed even in ancient times and it was only revived and encouraged during this period. See, G.M.D. Sufi, *KASHIR: being a History of Kashmir from the earliest times to our own*, 2 Vols. Light and Life Publishers, New Delhi 1974, II, 562.
40. Vigne, "Valley of Kashmir, Ghazni and Kabul", *JASB*, VI, 772 (cited hereafter as *Valley of Kashmir*), Moorcroft, *op.cit.*, II, 397-98.
41. On the basis of Baron Charles Hugel's untranslated accounts Dr. Dewan Chand Sharma asserts that 1,27,476 persons were engaged in this industry. Since there is gap of about fifteen years between the two observations, the increase seems to be very likely: *Kashmir Under Maharaja Ranjit Singh*, Atlantic Publishers & Distributors, New Delhi 1984, 85-86.
42. These were Bakal-i-Tibet (Tibet Merchant), Pasham Shawl farosh (Shawl wool sellers), Phewl Kater (Spinners), Pooemangod or Tar farosh (yarn sellers), Rangrez (Dyres), Alaka-bundor Kanare baf (Border maker), Tabgar (Silk Warp makers), Nakatoo (warp makers), Pennakam Guru (warp dressers), Berramgooroo (Warp threaders), Shaw Baf (shawl weavers), Baf Ustad Shawl-Baf (Teacher Shawl weavers), Naqash Shawl pattern drawers, Tarahguru (Colour caller), Taleemguru (Pattern masters), Pooroosgar (Shawl clearners), Wafarosh (Bookers), Mookim (Commission agent), Ruffugar (fine dranners) and Dhobee (washerman).
43. Moorcroft, *op.cit.*, 7, 13, 67, 186, 206; and 'A Journey to Lake Mansarovarain Undes', *Asiatic Researchers* 492.
44. Burnes, *op.cit.*, II, 397-98.
45. Vigne, 'Valley of Kashmir', *JASB*, VI, 772.
46. Moorcroft, *op.cit.*, 67; Burnes, *op.cit.*, II, 397-98.

47. Moorcroft, *op.cit.*, 383.
48. Vigne, *op.cit.*, I, 144, 197, 205, II, 23; Moorcroft, *op.cit.*, 119, 415.
49. Moorcroft, *op.cit.*, 369.
50. Moorcroft, *op.cit.*, 208.
51. Jacquemont, *op.cit.*, 29.
52. Moorcroft, *op.cit.*, 379, 382-84; Burnes, *op.cit.*, II, 400.
53. Burnes, *op.cit.*, II, 399, 400, 405-07, 415, 419, 434-35; III, 159; Moorcroft, *op.cit.*, 51, 85, 360; Masson, *op.cit.*, I, 99; Jacquemont, *op.cit.*, 84.
54. Burnes, *op.cit.*, II, 440-01, 406-07.
55. Moorcroft, *op.cit.*, 51.
56. Burnes, *op.cit.*, II, III, 405, 407.
57. *Ibid.*, II, 400.
58. *Ibid.*, II, 293-94, 419.
59. Vigne, *Travels,* II, 128-29; Burnes, *op.cit.*, II, 400.
60. Burnes, *op.cit.*, II, 399; III, 111.
61. *Ibid.*, II, 399-400; III, 111.
62. Jacquemont, *op.cit.*, 46; Masson, *op.cit.*, I, 3-4, 99; Vigne, *op.cit.*, II, 128-29.
63. Moorcroft, *op.cit.*, 51, 372-73; Jacquemont, *op.cit.*, 29, 57; Burnes, *op.cit.*, III, 111.
64. Vigne, *op.cit.*, II, 127, 131-32; Burnes, *op.cit.*, II, 398; Moorcroft, *op.cit.*, 356, 372, 373, 382.
65. Moorcroft, *Travels,* 374-75, 379, 380–84; Vigne, *op.cit.*, II, 133-34.
66. Hugel, *op.cit.*, 58, 99, 121, 219, 396-97; Masson, *op.cit.*, I, 411.
67. Hugel, *op.cit.*
68. Burnes, *op.cit.*, III, 164, 65.
69. Hugel, *op.cit.*, 396.
70. Moorcroft, *Travels,* 385, 389; Hugel, *Travels,* 121; Burnes, *Travels,* III, 155.
71. Moorcroft employed such artisans and got manufactured these swords. Later on, he sent them to England : Moorcroft, *op.cit.*, 395.

72. Masson, *Journeys,* I, 113.
73. Burnes, *Kabul,* 82.
74. Jacquemont, *Journal* 27; Masson, *op.cit.*, I, 410.
75. Hugel, *op.cit.*, 380.
76. Jacquemont, *op.cit.*, 57.
77. Hugel, *op.cit.*, 396; Jacquemont, *op.cit.*, 29.
78. Vigne, *op.cit.*, II, 123.
79. Vigne, *op.cit.*, II, 123.
80. Moorcroft, *op.cit.*, 369-70; Vigne, *op.cit.*, II, 122, 179, 460.
81. Vigne, *op.cit.*, II, 122.
82. Moorcroft, *op.cit.*, 66, 449.
83. Burnes, *op.cit.*, III, 128-29; *Kabul*, 368.
84. *Ibid.*, III, 128, 302, 327-28.
85. Burnes, *Kabul*, 320-28; *Travels*, II, 289; III, 178-79, 184, 302, 305-06.
86. The prices of boats made of deodar were as :

A Zohurq	*Cedar wood*	*Capacity mands*	*Cost Rs. Nanakshahi*
do	do	100	100/-
do	do	200	200-225/-
do	do	300	300/-
do	do	400	350/-
do	do	500	450/-
do	do	600	475/-
do	do	700	500/-
do	do	800	500-600/-
do	do	900	600-700/-

: Burnes, *Kabul*, 368.

87. Moorcroft, *op.cit.*, 347-48.
88. Moorcroft, says that 'a fabric of much greater importance to Great Britain than that of damasked sword-blades, is that of Yirak leather...Such pieces of this as came in our way were

usually old narrow slips employed as reins and head-stalls; but the leather was strong, solid, heavy and pliable, without any disposition to crack. Some of the pieces had been in use for eighteen or twenty years, and none the worse for constant wear : *op.cit.*, 395-96.

89. Vigne, *Travels*, II, 122; Moorcroft, *Travels,* 396.
90. Jacquemont, *Letters,* II, 30, 80; *Journal*, 69; Vigne, *op.cit.*, II, 115, 121; Moorcroft, *op.cit.*, 397, 411.
91. Moorcroft, *op.cit.*
92. Hugel, *Travels*, 292.
93. Jacquemont, *op.cit.*, II, 148; Moorcroft, *op.cit.*, 411.
94. Vigne, *op.cit.*, II, 102, 306-07.
95. Burnes, , *op.cit.*, II, 408.
96. Moorcroft, , *op.cit.*, 108-109.
97. In this 'devils drink' says Hugel, were mingled sauces compounded from flesh of every kind of animal, except beef, pearls and jewels, musk, opium and plants of various kinds : *Travels*, 298.
98. Moorcroft, , *op.cit.*, 358-359.
99. Vigne, *op.cit.*, I, 322, II, 102; Jacquemont, , *op.cit.*, II, 64-65.
100. Burnes, *op.cit.*, I, 402; II, 402.
101. Vigne, *Valley of Kashmir*, 771; Moorcroft, *Travels*, 348, 357; Burnes, *op.cit.*, I, 402.
102. Moorcroft, *op.cit.*, 357; Vigne, *op.cit.*, 771.
103. Moorcroft, *op.cit.*, 357-58.
104. Vigne, *op.cit.*, II, 121-122; *Valley of Kashmir,* 772-73.
105. Moorcroft, *op.cit.*, 357.
106. Vigne, *op.cit.*, II, 87, 109-10; Jacquemont, *op.cit.*, 57; Moorcroft, *op.cit.*, 51.
107. Moorcroft, *op.cit.*, 343.
108. *Ibid.*, 374.
109. Hugel, *op.cit.*, 120-121.
110. *Ibid.*
111. Moorcroft, *Travels*, 372.

112. *Ibid.*, 370.

113. *Ibid.*, 371.

114. Burnes, *Travels,* I, 50, 51-56, 84; II, 327, 401-02; Moorcroft, *Travels*, 45-46, 96, 104; Vigne, *op.cit.*, I, 100-01; II, 191; Jacquemont, *Letters,* II, 145-46, 191; Hugel, *op.cit.*, 246.

115. Moorcroft, *op.cit.*, 84, 104, 365; Burnes, *op.cit.*, II, 327-28, 401; Vigne, *op.cit.*, I, 100; Jacquemont, *op.cit.*, II, 161.

116. Vigne, , *op.cit.*, I, 112, 207; II, 184, 207, 397; Hugel, *op.cit.*, 161-62, 190.

117. Moorcroft, *op.cit.*, 365; Vigne, , *op.cit.*, II, 5; Burnes, *op.cit.*, II, 327.

118. Burnes, *op.cit.*, I, 52; II, 402.

119. *Ibid.*, I, 80; II, 327.

120. *Ibid.*, II, 401-02.

121. Burnes, *op.cit.*, II, 327.

122. *Ibid.*, III, 307.

123. Moorcroft, *op.cit.*, 328-30, 333, 340-44, 347, 359-62, 396-07, 401-02, 406-10, 412, 416-17, 431, 433-34; Vigne, *op.cit.*, I, 335; About one thousand ass loads of roots of costs were annually collected.

124. Moorcroft, *op.cit.*, 51, 85, 102, 119, 124, 207, 211-12, 314, 454, 468-69, 480; Burnes, *op.cit.*, I, 74; II, 395-412, 415; III, 119, 130, 159, 282-83, 307-08; Jacquemont, *op.cit.*, 12, 46, 86; Hugel, *op.cit.*, 220, 391, 393; Masson, *op.cit.*, I, 32, 52, 357, 395, 416.

125. Burnes, *op.cit.*, I, 54; II, 167, 325, 402, 435-36; Moorcroft, *op.cit.*, 361.

126. Moorcroft, *op.cit.*, 51, 85; Burnes, *op.cit.*, Ii, 399-401, 405, 407, 416, 419, 434-35; II, 111, 293-94; Also *Kabul,* 81-93.

127. Vigne, *op.cit.*, II, 457.

128. Burnes, *op.cit.*, II, 167, 435-36; also *Kabul*, 83.

129. Vigne, *op.cit.*, II, 235; Jacquemont, *op.cit.*, II, 299; also *Journal,* 17, 29, 80; Moorcroft, *op.cit.*, 213, 232-33, 331-32, 366-67, 382-83, Burnes, *op.cit.*, II, 397, 398-99, 403-04, 416, 418, 435; III, 69, 177; Hugel, *op.cit.*, 390.

130. Moorcroft, *op.cit.*, 67-68, 119, 151, 206-08, 268, 312-13, 361, 367; Burnes, *op.cit.*, II, 175-76, 180, 439-40; Vigne, *op.cit.*, II, 14, 344, 369-70.

131. Hugels, *Travels,* 148-49; Jacquemont, *op.cit.*, II, 141; Vigne, *op.cit.*, II,

132. Burnes, *op.cit.*, II, 405-06, 416; III, 282-83; Vigne, *op.cit.*, II, 344; Moorcroft, *op.cit.*, 134, 151, 211-12, 372-73, 396.

133. Jacquemont, *op.cit.*, I, 263; Moorcroft, *op.cit.*, 58-59, 151, 207, 212; Burnes, v I, 123, 153, 155; II, 275-76, 416; also *Kabul*, 78-93.

134. Moorcroft, *op.cit.*, 151, 212; Jacquemont, *op.cit.*, 46; Burnes, *op.cit.*, II, 407-08, 419.

135. Jacquemont, *op.cit.*, 10,12.

136. Burnes, *op.cit.*, III, 282-83.

137. *Ibid.*, 399-400; Moorcroft, *op.cit.*, 51.

138. Moorcroft, *op.cit.*, 13, 85, 102.

139. Vigne, *op.cit.*, I, 196-97, 217, 218; II, 345; Jacquemont, v I, 263; also *Journal* 29; Burnes, *op.cit.*, II, 289-90; III, 128, 302; Moorcroft, *op.cit.*, 361, 365 373. 387, 405.

140. Burnes, *op.cit.*, I, 168-69; III, 94-95, 277; also *Kabul*, 56-57, 77-78; Jacquemont, *Journal*, 12, 86; Vigne, *Travels*, I, 217; II, 43, 345; Moorcroft, *op.cit.*, 47, 331; Hugel, *op.cit.*, 220; Masson, I, 32, 48, 52, 58, 67, 69, 71.

141. Moorcroft, *op.cit.*, 370-74; Hugel, *op.cit.*, 120-21.

142. Moorcroft, *op.cit.*, 370-74; Hugel, *op.cit.*, 120-21.

143. Other coins in circulation were : Bhawalpur rupee, Ahmedpur rupee, Shikarpuri and Khairpuri rupee, Bijashahi rupee, Shah Shujah rupee, Chiki and Mehrabi rupee and Hari Singh rupee etc.

144. Hugel, *op.cit.*, 396; Jacquemont, *op.cit.*, 29; Vigne, *op.cit.*, II, 74, 123; Moorcroft, *op.cit.*, 54, 370-71.

145. Morcroft, *op.cit.*, 209, 211-12, 350, 369, 370-71, 367, 441; Hugel, *op.cit.*, 74-75; Vigne, *op.cit.*, II, 426.

146.

Horse load	=	22 *taraks*
Ass	=	16 *taraks* (96 pounds)
Tarak	=	6 *sers*
Ser	=	20 pals.

According to Moorcroft the actual *ser* at Kashmir was not above one pound avoidupois, whereas, Hugel put it as equal to two pound. According to him a *kharwar* was equal to 192 pounds: Moorcroft, *op.cit.*, 350, 357, 368-69; Hugel, *op.cit.*, 162; See also, Vigne, *op.cit.*, II, 426.

147. Vigne, *op.cit.*, I, 77, Hugel, *op.cit.*, 74.

148. Moorcroft, *op.cit.*, 2, 66, 96, 104, 119, 207, 330, 331, 336, 339, 398, 400, 431-33, 443-44; Vigne, *op.cit.*, I, 68, 78, 163, 197, 292, II; 344-45, 440; Hugel, *op.cit.*, 73, 115, 140-41, 155, 168, 187; Burnes, *op.cit.*, II, 283; Jacquemont, *op.cit.*, II, 9, 56.

149. Burnes, *op.cit.*, III, 128-29, 178-79, 184, 243-45, 283, 302, 305-06, 315.

150. Moorcroft, *op.cit.*, 330, 336, 339, 400.

151. Burnes noted in the 1830s that the roads from one extremity of the country to the other could admit of wheeled carriages, except in the mountains. All the five rivers of the Punjab, including the Indus were navigable : *Travels,* II, 288-89; III, 119, 298, 411-12. Serais were built along the imperial route from Lahore to Hassan Abdal to Kabul at intervals of every six *kohs* from each other : Hugel, *op.cit.*, 226.

152. Vigne, *op.cit.*, II, 100.

153. Moorcroft, *op.cit.*, 331; Jacquemont, *op.cit.*, I, 406; Hugel, *op.cit.*, 155.

154. Moorcroft, *op.cit.;* Jacquemont, *op.cit.*, 1, 263, 400, 403; *Journal,* 46; Burnes, *op.cit.*, III, 169.

155. Burnes, *op.cit.*, III, 169.

156. Moorcroft, *op.cit.*, 58, 67, 124, 209.

157. Burnes, *op.cit.*, II, 324; *Kabul,* 83-84.

158. Burnes, *op.cit.*, II, 275, 324; III, 111; *Kabul* 83-84; also Moorcroft, 51, 92, 120, 471; Vigne, *Travels,* I, 196.

159. Vigne, *op.cit.*, I, 309; Burnes, *op.cit.*, III, 298-99.

160. Moorcroft, *op.cit.*, 358.

161. Burnes, *op.cit.*, II, 397-98.

162. Moorcroft, *op.cit.*, 374, 375.

163. Moorcroft, *op.cit.*, 369-71, 375, 386.

164. Burnes, *op.cit.*, II, 288-90, 396–412.

165. In the 1820s, Moorcroft estimated the population of the valley at 800,000. Hugel, who was visiting the valley three years after

the famine of 1833 gives the figures at 200,000: Moorcroft, *op.cit.*, 328, 330, 341, 343, 344, 345, 346, 406, 408, 409, 436, 440, 442; Vigne, *op.cit.*, I, 308, 310, 311, II, 318; Hugel, 'Visit to the valley of Kashmir', *Journal of Asiatic Society of Bengal,* V, 185; Jacquemont, *op.cit.*, 65, 66, 70, 79, 82; also *Letters*, II, 58, 76, 87.

166. Burnes, *op.cit.*, II, 411-12, 414-15, 418-19. Also Moorcroft, *op.cit.*, 46-47; Jacquemont, *op.cit.*, 59.

167. Vigne, *op.cit.*, I, 257, 282; II, 118; Hugel, *op.cit.*, 405; also 'Visit to the valley of Kashmir', JSAB, V, 185.

168. Vigne, *op.cit.*, II, 120-121.

169. Burnes, *op.cit.*, III, 111, 169; Jacquemont, *Letters,* I, 263, 400, 403; also *Journal,* 46.

170. Moorcroft, *op.cit.*, 55; Burnes, *op.cit.*, I, 11.

171. Fauja Singh (ed.), *Punjab da samajik Itihas,* Punjabi University, Patiala, 1979, 65; Fauja Singh & A.C. Arora (eds), Maharaja Ranjit Singh : *Politics, Society and Economy,* Punjabi University, Patiala 1984, 174, 191.

172. In 1820s Moorcroft noted the value of shawls and shawl goods manufactured as Rs. 35,00,000 and Burnes in 1830s estimated the revenue from shawl industry as Rs. 18,00,000. The state duty being 25% to 26% upon the estimated value of the goods, it comes to the amount of about Rs. 72,00,000: Moorcroft, *op.cit.*, 384; Burnes, *op.cit.*, II, 397-98.

173. Moorcroft, *op.cit.*, 28.

6

Evidence of Society

Besides evidence on polity and economy, the travel literature provides us ample information on the society of the Punjab under Maharaja Ranjit Singh. Almost all the aspects of the Punjabi life are covered. It tells us about the three major communities of the Punjab, their faith, believes and superstition. Their dwelling, food, means of amusement and their art and craft are also taken up in the literature. In the chapter, the evidence on society will be studied not only to estimate its significance but also to underline its major concerns.

I

Alexander Burnes is the only traveller who provides estimation of the population of the Punjab under Maharaja Ranjit Singh. In his view the population was about 30,00,000 in all, and of these about 5,00,000 were the '*Khalsa*'. The bulk of the population was constituted of the Muslims and the Hindus. However, Burnes does not make it clear, what he meant by the term '*Khalsa*'. Does it include the whole population professing the Sikh faith or the '*Singhs*' of Guru Gobind Singh alone?[1] Even if it includes the whole Sikh population, the proportion of the Sikh population does not seem to be satisfactory in the light of his own observation. Burnes observed that the Sikh population was on the whole quite low. "The paucity of the 'Sikhs', was so striking in some areas that their number was confined to garrisons alone which did not exceed 500 men in the city like Multan".[2] There were very few Sikhs beyond the river Jhelum. Even to the east of Lahore, where there was a concentration of the Sikh population, there proportion in the total population was not more than one third.[3] However, Burnes opinion that political ascendancy of the Sikhs was securing new converts to the faith, probably, at the rate 5,000 a year, seems to be an exaggeration.[4]

Peasantry constituted the bulk of the population. It was composed of all the three communities : the Muslims, the Hindus and the Sikhs. However, the *Jats* were predominant among them.[5] A considerable number of artisans living in the cities, towns and large villages belonged to the Mohammedan and Hindu faiths. Labourers, both in urban and in the rural areas, however, were mostly *chamars* or Hindus of low caste.[6]

The Sikhs, as a people, were of special interest to these travellers. Burnes views them as a 'robust and athletic race of sinew limbs and tall stature. They were the most rising people of modern India.[7] To Jacquemont they were unsophisticated but simple and honest in manners, which made them 'a good sort of people'[8] Hugel mentions them as 'strongly built' people.[9] Masson describes them as 'frank, generous, social and lively', which certainly made them 'a fine race of men'.[10]

They were exclusively a military and agricultural people.[11] They loved horses and arms. There was scarcely a Sikh who did not have one or more brood mares.[12] A large portion of the population was serving either in the *Maharaja's* army or under different chiefs and they were not 'the worst clothed and worst bed'.[13] However, they made a good soldier and were incurred to long marches and every fatigue. The 'coolness and courage' surpassed belief : they have a great encouragement from their chief.[14] The tract of Majha was celebrated for the bravery of its soldiers as it was for the breed of horses.[15] Jacquemont commented upon their bravery as: "They are like hunting leopard which are taken out for hunting in an iron cage and only released when the game is in sight."[16]

The Akalis were a part of the Sikh society. Besides Amritsar, Lahore was their favourite headquarter during the reign of Maharaja Ranjit Singh.[17] They were 'a class of military fanatics', who clothed themselves in black, and were always armed in a most profuse manner. Some of them have half a dozen swords struck about them and their houses and as many pistols and other arms. They carried around the top of their *pagri* (turban) a circular steel disc, with a rim, nearly in inch broad the edge of which being very sharp. Thrown by the hands, it could be an offensive weapon.[18] Masson makes us believe that, "these men could eject it with such force that they could divide the leg of a horse or even of elephant".[19] These travellers are of the opinions that their fighting spirit was wisely turned into an advantage of the state by the *Maharaja* by employing them preferably against the Muslim enemies. Around 1830s, about 4,000 to 5,000 of them were deployed at Attock, to check the activities of a Mohammedan fanatic, Sayyid Ahmed who was fighting against the Sikhs, in the name of Islam.[20]

The Akalis had a strong disliking for the British and other European servants of the *Maharaja* and visitors to the kingdom of Lahore alike. For instance, General Allard was once attacked by them with showers of stones. Jacquemont was threatened, while he was on his excursion around the city of Lahore, but for his escort.[21] He was not allowed to go into the *Harimandar Sahib* for the fear of the Akalis.[22] Perhaps for these reasons they are described as 'armed beggars', robbing for subsistence', 'wrong-headed', 'short-sighted', etc.[23]

The Sikhs revered *Guru Granth*. Burnes saw priest waving a *chauri* (Tibetian cow's tail), over *Guru Granth* as a mark of reverence.[24] They addressed themselves as *Khalsa Ji i.e.* a member of the *Khalsa Panth*.[25] Their popular way of exclamation was *Wah Guru Ji Ki Fateh*[26] Next to *Guru Granth*, the Sikhs revered and respected the Bedis and the Sodhis as descendents of the Sikh Gurus. Burnes tells us that even Maharaja Ranjit Singh respected Baba Sahib Singh Bedi and used to receive him with distinction.[27] *Bhais* and *Granthis* were not only respected their advice was too sought for.[28]

Amongst the Sikh places of pilgrimage, Harimandir Sahib drew special attention of these travellers. Both Hugel and Jacquemont gives us to understand that the 18th century Sikh struggle against the state was mainly centered around the possession of Sri Harimandir Sahib. For the state had seen clearly its importance in the religious life of the Sikh community. Therefore, the state thought not only to destroy it, but also aimed 'a fatal below at the faith.'[29] A number of measures were taken to achieve the desired end including persecution and prohibition of visit to the Harimandir and bathing in the Amrit-sarovar, particularly on the occasion of *Diwali* and *Baisakhi*.[30]

It profanation by the state was strongly reacted by the Sikhs and they were not slow in restoring it to its farmer splendour. Commenting upon the reaction of the Sikhs to the profanation done by Ahmad Shah Abdali to the temple and the tank, Hugel observes: ' Ahmed Shah had not reached Atock before a second *gurmata* was held in Amritsar, where the profanation of this sacred spot animated all the spectators to deeds which brought about, perhaps sooner than might otherwise have happened, the downfall of the Mohammedan power in the north of India, At the same time the Sikhs began to cleanse their dishonoured tank, and (a rare example for Hindus) it was restored to greater splendour than ever."[31]

Burnes describes it as a 'national temple' of the Sikhs.[32] It stands in the midst of a tank Amrit-sarovar. To Hugel Amrit-sarovar appears to be a unique object containing immense body of water 'as clear as a mirror', 'a rare occurrence in such places in India'.[33] A narrow marble bridge, on the western side, connect it with pavement around the Amrit-sarovar. Its 'mysterious and romantic' character appeals forcibly to the imagination of a visitor. It is 'far surpassed to other Indian temple.[34] Its golden roof; designed very beautifully and skillfully, in laid with marble, adds to its beauty. A large golden door opens into the temple, all the four golden doors are surrounded with little vestibules; the ceilings being supported by richly ornamented pillars. Right in the centre of the temple is placed *Guru Granth Sahib*, under canopy of gold cloth cost 10,000 pounds. A *granthi* sits in presence of the Guru Granth. A *chauri-bardar* wave the *chaur* over the *Guru Granth*, to keep away the impurities. The lower portion of the interior walls were covered with a handsome carpet worked in gold. The ground was covered with Kashmir shawls stuff. Devotees sit in a circle around the *Guru Granth*, leaving an open space, which is never encroached upon, it being customary that the Guru should be viewed from a certain distance with due reverence.[35]

Facing the gateway to the temple, stands Akal Bungh (Akal Takht). Here Guru Sahib (*Guru Granth*) rests during night hours. It is a repository of Guru's belongings; and baptistery of the Sikhs. Near the Akal Takht stands two large Sikh standards. Hugel describes these of red colour. On one of these was written *Wah Guru Ji Ki Fateh* and on the other, the name of the excavator of the Amrit-sarovar and founder of Ramdaspur-Ram Dass. Letters were in white colour. These flags were from 129 to 150 feet long; stretched on masts and confined with iron chains.[36]

Observations of these travellers communicate to the reader that politics was discussed at Harimandir, even during the reign of Maharaja Ranjit Singh. Also, *Maharaja's* control over the affairs of Harimandir was quite strong. Yet visits of the Europeans to the temple were not liked by the Akalis. For instance, Alexander Burnes, a state guest, while visiting the Harimandir wished to see the Akal Bunga. He offered rupees two hundred and fifty to the Akal Takht. But for fear of the Akalis, he was not allowed to go in. Desa Singh Majithia, who had been ordered by the *Maharaja* to make his visit secure, was so solitious about his safety that he led Alexander Burnes by the hand which he grasped firmly through the assembled crowd. Such examples are multiple.[37]

Generally, the Sikhs were more liberal even in regard to the admission of other communities into their *Gurdwaras* (Sikh temples). Hugel comments that, "the same idea of profanation do not exist in the Sikhs as in the Hindu faith and they admit Europeans into the interior of their temples".[38] Most of the *Gurdwara* provided shelter to the travellers.[39] The Sikhs were considered to the most tolerant people.[40] Flushed by a series of victories, they had a zeal and buoyancy of sprit and the power of taking revenge but they remained lenient.[41]

However, the Sikhs were not free from Bramanical influence. Almost all the chiefs have had a *pandit* in their establishments. For instance, Vigne found Raja Suchet Singh consulting to his *pandit,* who was an astrologer, even going out for hunting.[42] Sardar Thakur Singh, for example, used to repeat some prayer over a basin of warmed ghee, produced by the Brahmin, who alike mubbled something and at the conclusion dropped into the fluid some copper coins.[43] Particularly, the Kashmiri *pandits* were held in such an estimation that the Sikhs thought it repugnant to take any part in their punishment. To "kill a *pandit* was nearly as bad as to kill a bullock".[44]

Many kinds of superstitions were prevalent among the Sikhs. Vigne observed a singular display of superstition by the *Maharaja* himself, who had sent Pandit Radha Krishan to Jwalamukhi to offer prayers for his recovery from illness. A sum of 15,000 rupees was given to the said person to purchase *ghee* to be consumed by the sacred flames of Jwalaji.[45] When Vigne presented a bottle of water to the *Maharaja* denoting the same from Gunga Bal; the *Maharaja* was much pleased an Naunihal Singh dipped his finger into it and reverently moistered his forehead with it.[46] Cow was sacred to them and its slaughter was forbidden. If any one found guilty of slaughtering the cow, was beaten up by the Sikh peasantry even, alongwith the seller of the beef.[47] Also caste prejudice was not less strong than the Hindus. Their priests were always of high caste Hindu descent and they had much contempt for the lower castes.[48] In the ordinary intercourse with the Hindus, the *banias* did not receive much courtesy.[49]

Though the Sikhs were to be distinguished from the Hindus and the Muslims, yet some of the manners and customs appeared to be strikingly similar. On this basis, Jacuqemont suggested that their common ancestry was not many generations back. Hugel also seems to suggest the same idea in a slightly different manner. He says that generally speaking 'they (Sikhs) are descendants from all the lowest castes of Hindus'.[50]

Burnes observed a general change in the habits of the Sikhs

as a result of their political ascendancy. In Burnes' opinion this change was not for the better. The peculiar tenants of Sikh religion made them a distinct people from the Hindus and the Muslims. But the change might effect the energies of the community adversely. Here, Burnes had in mind the suspension of bi-annual meetings of the Khalsa brotherhood at Amirtsar, where decisions were taken by general consent through the institution of *Gurmata* about issues of utmost importance relating to the Sikh community. He observes : "so entirely had the Seik (sic) nation altered its constitution, under this chief, that, within a period of twenty years, it has passed from a pure republic an absolute monarchy. The genius of one man has effected this change, though contending with powerful opposition, from a religion that inculcates, above every other, democracy and the equality of all.[51]

The political change, which Burnes noted, from a 'democracy' to a 'monarchy' did have social implications. For example, to consolidate his rule a monarch needs help of all the sections of the society. Thus with the ascendancy of the Sikhs to political power, there started a process of wooing the other communities. In this process, several Hindus beliefs and practices entered into the Sikh way of life implicitly or explicitly.

II

In the Hindus society traditional system of *varna* was observed. Hugel mentions, Brahmin, Kashatrya and Sudra and omits Vaishya without giving any explanation.[52] Many sub-castes did exist but the most superior of these were the *Pandit* (Brahmin). Being a priestly class, they enjoyed much respect even from the Sikhs. Almost all the Sikh chiefs had kept a family priest in their establishments.[53] However, many of them were quite ignorant about their knowledge of the Hindu *shastras.*[54] Some of the travellers failed to understand the Hindus social order. For example, Vigne intermingle castes and tribes. He observed that the Hindus were divided into different tribes such as *Pandits*, Rasdum, Kol, Kabuta etc. These were arranged under the two names : the Malamasis and Baruhmasis.[55]

Varna and caste system were very rigid among the Hindus. It was a singular feature of the Hindu society. No proselyte could be admitted into the fold of Hinduism. *Varna*, in which one has taken one's birth can not be changed. A *Brahmin* must be a child of a Brahmin. The Hindus, particularly the *Brahmins* and the *Rajputs*, did not eat with other castes. Furthermore, it confined to its votaries to the soil and air of Hindustan. A penalty of the utter loss of caste was imposed upon those who crossed to the westward of the Indus.[56] However, inspite of the prohibition against the Hindus crossing the Indus, the Hindus of Peshawar and Kabul intermarry with their co-religionists of the same caste. Also we find that no class of Hindus refused to cross the Indus when Ranjit Singh made his Peshawar campaign and there were many Hindus of the highest caste in his army.[57]

Shiva, Vishnu, Surya (sun), Ganesh (Ganpati), Bhawani (the mother of gods), and Lakshmi (goddess of plenty), appear to be the main deities to be worshipped by the Hindus.[58] These deities had different denominations in different regions, as Bursla Devi, Ashatbuza (goddess with eight arms), Troki Devi, etc. were worshipped in the valley of Kashmir as also in the submountane regions.[59] Two most important sects of Hinduism in the Punjab were Shaivite, the votaries of Lord Shiva and Vaishnavite, the votaries of Vishnu. The former were the largest in number than the latter.[60]

Numerous temples belonging to the Hindu faith have been enumerated. They were found in the hills as well as in the plains.[61] However, the temples of Amar Nath, Jwalamukhi and Naina Devi, all in the hills and the temple at Katas appears to be most famous amongst them. An annual fair, about 10th or 12th of April was held at Katas in which both the Hindus and the Sikhs participated alike.[62] Similarly, the temple of Naina Devi and Jwalamukhi was visited by both the communities. The golden roof of both, the small and large buildings of the temple of Jawalamukhi was a gift from Maharaja Ranjit Singh.[63]

Apart from these places, Hardwar was a sacred place for the Hindus. A visit to it, particularly on the festival of *Kumbh*, was of great importance.[64] Similarly, a visit to Kali Sangam, and Gunga Bal in the valley of Kashmir was held sacred by the Kashmiri Hindus.[65] Besides, the passes too were worshipped in the mountains. For instance, at Pir Panjal Pass, Moorcroft found poles with voting offering to the mountain spirits. Amongst them he describes two shawls presented by Diwan Moti Ram when he had ascended the Pass on his way to the conquest of Kashmir.[66]

The Hindus considered a dip into the *Sangam* sacred. Belief in another world and another life was popular among all the sections of the society and so was the faith in destiny, lucky and unlucky days. Like animals threes like papal (ficus religiosa) were considered sacred.[67]

The Hindu ceremony of marriage was observed by Vigne as : "when the parents have arranged the match, the barber brings some trinkets from the bride and her parents, to the bridegroom's father, who accepts them as a matter of course; and this custom is continued from time to time until the days of marriage. On that day Brahmin attends; the hems of each of the parties garments are tied together; the Brahmin forms a circle with flour round a small fire, and calls upon the name of his favourite divinity; another says a prayer; at the same time throwing flowers into the fire, and then the parties walk seven times round the floor, and until the sixth round is completed she is not his wife. She then retires with two or three other women, and when she is unveiled, they commence teasing and abusing her after which the husband takes her home".[68] However, in Kashmir they ceremony differed though slightly : heaps of money was used to form the circle instead of flour and the parties were linked by their little fingers instead of their garments.[69]

Posthumous rites of the Hindus, who like the Sikhs burnt their dead bodies were observed by Vigne rather minutely. Two days after the cremation bones were picked from the ashes and put into an earthen pot alongwith some coins. The vessel was deposited in a niche over the door with a *chirag* (oil lamp). Before sun rise, the relations of the deceased assembled and turning towards vessel, all loudly asked the departed whether, he be hungry, thirsty, cold, warm, happy, unhappy etc. For ten days, very early in the morning they also carried an other earthen vessel to the river side, filled it with water lifted by the hand, carried it home and told the departed that it was for him and then throw rice, bread and flower into the sacred river alongwith the earthen vessel. On the tenth day, they shave their heads, and perform ablution, and earthen vessel was filled to the brim. As they usually believed that a *zin* had got into it, all the children, first turning away their heads, swing the jar into the water. After a few more prayers and hastly ablutions, they quickly returned home.[70]

Vigne attributes the habits, the prejudices and they apathy of the Hindus partly to the climate and partly to the force of their superstitions. Both, traditions and priest craft were enjoiner the observance of the most awful and imposing ceremonies, by the strength of which their souls were united to the faith of their father.[71]

The practice of *Sati,* to burn voluntarily herself alive on her husbands funeral pyre, was in vogue amongst the Hindus. It was no peculiar to the inhabitants of the kingdom of Lahore.[72] However, in the Punjab proper and in the valley of Kashmir, it was practiced rather rarely. If we believe Vigne, there had been only two *Satis* in the times of Sher Singh, and one in that of Kirpa Ram, in the valley of Kashmir.[73] But in the submountaneous regions it was commonly performed.[74] Child marriage and prohibition of widow remarriage appears to be the root cause of this social evil. In the Hindus marriages usually took place before the girl child get puberty, and it often happened that little girl of the age of 8 or 10 became a widow by the death of the child to whom she had been married, and to whom she had never seen, was condemned to celibacy for the rest of her life.[75] No ruler, before the British, ever dared to interfere with this social custom. Even this horrible practice of *Sati* embroiled the Sikh portion of the Punjabi society so far as the upper classes were concerned.[76]

III

A little information is available on the Muslim society. It was composed of mainly two sects : the *Sunis* and the *Shias*. The ratio in which these sects existed in the dominions of Maharaja Ranjit Singh is not know. However, in the case of the province of Kashmir, Vigne observed that the *Sunis* predominated. They were further divided into twenty different tribes and of these the *chakk* were the oldest and the most distinguished.[77] Moorcroft mentions that in the Bimber region most of the Mohammedans were formerly Hindus, and had marriage relations with those who were still Hindus.[78]

The Muslims were very strict in the observance of religious rites. Jacquemont appreciates their piety : "if there really be such a thing as faith, or true piety, in the world, it is among the Musalmans".[79] However, like the Sikhs and the Hindus, they too were not free from superstitions. Jacquemont found them praying for rain at Hazrat Bal.[80] They used to wear *taviz* (device) upon their arms.[81]

The travel literature contains stray references to the Muslim places of pilgrimages too. Burnes has mentioned the tomb of Lal Shah Baz at Shewan as a great place of pilgrimage. However, it was also visited by the Hindus.[82] In the Valley of Kashmir in Duchinpara *Paragana,* the tomb of Zainuddin, was a place of *ziarat.* An other place of *ziarat* was in Kishtwar.[83] A tomb of a Mohammedan saint at Katas attracted numerous visitors.[84] The tomb of Bahawal Haq at Multan was another sacred place of *ziarat.*[85]

Presence of *faqirs, yogis, barrages,* and *gosains* have been noticed by these travellers. Usually, they lived in or around the religious places such as Amritsar, Jawalamukhi, Katas and the tombs of Muslim saints. Jacquemont saw many *faquirs* at Amritsar around the Golden Temple and many *Baragis* and *Yogis* at the temple of Jwalamukhi.[86] Some of them go about nearly naked while some wore black, red orange and while coloured clothes. Some of them might be seen with long strings of berries about the throat while many of them simply covered themselves with ashes. In fact, the degree of 'nudity and dirt', was an indication of the degree of sanctity in which the man was held.[87] Hugel make us believe that these people were so popular that each village had a '*faqir*' and sometimes more than one village had a common *faqir* subsisted by the alms of the inhabitants. They did not pay their followers, who were a sort of apprentice *faqirs*, even servants except by liberal promises for the next world.[88]

IV

The life style of the chiefs or aristocracy was not different from the life style of the *Maharaja*. One may find a difference of degree but certainly not of kind. They went about attended by large retinue. Their apparel were gorgeous, and dwellings like mansion. They kept, though small, *zenana*, consumed much spirituous liquor, and listened to the *nach* girls.[89]

The Sikh women were not confined to their houses as strictly as the Mohammedan ladies, who strictly observed *parda*.[90] At many places, particularly in the hill tribes the women did all the out-door work, and even followed the plough.[91]

Slavery was very common among the women of the Punjab; nearly all the concubines and their servants were slave. In the *zenana* of General Ventura, observed Jacquemont, the ladies were being guarded and attended by female slaves, bought for from rupees sixty to eighty from the dealers, who brought them from the hills. Interestingly, it was uncommon among the men.[92]

Polyandry was practiced in the mountaneous regions. To Jacquemont, the practice was destitute of 'reason and moral sense.'[93] Masson tells us that it was common among the Sikhs to have one wife shared between brothers. But this custom was not imputable to them as Sikhs, for 'they were the remains of the ancient and rude state of society.[94] The wife was considered to be an impure creature for her husband. He hardly considered her as being of the same species with himself. However, Masson desired that "should they continue as an independent nation, it may be hoped that increased civilization would gradually remove these traces of barbarism and in the course of time, they would grow enlightened and become superior people."[95]

Prostitution as an institution did exist, and was not an irrespectable profession. We learn from Jacquemont that at Amritsar the prostitutes had their separate quarters. He found some of them squatting on the *verandas,* or on the balconies, neatly and tastefully dressed usually in white, pink or red muslim and adorned heavily with gold ornaments.[96] They were never exposed to insult, and it would have been a grave lack of good manner not to return their salutation which they never omit to give to a respectable passers by.[97] Jacquemont gives a vivid and bold description of their physical appearance : "they are fair enough; that is to say of a deep pallor with no more colour in their cheeks than in the rest of their faces. That are all very small, with good features and breasts, but their arms are too thin, their thigh thinner still, and their legs so thin as to be actually unsightly; their eves, naturally beautiful, have an added brightness and softness from the custom of slightly darkening the lower eye-lid with a preparation of antimony".[98]

The Sikh dress was usually consisted of *Pagri* (turban), a *jacket* and large bulky trousers, terminating at the knee, the legs from the knee onward remained naked. The chiefs occasionally wore full trouser, which was of latter introduction. A scarf was usually kept over the shoulders. It was usually trimmed with a coloured border. Sometimes scarlet shawls or to her showy fabrics were used for the purpose. The chiefs or wealthy wore *angraka* (coat), tied over the chest and reaching to the knee. Sometimes over the whole apparel a mantle, lined with skin, was thrown. Even the *Maharaja's* attendants used to clad splendidly and displayed a profusion of gold and jeweled ornaments. Usually, the Sikh dress was of white colour, except on the day of *Basant* when every body wore a yellow coloured garments. However, the Muslims liked blue colour.[99]

Vigne noticed the difference of tying turbans and wearing tunic between the Hindus and the Muslims. The Hindus smoothed their turbans over the right temple, while the Muslim on the left. They also wore a skull cap under the turban. The Muslim, tied their tunic on the right side, whilst that of the Hindu's was folded over to the left.[100]

In the hills the wealthy persons wore a sort of jacket and trouser, and latter very full above and tight at the ancle. Both the sexes wore wolle caps. Men's caps were flat, of red, with an upturned border of black or wholly black; the caps of the women were usually left undyed, but they had a fringe on the top, which hanged as a tassel on side.[101]

In the mountanous and mountainous regions, woolen garments were mostly used. Usually these were of the colour of the fleece but sometimes dyed of two colours.[102] The common garb of the poor classes was little else than a blanket, which was first wrapped round the waist; one end was brought over the shoulders and fastened across the breast with skewers and the other was passed round the things and secured to the waist; the legs and feet remained bare. However, when snow began to fall, a double coating was assumed alongwith trousers and "bootkings".[103]

There are references to the ornaments like *nath* (ring for nostril), *koka* (a small ornament to wear at the tip of the nose), *tikka* (an ornament for forehead), necklace, earring, armlets, anklets etc. These ornaments were of gold, silver and some other metals.[104] However, it appears that there was a much difference of size and metal used by the people of the plains, of mountaineers and of different tribes. For instance, Moorcroft observed the women of the hills districts wearing heavy rings in their ears and broad anklets of a metal of the appearance of a pewtar.[105] Burnes found women of the *jun* tribe wearing earrings of an enormous size, while Masson observed a Sikh lady carrying a profusion of trinkets.[106] The upper classes used to wear heavy jewellery.[107]

Dwellings of the upper classes were good enough to suit their status. The tranquility, that followed the conquest, made aristocracy to think of improving their places of residence. Consequently, the aristocracy inhabited in the houses which corresponded to 'baronial castle'. Burnes describes a family mainson of a chief named Jawala Singh as, "it stood in the centre, surrounded by a village, peopled by retainers, the whole being enclosed by a mud wall and out ditch. Within the space was to be found a *bazaar*, extensive stable, which were built on a plan of great regularity.[108] The richer bankers and merchants had houses three to four storeys high. These houses were built of bricks plastered with mud. In the hills, the houses were mostly made of wood for safety during the natural calamities.[109]

Both Burnes and Jacquemont observed that, thought the houses of the Sikh chiefs were 'the best', and had at a distance an 'imposing and respectable appearance', yet they were inferior to the fortified dwellings of the Rajput chiefs of Mewar.[110] Jacquemont found their houses at Amritsar "much inferior in design and construction to those at *Benares*".[111] However, it was common amongst the wealthy as well as the poor to whiten their houses and cover the front of these with 'coarse mythological pictures'.[112]

The common people in the plains lived mostly in *kacha* houses, made of sun-dried bricks. In the mountaneous regions, the houses wee usually a group of two or three cottages built of lose stones, wood and bamboo, interior being plastered with mud. In some places, these were flat roofed while in others, thatched with rice straw.[113] Near and on the river banks, the habitation was of temporary nature being mostly of pastoral tribes. So they never built any shelter beyond 'a movable hamlet'.[114]

There is little information about the food habits of the people. Common food items were *chapattis* made of a wheat flour, varieties of boiled rice, pulses, meat, chickens, eggs, milk, butter, *ghee*, fruits, sweetmeats, *sharbats* and varieties of other dishes adorned the dinning tables of the upper classes.[115] In fact, very sumptuous meals were taken by the aristocracy.[116] However, the thumb and fingers, used while eating, appeared to Burnes 'a poor substitute for knife and fork'.[117]

No information is available in the literature about the food of the common Punjabi folk of the plains. Bread made of wheat, buckwheat, 'chenopodium' and poppy seeds was eaten in the mountainous regions. *Satu* of barley (barley parched and ground to flour, mixed into a paste with a little water) was a popular diet of the mountaineers, particularly while travelling.[118]

Tea and coffee was mostly used in the hills, particularly the black tea made the best beverage in the mountainous regions.[119] However, Moorcroft noted in 1820 that the tea was becoming popular in the Punjab plains too.[120] *Sharbat* as a cold drink has been referred by Vigne.[121]

Opium, *bhang,* liquor, tobacco etc. were the main intoxicants. Tobacco was used mostly in *chillam* and *hooka* (hubble bubble). Opium was largely consumed by the rich section of the society particularly the aristocracy. A narcotic preparation of the juice of hemp or infusion of poppy heads and hemp was mostly used by the poor. *Buza* (a kind of spirituous liquor) was popular among the mountaineers.[122] Inspite of the prohibition of liquor in Sikhism, the Sikhs used it indiscriminately. The *Maharaja* himself was very fond of liquor and the Sikh aristocracy made no exception. No function, celebration of an event or a festival could pass without the introduction of a bout.[123] The commoners too used it. Vigne observed that "the Oriental have no idea of drinking unless they can drink too much".[124]

The Hindus did not eat with other castes; particularly the *Brahmins* and the *Rajputs*. Also they would not eat twice out of any vessel that cannot be cleaned with earth. Consequently, dishes of dock leaves sewen together were used for eating food. Even the drinking cups too were made of the same material.[125]

Like Hindus, the Sikhs were not restricted to certain food and drinks, but they were forbidden to eat beef.[126] However, jhatka (to sever the head of animals employed for food with one stroke of sword) was eaten by them.[127] Muslims were rather more prone to animal diet than the Hindus, who were mostly vegetarian. However, Jacquemont observed *pandits* (Brahmins) of Kashmir eating everything but beef and drinking *arrak* (somras).[128]

Observance of some etiquettes while receiving a guest was found expression in the travel literature. Vigne call it 'absurd and illiberal', but 'indispensable'. The advance to a meeting, or the remaining at home, the rising from the seat as the guest approaches and the distance at which he was placed, were all matters of etiquettes. These indicated the social position of the guest.[129] A person of consideration such as, Governors, priests, military personnel of ranks etc. were allowed a chair, while a *munshi* or a *thanedar* was offered *mura* or a stool. The next in inferiority of the same class would have been fortunate enough, if he was allowed to sit on the carpet. Rest of the visitors were not allowed to sit down at all.[130]

The norm of society demanded an inferior to advance first to a superior. He must offer some thing and took off his shoes at the entrance door. No man can approach a man of higher rank than himself without offering something to both master and men.[131]

The festival had an important role in the emotional life of the times. *Dushehra, Diwali, Lohri, Basant, Holi* etc. were celebrated both by the Hindus and the Sikhs alike. Even *Maharaja* himself used to celebrate these festivals with great enthusiasm.[132] On the day of *Dushehra,* the *Maharaja* also hold the annual review of his forces.[133] Though *Diwali* was a Hindu festival, the Sikhs celebrated it with greater noise and splendour. On the day Golden Temple was lighted with lamps, which presented 'the image of pandemonium'.[134] Festival of *Lohri* too was celebrated with similar zeal.[135]

The festival of *Basant* was celebrated with still more grandeur. Every one present in the court, nobles, commander of the forces, officers, hostages, dancing girls and the troopers, all had their apparel of yellow colour. Tents and carpets too were of yellow colour. Even *Guru Granth* was wrapped in a yellow coloured cloth to mark the celebration of the event.[136] The celebration started with the *Mukh wak* (opening and reciting a passage from the *Granth Sahib*). After listening *bani* for some time the *Maharaja* rewarded *Bhais* or *Granthis* for their services. Then hostages, chiefs and other officers presented themselves before the Maharaja and gave presents to suit their ranks. A parade of the army was held and the dancing girls presented themselves and sung the song of the day. The celebration ended with the introduction of a bout.[137]

The celebration of the *Holi* festival was not less magnificent. Vigne observed two battalions of Ranjit Singh's favourite troops creating a mimic smoke by throwing red power on each other's faces to the infinite amusement of the Maharaja.[138] The 'dirtiest' part of the celebration, Hugel feels was of sprinkling coloured water on each other. In the houses, the *holi* was often played in the *Zenanas* and the women were allowed to participate. However, drinking of spirit on the occasion was also a part of the celebration.[139]

The Punjabis were very fond of watching and listening to the dancers. Dancing was a popular recreation among the rulers, irrespective of their means, it was the general practice to have dancing girls. It was thought necessary to have proper reception of a guest to the court. Maharaja Ranjit Singh had the 'rarest beauties' in his court.[140] The dance as a profession was in vogue in the kingdom of Lahore. But it was looked down upon. The dancers were usually called as *Kanjri* rustic. However, polite person prefer to call them as nathe wali.[141] Maharaja Ranjit Singh had a regiment of the Kashmirian amazons, who could drank an incredible quantity of spirituous liquor without becoming intoxicated".[142] In fact, observed Hugel, they were, "so completely deadened by their course of life", that they appeared to be no longer alive to any excitement.[143]

Commenting upon the general life of the dancers Hugel said that they always moved in covered vehicles drawn by oxens. They were usually escorted by a party of armed police whom they pay for fear of being robbed of costly jewels with which they were commonly adorned.[144] However, they were in the surveillance of the ruler and were little better than slaves. They were generally not allowed to sing or dance without an adequate permission. An officer of the Government always accompanied them and whatever they received in lieu of the performance of their art, at least a part of that was taken of by that fellow.[145]

Imports of pretty Kashmirian faces to the Punjab, to adorn the harems of the chiefs and nobles, irrespective of their religious creed was underlined by Jacquemont.[146] The female child who promised to turn out pretty was sold at the age of about eight.[147] The prettiest of the dancing girls were from the Watul tribe. The sale of female children was considered a good source of income by their parents. These were sold from twenty to three hundred Francs, but average rate was fifty to sixty Francs.[148]

Gossip was an amusement. The Sikh passion for amusement was so strong, that, Hugel, found much truth in the proverb that, "you can take away the wife and children of a Sikh while he is listening to the adventures of Rustam and Surab and he would not miss them".[149]

The practice of medicine had drawn the attention of almost all the travellers. The medical practitioners pursued the indigenous system of medicing which Vigne called the system of 'Galen and Hipocrates'.[150] They distinguished diseases and their remedies into hot and cold, moist and dry. In fevers, for instance, they recommended that all around the patient should be of a green, as the most cooling colour. For diseases, they took the aid of mercury, substitute that of corrosive sublimate. In some cases, they obtained the benefits of an alternative medicine by persevering administration of decoction of *chob-i-chini*, the strength of which was increased at intervals of two or three days, until the cure was effected.[151] However, surgery was a well developed profession. Vigne mentions Budyan, a famous surgeon at Kangra, who was rewarded a land *jagir* by the Mughal emperor Akbar for his skill of providing a new nose to a man through means of operation. People came even from Persia to seek for a new nose.[152]

Burnes observed a peculiar way of curing a wound received from a tiger. The person undergoing treatment was furnished with the strongest stimulants and set people to prevent his falling asleep for five or six days. By that time, the wound assumed a certain appearance and they then permit the person to rest.[153]

We gather an impression from these travellers that majority of the people of all the communities, did not relish the idea of educating their children. This feeling was rather strong amongst the agricultural and labourer classes. While travelling in the Rachna Doab, when Burnes suggested to an agriculturist to send his boy to school, he replied that 'education was useless to a cultivator of the soil.[154] With few exceptions, this notion did prevail in the higher quarters of the society.[155]

Burnes observed much striking differences between the manners of Europe and Asia, as regards to correspondence. In the Punjab, as in the rest of Asian continent, the correspondence was entirely done by a secretary to whom it was simply told that he should write a letter of friendship, congratulation or whatever the subject might be, to which he affixed his master's seal, and that too sometimes without a perusal. If the signet was not legible, one might have tried often in vain to find out his correspondent; for he never named himself in his letters.[156]

V

References to the work of fine arts are not wanting in the travel literature. Transcribing books and illuminating their leafs with gold and silver was an important occupation of the artists. Jacquemont found in Srinagar alone about seven to eight hundred copyists in the 1830s. The majority of them were Muslims; working to order only. The Muslim artists employed seven to eight different techniques to transcribe the *Kuran* or *Shah Namah*; it contained 60,000 distiches. At the most 200 of these could be transcribed in a day which enabled a copyist to make three *annas* a day. However, the book business flourishing under the Afghans, declined under the Sikh rule. Non-familiarity of the Arabic languages coupled with the loss of political patronage made the *Kuran* script dearer. Its single copy cost not less than rupee one hundred.[157] Moorcroft during his stay at Kashmir got transcribed *Raja Tarangini* and *Nila Purana*, both Sanskrit works and presented to the Asiatic Society of Bengal.[158]

Another important art was painting. Walls, ceilings of rooms, palanquins, elephant houdas, work-boxes, pen-cases etc. were painted in different colours. The painting was mainly of two forms; raised and flat. The former could include of several diversities, according to the greater or less relief given to the performance.[159] Vigne holds that the painter had no oil colours, but flowers and other ornaments were raised on the surface by means of a composition paste, then painted and oiled two or three times until they joined the appearance of being varnished.[160] The brushes used were of the hair of shawl-wool-goat, and the pencils from the hairs in the fur of the cat. Some of the pigments used were native while other were imported.[161] Moorcroft is very appreciative of Kashmiri painters.[162]

Popular theme of the painter was religious and mythological pictures. For example, Hugel saw palace at Wazirabad, which had its outside walls as well as the apartment within adorned with fresco paintings illustrative of the Sikh religion. Among them were portraits of the ten Gurus. Hugel says that 'the chief painter of Maharaja's palace was certainly not a Raphael".[163] However, Jacquemont found some of the houses of the nobles having painted bad pictures.[164]

A good copyist used to make three *annas* a day, a calligrapher three and half *annas*, a carpenter four *annas*, a cutter eight *annas*, a gun-smith and a bow and arrow maker one rupee, a pen-case maker four *annas*, a good journeyman tailor two to four *annas*, a potter about nine *annas* a day.[165] Besides, every artisan was taxed. For instance, Moorcroft observed in the province of Kashmir that "nor are these imposts restricted to the artisans employed in the shawl fabric, every trade is taxed, butchers, bakers, boatmen, venders of fuel, public notaries, scavengers, prostitutes, all pay a sort of corporation tax".[166]

The information on society provided by the European travel literature suggests that its major concern is with the Sikh society. The Muslim society have drawn little attention. The treatment is suggestive of the social situation of these communities. With the rise of the Sikhs to power, their social position underwent a change. Sikhs were at the top of the social hierarchy. On the other hand, the social position of the Muslim went down. Much information on the Sikhs suggest that they were discussed as a ruling class.

The evidence on society does not reflect a serious concern. Though the Sikhs are discussed in detail, yet the description is cursory and lacks depth. Only those aspects are discussed which come under direct observation like, dress, dwelling, festivals, amusement and arts and crafts. These travellers do not make serious attempt to understand the *Punjabi* society and its social dynamism. For example, social order, social institutions and forces of change are not taken up adequately. Hugel discussed four varanas but omitted *Vaishya*. Some of the travellers failed to understand social order. Vigne inter mingle castes and tribes. In the name of Sikh society, only aristocracy of the Punjab is disucussed. On the other hand, evidence related to Kashmir deals with the common men. All this point out the specific concern of the literature.

All the travellers who visited the valley of Kashmir do not present a happy picture about the general condition of the weaker sections of the society. Moorcroft writing in the beginning of the Sikh rule, found them in utter destitution of dwellings and clothes to defend themselves against the cold.[167] Ten year latter Jacquemont observed that Kashmir 'surpassed all imaginable poverty'. There was "scarcely more chance of getting supper for him who tills, spins or rows all day".[168] Similar views were held by Hugel and Vigne who were writing about 1840s.[169] However, in reality, it appears that the position was not so bad. Elsewhere, Vigne, himself have observed that "a field labourer was paid in rice, of which he had his dinner in the middle of the day, and in the evening 6 ser (12leb) of unhusked rice, by selling the surplus of which after feeding a wife and a small family, he was a gainer of an *anna* day a or about two rupees of month"[170]

But the observation of these travellers about the people of the Punjab is different. Both Burnes and Hugel observed that the inhabitants of the kingdom were well fed and healthy, well-clad and happy, and not wanting even in ornaments.[171] Contradicting the observations of Jacquemont, Hugel says that "I confess I saw no such sign of misery, when a stranger can only get bearers at a high price and is forced to pay down the money in advance; when he sees the natives well clothed, and evidently well fed, nay, more independent, even proud in their bearing, how can be conclude that they are so wretched? On the Journey, I observed that, instead of carrying the produce of their fields on their heads, as usual, they had horses with them, which were well laden into the bargain".[172] However, the expenses of a poor man in the Punjab were about three larger rupees or 6s, a month, but the provisions on which he subsisted were six or eight times as cheap as those of eaten by an English peasant. The expenses of his counterpart in the valley of Kashmir did not exceed more than two Hari Singh rupee or 2s. 8d. a month.[173]

As Kashmir was under Maharaja Ranjit Singh, the treatment tries to suggest, though obliquely, that the rule of *Maharaja* was the sole cause of this miserable condition of the people. Also that the prosperity of the Punjab wa due to exploitation of other areas within the domain. But as placed the real fact betrays the contention. Both Jacquemont and Vigne themselves admit that half of the Sikh rule had been successively a prey to earthquake, the pestilence and the famine, which reduced the population to one fourth of its former number when the Sikh occupied the valley.[174] In fact, it was the famine and cholera and not the oppression of the Sikh rule, and the consequent flight of the inhabitants to other parts of the country which reduced the population. Vigne, himself confesses that the conditions of the peasants of Kashmir, as compared to the English and the Punjabi peasants of the early 19th century, was not bad.[175]

However, the information provided by the travel literature on the early nineteenth century Punjabi society is not without significance. The literature contains evidence on almost all the sections of the society; aristocracy, traders, artists, peasants and workers, dancing girls etc. The travellers noted the change which political ascendancy had brought about in the Sikh way of life. For example, Masson and Vigne observed *Brahminical* influence on the Sikhs. Any how, being brought up in a particular socio-cultural set up, the travellers observed those social institutions and practices which appeared to them peculiar and which wee generally overlooked by the native chronicles. For instance, these accounts provide us information on what we call the most inhuman practices like slavery, *sati*, child marriage, polyandry and prostitution. The significance of the evidence is due also to the fact that it is based on personal observation and not on heresy. Also, these accounts were written away from the scene without fear or pressure of any kind.

REFERENCES

1. Burnes, *Travels,* II, 286.
2. *Ibid.*, III, 110-11, 134.
3. *Ibid.*, III, 299.

4. *Ibid.*, I, 45.
5. *Ibid.*, I, 3-4.
6. Jacquemont, *Journal,* 4, 25.
7. Burnes, *Travels*, I, 45, 76; II, 285-86; III, 101, 140.
8. Jacquemont, *Letters,* I, 391–401.
9. Hugel, *Travels*, 331.
10. Masson, *Journeys*, I, 433-34.
11. *Ibid.*, I, 434; Burnes, *op.cit.*, II, 285; III, 143.
12. Masson, *op.cit.*, I, 434.
13. Jacquemont, *Journal,* I, 434.
14. Burnes, *op.cit.*, II, 288, III, 138-39.
15. *Ibid.*, I, 10.
16. Jacquemont, *op.cit.*, 53.
17. *Ibid.*, 28, 53.
18. Masson, *op.cit.*, I, 436-37, 451; Jacquemont, *Letters*, II, 186; *Jounal*, 28, 53, 61; Burnes, *op.cit.*, III, 177.
19. Masson, *op.cit.*
20. Jacquemont, *op.cit.*, 28, 53-54; Hugel, *op.cit.*, 268.
21. Jacquemont, *op.cit.*, I, 408; II, 330; *Jounal,* 30, 53.
22. *Ibid.*, II, 182-83.
23. Burnes, *op.cit.*, I, 8-9; Jacquemont, *op.cit.*, I, 408.
24. Burnes, *op.cit.*, 118.
25. Masson, *op.cit.*, I, 425.
26. Burnes, *op.cit.*, III, 117; Jacquemont, *op.cit.*, II, 33.
27. *Ibid.*, I, 69-70; II, 286; Jacquemont, *op.cit.*, II, 186; Hugel, *Travels*, 338.
28. Hugel, *op.cit.*, 169.
29. Hugel, *op.cit.*, 392.
30. *Ibid.*
31. Hugel, *op.cit.*, 392-93.
32. Burnes, *op.cit.*, III, 176.
33. Hugle, *op.cit.*, 393.

34. *Ibid.*, 394.
35. Hugel, *op.cit.*, 394.
36. *Ibid.*, 393-94.
37. Hugel, *op.cit.*, 394-95; Burnes, *op.cit.*, III, 175-78; Jacquemont, *op.cit.*, 182-83.
38. Hugel, *op.cit.*, 43; Burnes, *op.cit.*, I, 11-12; Jacquemont, *op.cit.*, 51-52.
39. Hugel, *op.cit.*, 169.
40. Burnes, *op.cit.*, II, 286; Jacquemont, *op.cit.*, 25.
41. Masson, *op.cit.*, I, 435.
42. Vigne, *Travels*, I, 191-92; Masson, *op.cit.*, I, 424.
43. Masson, *op.cit.*, I, 450-51.
44. Jacquemont, *op.cit.*, 81-82.
45. Vigne, *op.cit.*, I, 135.
46. Vigne, *op.cit.*, II, 153.
47. Jacquemont, *op.cit.*, 21.
48. *Ibid.*
49. Masson, *Journeys*, I, 436, 474.
50. Jacquemont, *op.cit.*, 54; Hugel, *op.cit.*, 821.
51. Burnes, *op.cit.*, III, 295-96.
52. Hugel, *op.cit.*, 185.
53. Jacquemont, *op.cit.*, II, 59, 66; Masson, *op.cit.*, I, 424, 450-51.
54. Jacquemont, *op.cit.*, II, 66.
55. Vigne, *op.cit.*, I, 199-92; II, 139.
56. Vigne, *op.cit.*, II, 54-55; Hugel, *op.cit.*, 216.
57. Jacquemont, *op.cit.*, 86; Vigne, *op.cit.*, II, 54.
58. Vigne, *op.cit.*, I, 219; II, 3, 4, 132; Hugel, *op.cit.*, 37.
59. Vigne, *op.cit.*, I, 200–02, 206, 216.
60. *Ibid.*, II, 139-40.
61. Masson, *Jouneys, I,* 410; Vigne, *op.cit.*, I, 55, 200–02, 206, 216; II, 3-4, 6-8, 10-11, 29, 78; Jacquemont, *op.cit.*, 27, 62; Hugel, *op.cit.*, 42-46.

62. Vigne, *op.cit.*, I, 55; Jacquemont, *op.cit.*, 62; Hugel, *op.cit.*, 42, 45-46.
63. Hugel, *op.cit.*, 45; Vigne, *op.cit.*, I, 55.
64. The festival of *Kumb* occurs after every twelve years. Burnes saw many Hindus returning from Hardwar after attending this festival: *Travels*, I, 69.
65. Hugel, *op.cit.*, 110; Vigne, *op.cit.*, II, 152.
66. Moorcroft, *op.cit.*, 443.
67. Burnes, *op.cit.*, III, 147; Jacquemont, *op.cit.*, II, 191; *Journal*, 41; Vigne, *op.cit.*, I, 175.
68. Vigne, *op.cit.*, 259-60.
69. *Ibid.*, 260.
70. Vigne, *Travels*, II, 151-52.
71. *Ibid.*, II, 54.
72. Jacquemont, *Journal*, 56.
73. Vigne, *op.cit.*, I, 83-84, 86; II, 12, 151; Jacquemont, *op.cit.*, 55-56, *Letters*, II, 207.
74. Jacquemont, *op.cit.*, 55.
75. *Ibid.*, 5; Vigne, *op.cit.*, II, 11-12.
76. Vigne, *op.cit.*, I, 83-84, 86; II, 151; Jacquemont, *op.cit.*, 207.
77. Vigne, *op.cit.*, II, 137, 139.
78. Moorcroft, *op.cit.*, 447.
79. Jacuqemont, *op.cit.*, II, 133-34.
80. The palce is in the vale of Kashmir and it said Jacquemont, *op.cit.*, II, 133.
81. Vigne, *op.cit.*, II, 140.
82. Burnes, *op.cit.*, III, 55-57.
83. Vigne, *op.cit.*, I, 205.
84. Jacquemont, *op.cit.*, 62.
85. Burnes, *op.cit.*, III, 111-12.
86. Jacquemont, *op.cit.*, 27, 62-63; Hugel, *op.cit.*, 42, 45-46. Also Vigne, *op.cit.*, I, 227-28.
87. Hugel, *op.cit.*, 45-46; Jacquemont, *op.cit.*, 62.
88. Jacquemont, *op.cit.*, 63; Hugel, *op.cit.*, 29.

89. Burnes, *op.cit.*, I, 13-14; III, 101, 146; Jacquemont, *op.cit.*, I, 393-94, 396, 401; II, 71-72, 163; *Journal*, 34; Vigne, *op.cit.*, II, 102-03, Hugel, *op.cit.*, 115,191.
90. The Muslim ladies concealed their body in such a way that one could not see even their countenance. They could be seen throwing white robe over their entire body leaving netted orifice before the face and the mouth: Burnes, *Travels,* I, 62; III, 82, 85, 146.
91. Burnes, *op.cit.*, II, 212-13.
92. Jacquemont, *op.cit.*, 34-35.
93. *Ibid.*, 73; *Letters,* II, 91, 98.
94. Masson, *op.cit.*, I, 435.
95. *Ibid.*, 436.
96. Jacquemont, *op.cit.*, 27.
97. *Ibid.*
98. Jacquemont, *op.cit.*, 27.
99. Masson, *Journeys,* I, 433-34, 443; Jacquemont, *Journal,* 25, 40; Hugel, *Travels,* 380; Burnes, *Travels,* I, 61; III, 102, 136; Vigne, *Travels,* II, 140.
100. Vigne, *op.cit.*, II, 140; Jacquemont, *op.cit.*, 25.
101. Moorcorft, *op.cit.*, 108.
102. *Ibid.*
103. *Ibid.*, Hugel, says that white woolen too was used : *Travels*, 55.
104. Hugel, *op.cit.*, 57-58.
105. Moorcroft, *op.cit.*, 108.
106. Burnes, *op.cit.*, III, 133; Masson, *op.cit.*, I, 404.
107. Burnes, *op.cit.*, I, 146; Jacquemont, *op.cit.*, 61.
108. Burnes, *op.cit.*, I, 13, 14; also Jacquemont, *op.cit.*, II, 16; *Journal*, 26, 27, 57-58; Vigne, *op.cit.*, I, 220, 236-37, 246; II, 187-188; Hugel, *op.cit.*, 207.
109. Jacquemont, *op.cit.*, 26, 57; Burnes, *op.cit.*, I, 10-11, 50; Vigne, *op.cit.*, I, II, 210, 212, 220.
110. Burnes, *op.cit.*, I, 14.
111. Jacquemont, *op.cit.*, 26.
112. *Ibid.*, 26, 57-58.

113. Moorcroft, *op.cit.*, 409; Vigne, I, 174-75, 205; II, 189.

114. Burnes, *op.cit.*, III, 287-88, 307.

115. Burnes, *op.cit.*, III, 134, 166; In the hot climate *suji* (heart of the wheat), beaten with an egg or two alongwith milk; varied by another dish commonly known as *dal bat*: to which a fluid pease pudding, curried and mixed with boiled rice, made a breakfast of the well to do classes : Vigne, *op.cit.*, I, 72, 81.

116. Jacquemont was served with a splendid dinner by M. Allard, by a host of servants richly dressed in silk : *Letters*, I, 394-95.

117. Burnes, *op.cit.*, III, 166.

118. Moorcroft, *op.cit.*, 108-09.

119. Vigne, *op.cit.*, I, 72.

120. Moorcorft, *op.cit.*, 197.

121. Vigne, *op.cit.*, 181.

122. Moorcroft, *op.cit.*, 53, 108-09; Jacquemont, *op.cit.*, 9.

123. Hugel, *op.cit.*, 311; Burnes, *op.cit.*, III, 166.

124. Vigne, *op.cit.*, II, 102.

125. *Ibid.*, I, 108-09; Burnes, *op.cit.*, III, 166.

126. Hugel, *op.cit.*, 283.

127. Masson, *op.cit.*, I, 424; Burnes, *op.cit.*, III, 141.

128. Jacquemont, *op.cit.*, 21; *Letters*, II, 59; Vigne, *op.cit.*, II, 140-41.

129. Vigne, *op.cit.*, I, 56.

130. *Ibid.*, 57.

131. Jacquemont, *op.cit.*, II, 36, 71-72, 167, 171; Vigne, *op.cit.*, I, 56.

132. Hugel, *op.cit.*, 283, 310-11, 338-40; Masson, *op.cit.*, I, 445-46; Jacquemont, *op.cit.*, I, 329; II, 182-83, 198; Vigne, *op.cit.*, I, 43; II, 94; Burnes, *op.cit.*, I, 26-27.

133. Masson, *op.cit.*, I, 445-46; Jacquemont, I, 329.

134. Jacquemont, *op.cit.*, II, 182-83, 198.

135. Hugel, *op.cit.*, 283.

136. Hugel, *op.cit.*, 338–40; Burnes, *op.cit.*, I, 26–28.

137. Burnes, *op.cit.*, I, 27-28.

138. Vigne, *op.cit.*, I, 43; Hugel, *op.cit.*, 310-11; Masson, *op.cit.*, I, 47.

139. Hugel, *op.cit.*, 311.

140. Hugel, *op.cit.*, 310; Jacquemont, *op.cit.*, I, 391. II, 16, 55-56, 65-66; *Journal*, 44-45.

141. Hugel, *op.cit.*, 146.

142. *Ibid.*, 309.

143. Jacquemont, *op.cit.*, II, 213-14; Hugel, *op.cit.*, 309-10.

144. Hugel, *op.cit.*, 311.

145. *Ibid.*, 146.

146. Jacquemont, *op.cit.*, II, 74-75.

147. *Ibid.*, II, 65.

148. Vigne, *op.cit.*, II, 144-45.

149. Hugel, *op.cit.*, 145-46, 339.

150. Vigne, *op.cit.*, II, 123.

151. *Ibid.*

152. *Ibid.*, I, 140-141.

153. There was a popular belief that if a person, who had been wounded, be allowed to sleep, he would see the tiger in his dreams, and thus lost his heart, and consequently die; Burnes, *Travels*, III, 140.

154. Burnes, *Travels*, I, 44.

155. Hugel, *op.cit.*, 221, 281; Burnes, *op.cit.*, I, 44; III, 140-41.

156. Burnes, *op.cit.*, III, 84-85.

157. Jacquemont, *op.cit.*, 69-70.

158. Moorcroft, *op.cit.*, 347.

159. Vigne, *op.cit.*, II, 122; Moorcroft, *op.cit.*, 396-97.

160. Vigne, *op.cit.*, II, 122.

161. Moorcroft, *op.cit.*, 396.

162. He says that Kashmiri painters were esteemed for the variety and elegance of patterns, the brilliancy of their colours and the beauty of the varnish: Moorcroft, *op.cit.*, 396.

163. Hugel, *op.cit.*, 250; Jacquemont, *op.cit.*, 26, 57-58.

164. Jacquemont, *op.cit.*, 58.

165. Vigne, *op.cit.*, II, 121, 126-27; Jacquemont, *op.cit.*, 169.

166. Moorcroft, *op.cit.*, 345.

167. Moorcroft, *op.cit.*, 406, 442.

168. Jacquemont, *op.cit.*, II, 76,87.

169. Hugel, *op.cit.*, 321; Vigne, *op.cit.*, II, 118.

170. Vigne, *op.cit.*, II, 121.

171. Burnes, *op.cit.*, I, 3-4; Hugel, *op.cit.*, 38, 68, 232.

172. While travelling in the Deccan, Hugel saw number pay *kos*; but in the Punjab, he was forced to eight *annas* for the day's work; Hugel, *op.cit.*, 73-75.

173. Vigne, *op.cit.*, II, 120.

174. Jacquemont, *op.cit.*, II, 125-26; Vigne, *op.cit.*, I, 202, 257; II, 118; Hugel, *op.cit.*, 158.

175. Vigne, *op.cit.*, II, 120; Hugel, *op.cit.*, 305.

7

Conclusion

The European travellers remained active in the kingdom of Lahore for about two decades *i.e.* 1820 to 1840. The period of travel activities coincides with the period of consolidation as well as expansion of the dominions of Maharaja Ranjit Singh in the North and West. The Amritsar Treaty (1809) gave him free hand in the North and West. Consequently, within two decades, the *Maharaja* pushed his frontiers up to the river Indus. However, his arms did not stop at the Indus. His forces continued their marches up to the Sulaiman mountains. For the *Maharaja* knew that unless firm control was established over the whole territorial belt between the Indus and the Sulaiman, the Afghan hordes could easily make their way through the passage in the mountains and concentrate on the right bank of the Indus thereby threatening the peace of Sikh dominions.

By 1830s, the *Maharaja* had extended his control across the Indus, but the process of consolidation was yet incomplete. He had to contend with a fierce opposition of Sayyid Ahmad from 1826 onward. Significantly, the British were helping him though indirectly. In 1831, the Sikh forces emerged all powerful by defeating and slaying Sayyid Ahmad at Balkot. Thus a great dancer to the security of the Sikh possessions from the West was over. Henceforward, the whole country from Peshawar to the borders of Sindh along the left bank of the Indus became secure and the *Maharaja* was free to turn his attention towards Sindh. Having control over this region the Sikh ruler could have an outlet to the sea and through this channel he could have established relations with other powers. The British considered it an effort to make a power-block against them. However, the expansionist design of the *Maharaja* was an apparent danger to the British design as well.

While the *Maharaja* was busy in conquests and consolidation in the north and West the British were involved in their campaigns against the *Pindaris*, *Marathas* and *Gurkahs*. They were hardly free from their entanglements in Central and Northern India when war broke out with Burma in 1824, which dragged on for two years. However, the British came out victorious. About the same time the famous fort of Bharatpur too was mastered. Thus by the middle of the twenties, the British had become undisputed masters of India. The only parts of the country lying outside their jurisdiction were Sindh and the Punjab. The great success they had achieved and the absence of any more serious challenge to their sway brought about a marked change in their internal as well as external policies. This change became noticeable from 1826 onwards in their policy towards Ranjit Singh even though outwardly every respect continued to be shown to the Treaty of Amritsar (1809).

A more crucial factor which changed British attitude towards the Kingdom of Lahore was the increased Russian influence, both commercial as well as political in the Central Asian countries, particularly in the court of Persia. The Russian advance towards Persia had started in the opening decades of the nineteenth century. The treaty of Gulstan (1813) virtually turned the Caspian sea into a Russian lake by depriving Persia of 'the right to maintain any warships' in the sea. Consequently, Persia concluded a treaty with Great Britain in 1814 at Tehran. The British pledged to go to the aid of Persia if she was attacked by a European power, either by sending arms or by providing a subsidy.

Undeterred by this pledge the Russian troops occupied Gokcha and the British did not help the Shah. The Russians utterly routed the Persians at Tabriz and imposed a humiliating treaty of Turkomanchi (Feb. 1828), on Persia.

Besides consenting to pay a huge indemnity, the Persians ceded Azarbijan and some other fertile provinces to Russia. Henceforth, Persia became subservient to Russia. In order to prevent Persia to brood over her losses to Russia, a deliberate attempt was made to coax and encourage the Shah of Persia to entertain ideas of expansion towards Afghanistan, Khiva, Khorasan and Bokhara. Soon a plan was crystallized into a campaign against Heart. Heart was the key to Kabul and a combined Russo-Persian campaign for its possession was considered a big possibility. Though India was much more remote, yet it was thought if Heart was occupied by Persia, her ally Russia may pose a serious threat to British India. Consequently, a great fear came to grip the minds of the British who in all seriousness engaged themselves in devising counter-measures in self defence. One such measure was to secure the natural and traditional line of defence of India–the Indus. It was considered useful for commercial as well as from strategic point of view.

Coupled with this was the British commercial interest. They wished to occupy the Central Asian markets for their produce. For the *bazaars* of Bokhara, a central mart between Asia and Europe, were being supplied by over land route from Russia. Numerous fairs were annually held on the Southern frontiers of Russia, on the banks of Volga, lasting for forty days. The central Asian merchants made most of their sales and purchases on these fairs but there was no party to counter the Russian exports to Bokhara. Likewise, Russia was carrying on an extensive trade with China through Kashgar and Yarkand. Even Russian goods find their markets as far as Kabul and the Punjab. Russians had the advantage of using Volga, the greatest of the European rivers, for commercial purposes. Therefore, to compete Russia it was imperative that the British goods should have been cheaper and in plenty in the Central Asian markets. The British thought that "if Russia navigates the Volga, Britain can command like facilities, by the two more grand and equally navigable streams the Ganges and the Indus". For this exigency the revival of the ancient channel of commerce–the Indus was thought expedient. An inquiry into the condition and manufactures of every region which adjoin the Indus, as well as those situated between it and the Caspian sea, too was though necessary.

Equal interests of the British were in the military resources of the Punjab, Sindh, Afghanistan and other countries lying between it and the Caspian Sea. They were interested to know the feasibility of any threat to their Indian possession which these powers could have formed together with Russia from the North-West. Therefore, they were driven to know "the then state and condition of these tribes who, at different period of history, had sent forth successive hordes to overrun and occupy the fairest regions of Asia".

Thus, to check the Sikh move towards Sindh, to arrest the growth of Russian empire, to open Central Asian marts for British commerce, to immunize Persia and Afghanistan against Russian influence and thereby avert an opportunity to Russo-Persian invasion on British India, were the motives of the British expansionists in the 1830s. To meet successfully to these problems, it was thought by the statesman, both in England and India alike, to enhance the British influence beyond Indus. This needed much information of 'political and geographical' nature. Hence, to penetrate diverse regions and courts, the commerce and diplomacy was an instrument. In this backdrop, the accounts of these travellers played a significant role.

All the six travellers under analysis belonged to distinct nationalities. Four of them were English, one a French and one a German. Like their nationalities their purpose to visit the Kingdom of Lahore too was varied. Two of the English, William Moorcroft and Alexander Burnes were actually in the service of East India Company. Charles Masson had deserted the Company's Army in 1826. However, later on he became an accredited agent at Kabul. But Godfrey Thomas Vigne was not in the service of the Company. However, his visit to the dominions of Maharaja Ranjit Singh was not without political connection. He visited the kingdom in concert with C.M. Wade, the Political Agent at Ludhiana. Victor Jacquemont was in the service of the French Government while Baron Charles Hugel had served in the Austrian Army as Colonel before taking up his Asian travels. Both the non-English travellers were visiting the dominions of the Maharaja with the prior knowledge and recommendations of the higher officials of the East India Company both in England and in India alike.

There is a marked dichotomy in their explicit and implicit purpose which was maintained persistently for diplomatic reasons. For example, when Moorcroft made political arrangement with the ruler of Ladakh, assuring the British protectorate against the Sikhs, the Company's officials not only disapproved of his conduct but informed the *Maharaja* that Moorcroft was doing all that without the sanction of the Company. Furthermore, when Moorcroft asked for an official letter of introduction to the ruler of Bokhara, he was flatly refused by Lord Hastings, who otherwise had a 'strong interest' in the Bokhara project. When Alexander Burnes started exploring *Rajputana* desert in 1829, he was not allowed to do so for diplomatic reasons. But the year following when the Company's officials got an excuse of conveying horses to *Maharaja* Ranjit Singh, they were not slow to use the occasion for exploring the Indus–a plan which they had shelved since 1820s when Moorcroft first made mention of its advantage for the extension of British commerce in the Central Asian countries.

This purposeful dichotomy served a device to keep the hidden motives ambiguous. It helped the British to frame a precise, broad-based, farsighted and complex diplomatic policy under constantly changing circumstances. Also, this dichotomy was maintained between the diplomatic policy of the government and the popular impression in the form of travel literature. For instance, Godfrey Thomas Vigne was of the view that the occupation of Kashmir would be of great value to solve the problem of defence of British India from the North-West. But the British diplomat thought it otherwise *i.e.* to extend British frontier up to the Indus. The complexity of the British policy was such that even Jacquemont failed to understand it. For example, commenting upon the Ropar meeting which took place between the *Maharaja* and Lord William Bentinck he says, "what Lord William Bentinck wants with Ranjit Singh I am unable to guess, to frighten him, and show him how easy it would be to annihilate him". Alexander Burnes who was incharge of the horses to be conveyed to the ruler of Lahore was not informed of by the higher officials as if the horses intended for Ranjit Singh were from the king of England or from the Directors of the Company or form the Governor-General himself.

Though, the travel literature does not discuss the policy of the East India Company towards Ranjit Singh, yet it helps us to have a feel about its complex nature and broader implications. Apparently, it was not a policy of confrontation but of conciliation, leading though slowly, yet surely to the 'desired ends'. For it did not remain static. The earlier impression of friendship, cooperation and neutrality underwent a change with the changing conditions at the national and international and international level. For instance, in the 1820s Moorcroft was being rebuked for his political activities in Ladakh. But in the 1830s, when Ahmad Shah, the *Balti* chief implored for British protection Vigne promised him to give a favourable report of him to C.M. Wade. Even he took with him Nasim Khan as an Agent of the *Balti* ruler to stay with Wade at Ludhiana. The idea was to give impression to the Lahore Durbar that the *Balti* chief was under their protection. Through this move, the British Indian Government wanted to prevent Sikh conquest of Iskardo without having any apparent confrontation with the Sikhs. However, it becomes clear from the travel literature that the British policy was aimed at exerting psychological pressure on the Lahore Durbar without explicit change in their attitude towards the Treaty of Amritsar (1809).

However, the observations of these travellers should not be confused with the officials policy of the East India Company. For there is a difference between the professed policy of the Company and the personal opinion of an individual traveller. For instance, Burnes was in favour of keeping Dost Mohammad on the throne and did try to prove in his account his capability as a strong and pro-British ruler on the throne of Kabul. But the company's officials were prone to help Shah Shujah to be a ruler of Kabul instead of Dost Mohammad for it suited to their purpose. Inspite of the difference of opinions between the travellers and the Company's officials policy, the travel literature played a significant role in the process of framing a precise diplomatic policy by the East India Company in order to achieve 'desired ends'.

The travellers have commented upon many facets of life in the Kingdom of Lahore. They discuss Maharaja Ranjit Singh's person, his courtiers, his possible successor, his army, administration of revenue and justice. Above all speculating on the probable termination of the Kingdom of Lahore, they dwell on the Anglo-Sikh and the Sikh-Afghan relations. The economic potentialities of the states; its agricultural and industrial products, its natural resources, its trade and commerce with due focus on some important urban centres like Multan, Lahore, Amritsar, Kashmir and Peshawar etc. are keenly observed. Besides, some social customs, beliefs and practices of the Hindus, the Sikhs and the Muslims, their fairs and festivals as well as social institutions like slavery, prostitution, child marriage and *sati* too became a foci of their attention.

But all the three aspects *i.e.* polity, economy and society have not been treated with equal interests which in turn largely depended upon the purpose with which they travelled and wrote. Besides, each one of them had his own idiosyncrasy and a particular situation for observing the some object. For instance, William Moorcroft could better comment on the stud of the *Maharaja* than Alexander Burnes or Vigne, for each one of them had a different motive to come to Lahore and were trained in different professions. Also there is a gap of about a decade between the observations of Moorcroft and Jacquemont and Burnes, between the latter and Masson, Hugel and Vigne. Any way, the English travellers were writing for their masters and contemporaries in Western Europe alike while both the non-English travellers were writing to gratify the curiosity of their countrymen about the polity and economy of an Asian ruler in close contact with the expanding European colonialism. Therefore, all the six reflect some common interests in the polity, economy and society of the Kingdom of Lahore. Their collective evidence on these aspects are quite impressive, though their scope is limited to some institutions which were functioning at the time of their visits. However, travellers do not go into the historical background of the these institutions.

This limited scope not only is indicative of their purpose but also express the British diplomatic interests. At times, they do not trace the historical background as it had been covered by some other scholars. The historical background of the kingdom of Lahore is left precisely because the ground had been covered by H.T. Prinsep in his work *Origin of the Sikh Power In The Punjab and Political Life of Maharaja Ranjit Singh*. The work covered the history of the Sikhs up to the year 1831. In regards to Sikh-Afghans or the State of Afghanistan, Burnes took up the events which happened since the year 1809, the year in which Elphinstone closed his narration. Burnes have discussed the affairs of Afghanistan up to the year 1824 and we find in Masson's work a regular account of the affairs of Afghanistan since the death of Wazir Fateh Khan up to 1841. In fact each one of them was conforming and expanding the information of his predecessors. Also, it appears that each one of them was trying to answer the question raised by the earlier and thereby filling the gap. For instance, Moorcroft devoted much time and space to Kashmir and Ladakh and general condition of commerce in these regions including Central Asia. He referred to the utility of the revival of the Indus route for the expansion of British commerce in Central Asia. Burnes devoted more space to the Indus, the Punjab and commerce of Central Asia and did not touch Kashmir. Masson devotes few pages to the affairs of the Punjab and bulk of the work is devoted to Afghanistan. If we find less evidence in Vigne's works, it is simply because the ground had been covered by his predecessors. Therefore, he devoted more space to Kashmir and Iskardo than to the Punjab and Afghanistan. Both the non-English were curious to know about the Sikhs that is why Hugel inserted much of Prinsep's work in his narration about the historical development of the

Sikhs leading to the formation of an independent Sikh state under Maharaja Ranjit Singh.

Besides being sketchy in nature, the evidence on polity lacks systematic presentation which can be explained due to the scope and nature of British interests in the kingdom of Lahore. The British policy makers wanted to know the then state of the kingdom of Lahore. Their interest was more in the working of certain institutions such as military, revenue, justice etc. For instance, Burnes was keen in noting the composition of the nobility, besides counting the strength of the armed forces. By doing this he was perhaps trying to single out those chiefs which could easily be persuaded against the *Maharaja*. Referring to the power and resources of the Jamwal brothers in the Alpine Punjab, Vigne advocated that the surest way of gaining the popularity of the people as also of the establishment of peace in that region, the restoration of the old *Rajas* whom *Maharaja* had dispossessed, was necessary.

The observations of the travellers on economy underlies varied nature of interests interlocked with the general interest of the East India Company. Moorcroft, Jacquemont, Hugel and Vigne appears to be more concerned about the peasantry and working classes in the province of Kashmir. On the other hand Burnes is more concerned with the Punjab. Amongst all of them Moorcroft alone covers almost all the aspects of the economy discussed by the travel literature. The evidence of economy seems to give impression that their main purpose was to condemn the Sikh rule. The fiscal policy of the *Maharaja* became a centre of their criticism, for they asserted that the excessive duties levied by the state was the main cause of the depressed state of the commerce of the Punjab. But the criticism does not conform the reality. Even at places the information provided by these travellers contains contradictions. For instance desperate plight of the peasantry of Kashmir and their consequent flight to neighbouring regions was not the result of the oppressive policy of the state alone. There were numbers of other factors too. Also, exactions were carried to a certain point. The administration of the Sikhs was not so bad as compared to the Afghans. The low return of the revenue appears to be the result of the withdrawl of certain cases after the famine of 1833. Above all, it was the natural calamities like earthquake, famine and cholera which reduced the population of Kashmir. As regard to the fiscal policy we finds in other sources that the custom duties prevalent in the kingdom of Lahore were less than those of Afghanistan and British India. The *Maharaja* was encouraging the indigenous manufacture in several ways which boosted the industrial productions making the Punjab to a great extent self sufficient economic unit. The evidence on society is not less significant. They shed light on many aspect of the early nineteenth century Punjabi society. The change that the Sikh community was undergoing has been observed. For example, Masson tells that many Hindu beliefs and practices had crept into the Sikh way of life, implicitly or explicitly. But these evidences lacks systematic exposition. The early nineteenth century Punjabi society and its social dynamism have not been understood properly. Even some of the travellers failed to understand the social order. For instance, Vigne inter mingles caste and tribes. In their discussion of the Sikh part of the Punjabi society only the aristocracy has been discussed. Here again description is cursory and lacks depth. Only those aspects have been taken up which came under direct observation like apparel, dwellings, festivals, amusements and arts and crafts. However, in the province of Kashmir, the common men became a theme of their discussion.

All the travellers who visited the province of Kashmir have tried to give impression that the lot of the common people was too bad to live; they, 'surpassed all imaginable poverty'. But the position of the inhabitants of the Punjab have been described quite differently. Hugel observed that the inhabitants of the Punjab were 'well-fed and healthy, well-clad and happy, and not wanting even in ornaments'. As Kashmir was under Maharaja Ranjit Singh, the treatment tries to suggest, though obliquely, that the rule of the Maharaja was the sole cause of the miserable condition of the people. Also, the prosperity of the Punjab was due to the exploitation of other areas within the domain. However, the real facts betrays the contention. Vigne himself admits that condition of the peasants of Kashmir, as compared to the English and the Punjabi peasants of the early nineteenth century, was not bad.

However, these shortcomings do not diminish the significance of the evidence on early 19th century Punjabi polity, economy and society. Being foreigners and brought up in a particular socio-cultural set up, the travellers observed those aspects which were peculiar to them and were generally overlooked by the contemporary Persian chroniclers. Unfortunately, some historians of Maharaja Ranjit Singh's period advocate the utility of the Persian sources and condemn the use of travel accounts simply as these were written 'with a motive particularly keeping before them the interests of the British in India'. Perhaps, these historians did not realize that a historical work has its own specific function. The significance of travel literature does not diminish because they underlies the specific purpose of providing information to the East India Company for his expansionist design and on the other hand it is not in the interest of the Kingdom of Lahore. The real historical significance of travel literature lies in the process of translating the purpose by providing desired information for propounding a complex diplomatic policy. In fact, the travel literature was also the product of well-advanced Western diplomatic processes for which Oriental diplomacy was no match.

Glossary

Abwab	:	generally, cesses paid by the cultivator to the officials in addition to the land revenue: also called *Kharch.*
Akali	:	literally 'an immortal', also a member of a militant sects of the Sikhs.
Amir	:	A nobleman, a Mohammedan of high rank.
Anna	:	1/16th part of a rupee.
Arrak	:	literally juice, abstract distillate; generally used for distilled rose water also distilled water.
Asli Tus	:	a kind of wool, particularly the fleece of the wild sheep and other animals.
Attar	:	scent, otto
Bafta	:	a cloth woven with gold thread, brocade.
Bairagi	:	a member of the *Vaishnava* order of ascetics.
Basant	:	A seasonal festival of India marking the decline of severe winter and heralding the advent of spring, falling generally towards the end of January or the beginning of February.
Batai	:	division of produce between the cultivator and the state : also called *ghalla-bakhshi; batai-lutai* : a saying embodying the idea that , from the view point of state, *batai* is throwing away much of its share.

Batti (vatti)	:	a measure of weight equal to two *sers*.
Begar	:	forced or unpaid labour.
Bhai	:	literally a brother; an epithet generally used for a Sikh formally connected with religious affairs; also epithet of respect.
Brahmin	:	the first of the four *varanas*.
Chakk	:	a war like tribe in Kashmir, also a caste amongst the Muslim peasants.
Chakmak	:	a stone which gives out sparks on rubbing a flint.
Chamar	:	a leather worker by caste.
Chauri	:	a flying-whisk made of the tail of the yak and used generally for deities and royalty.
Chaudhri	:	the hereditary headman of a *tappa*.
Chawal	:	a unit of small weight equal to $1/8^{th}$ part of a *Ratti*.
Chhatak	:	a measure of weight, consisting of 5 *tolas* and equal to 1/16 of a *ser*.
Chikun	:	embroidered fine muslin, lappet.
Chillum	:	the part of hubble-bubble which contains the fire and tobacco placed in it.
Chupan pal	:	used for a person who takes care of the flock and herds of other people in Kashmir.
Daftar-i-mu'alla	:	the central office.
Darbar	:	the royal court.
Dhani	:	a tract of land in the Jhelum district particularly in Chakwal sub-division.
Dharmarth	:	literally, by way of religious duty; land revenue alienated in favour of a religious personage or institution by a ruler or acting in his place, by a *jagirdar*.
Diwali	:	The Indian festival of lights celebrated in

		commemoration of the return of Lord Rama from his exile and usually falling towards the end of October or the beginning of November.
Doab	:	a region lying between two rivers.
Dokan	:	literally shop; in Kashmir it was used for shawl manufacturing.
Doshala	:	shawls in pairs.
Dunga	:	a sort of boat used in the lower portion of the Indus; it was clumsy as compared to *Zohruq* but stronger built.
Durri	:	cotton carpet.
Dushehra	:	An Indian festival commemorating the victory of Lord Rama over the forces of Ravana, celebrated by burning the effigies of the latter generally falling in October.
Faqir	:	a Muslim medicant.
Gaz	:	a measure of distance consisting of 16 *girah, girha* generally used for measuring cloth.
Ghee	:	clarified butter.
Ghumaon	:	a measure of land, varing in different part of the Punjab, and consisting of 8 *kanals*; also equal to 2 *bighas* or about an acre.
Ghurchara	:	literally, a horse-rider; one of the irregular horseman of the kingdom of Lahore; also the *ghurchara* horsemen of Ranjit Singh organized into a separate regiment and recruited from amongst the aristocracy of the Punjab..
Girha	:	a measure equal to 2½ inches in length.
Granth	:	literally a book; here used for the sacred book of the Sikhs.
Granthi	:	Reciter of Sikh scripture (Granth Sahib).
Gujar	:	a clan whose occupation was rearing cattle,

		the *Gurjars* are said to have come originally from Gujrat.
Gulbadan	:	used for flockman who takes care of horses.
Gurmata	:	a unanimous decision arrived at by the Sikhs present before the Guru Granth Sahib.
Harimandir	:	the Golden Temple at Amritsar.
Hath	:	a cubit or a scale of length, measured from the elbow to the tip of the middle finger, or abouts 18 inches.
Hindustan	:	India; the land of the Hindus; generally referring to the U.P. in the 18th and 19th centuries.
Holi	:	One of the ancient festivals of the Hindus, also known as festival of colours, it usually falls in the month of March.
Hooka	:	a hubble-bubble.
Howdah	:	a litter, a seat on an elephant.
Hundi	:	a bill of exchange.
Jagir	:	an assignment of land revenue in lieu of salary.
Jhalar	:	a wheel fixed on the bank of a river, a stream or a canal to draw water for irrigation.
Kaccha maund	:	a measure of weight equal to 16 *sers*.
Kalga	:	plume adorned on the turban by the nobles and the chiefs.
Kamarband	:	waist cloth.
Kangri	:	warming pan used in winter in the hills.
Kankut	:	a method of assessment based on the appraisement of the standing crops by measurement of land and inspection of the crop.

Kardar	:	an agent; an official; a revenue collector of a *ta'ulluqa* or a *pargana.*
Karkhana	:	workshop or a place of manufacture.
Kasba	:	townlet; like small town.
Khalsa (Khalisa)	:	literally land held directly by the state; here used to denote the fighting brotherhood of the Sikhs, particularly the followers of Guru Gobind Singh.
Kharch	:	cesses paid by the cultivators to the officials in addition to land revenue, also an interest paid on loan advanced to the cultivators for the development of agriculture.
Kharif	:	the autumnal harvest, sown in June-July before the commencement of the rains and reaped in October-November.
Kharwar	:	literally, an ass load, signifying a measure of weight as well as of land in Kashmir.
Khil'at	:	a robe of honour, containing articles of costume generally numbering three to twenty-one, including even arms or horses, and bestowed by a superior on an inferior as a mark of distraction.
Kiladar (Qiladar)	:	the governor or commandant of a fort.
Kimkhob or Kinkhob	:	Gold cloth.
Kohs	:	a measure of distance, variously estimated at about one and a half or two miles.
Kotwal	:	the chief officer of the police for a city or town or camp.
Kumb (Kumbh)	:	water-pot; religious congregation after every 12 years at Hardwar, the eleventh sign of Zodiac, son of Prahlad.
Kuran	:	commonly, but incorrectly, *Koran* and *Coran*; the sacred book of the

		Mohammedans, the supposed revelation made to Mohammad and delivered by him orally, collected and committed to coriting by the Khalif.
Lungi	:	a piece of cloth worn tied to the waist and flowing down to ankles.
Majha	:	literally the middle country, usually refereeing to the territory of Lahore and Amritsar districts.
Masha	:	a unit of small weight consisting of 8 *rattis* and equal to 1/12th part of a *tola* or 1/80th part of a *chhatak*. It is generally used for weighing precious metals and stones.
Masand	:	a seat; a throne.
Manwatta	:	a unit of weight prevalent in Kashmir equal to 1½ *ser* but said to have been actually of varying weight.
Muqaddam	:	the headman of a village.
Mullas (Mulana) (Maulvi)	:	a Mohammedan lawyer, but usually applied t a Mohammedan village school master.
Mura	:	stool made of reeds, thick mat.
Nach	:	Dance; dancing.
Nach wali	:	dancing girl.
Nath	:	an ornament worn in nostril.
Nanakshahi	:	literally, the followers of Guru Nanak; here in a coin current in the Sikh times of the value of 16 *annas*.
Nazim	:	the governor of a province; an administrator.
Nazrana	:	the tribute paid by a vassal; also paid by an official on a regular basis or on special occasions.
Pacca Maund	:	a measure of weight-eqaul to 40 *sers*.

Padshah : a king.

Pagri : a turban.

Pahi-Kishti : in Kashmir the term was used for lands more remote from the city; less productive and requires much labour.

Paji : a unit of measure in Kashmir said to be equal to 6 *sers*; generally it was used for measuring oil.

Pal : a measure of weight equal t 3½ Mahmood Shahi Rupaiya.

Palangposh : a bed sheet or coverled or bed cover.

Panchayat : a village council consisting of five members for the purpose adjudication forming the lowest rung in the hierarchy of judicial administration.

Pandit : a *Brahmin*, whether learned or not.

Pao : a unit of weight equal to four *chhtak* or quarter of a *ser*.

Parda : a veil, a screen, a curtain, especially one which excludes the women of a family from the gaze of men.

Pargana : the administrative sub-division of a Sarkar under the Mughals and of a *suba* under Ranjit singh, and thus interchangeable with *ta'alluqa*.

Pashmina : a kind of fine wool; woolen goods.

Pashm : wool.

Patka : turban cloth; it used to be from 8-10 *gaz* in length and twelve *girhas* to one *gaz* in breadth.

Pattu : strong shawl-cloth of inferior manufacture, also used for a coarse blanket.

Patwari : the village accountant.

Piada	:	a foot soldier.
Phiri	:	second class wool or in the process of cleaning, the wool left behind.
Phulkari	:	embroidered cloth, flower cloth only used for betrothal.
Qanungo	:	a hereditary keeper of the revenge records at the *Pargana* or the *ta'alluqa* level.
Qazi	:	an official appointed by the government to administer civil and criminal justice according to the Islamic Law.
Rabi	:	the spring crop generally sown in October-November and reaped in April-May.
Ratti	:	a unit of small weight equal to 8 grains of rice or $1/8^{th}$ of a *masha.*
Sangam	:	meeting, place of meeting, the confluence of two rivers, the debouch of a river in the sea.
Sar-Kishti	:	in Kashmir the term was used for lands near the city or habitation and more productive.
Sarsai	:	the small unit of area in the *ghumaon* system of land measure, equal to one square *karam* or about $1/9^{th}$ of a *marla.*
Sati	:	a widow how immolates herself on the funeral pyre of her deceased husband.
Sayyid	:	a descendant of prophet Mohammad, especially one of his grandson, Hussain, and held venerable by the rulers and people alike.
Ser	:	a unit of weight equal to four *pao* or 16 *Chhataks* under the Sikh rule the *ser* was equal to 96 rupees weigh of Nanakshahi coins.
Sarbat (Sharbat)	:	beverage used as cold drink.

Shali	:	the words was used for paddy in Kashmir.
Shastras	:	religious books of Hinduism.
Singhara	:	the water chestnut, an edible water root.
Suba	:	a province or the primary division of an empire.
Subadar	:	the governor of a province.
Susi	:	a kind of cloth with lining, mostly used by women folk.
Ta'alluqa	:	literally, a dependency denoting connection with, or possession of a given area; the term was most commonly used under Sikh rule for the administrative unit next to the province, and as such had become interchangeable with *pargana*.
Tahli	:	the Indian rosewood tree, dalkergia siss.
Taqavi	:	literally, strengthening or assisting; the money advanced to cultivators for implements, seeds and digging well, etc.
Tavis (Tawiz)	:	An amulet, a char, especially a verse of the *Kuran* engraved on a stone or a piece of metal, inclosed in a case and strung on a thread worn round the neck, also a platform or slab of stone placed over a grave.
Tikka	:	an ornament for forehead.
Thanadar	:	an officer incharge of a *Thana*, formerly an officer under the *faujdar* employed with a small irregular force, in protecting the country and enforcing payment of the revenue; also a petty police-officer subordinate to a *darogha*.
Thathiar	:	utensil maker.
Tola	:	a unit of small weight equal to 12 *mashes* or 96 *rattis*. It is generally used for weighing precious metals.
Trak	:	a unit of weight in Kashmir, equal to about

		4½ Lahore *sers* or 1/16th of a *Kharwar*.
Trukee	:	it was a sort of interest on the advances of grain which was provided to the farmers to overcome famine conditions during the governorship of Raja Sukhjeevan Mal; In the times of the Sikh the term continued to be used for the interests on *Taqavi* given to the peasants for the development of agriculture.
Varna	:	the Hindu Caste system.
Yogi	:	a renucient belonging to one or another of the twelve Gorakhnathi orders.
Zamindar	:	Feudal tenures of the nature of conditional *jagirs* conferred on certain of the frontier Zamindar of Bengal by the Mohammedan government.
Zamindari	:	the office and rights of a *zamindar*, tenure of a *zamindar*, whether individual or coparcenary; the tract of land constituting the possessions of a *zamindar* or of coparcenary *zamindar*; it maore usually designates the former.
Zanana	:	women's apartment.
Ziarat	:	Pilgrimage, going on pilgrimage to any holy shrine among the Mohammedans.
Zohurq	:	a kind of boat rounded at both ends.

Index

I

L

M